T0311311

truth. growth. repeat.

truth. growth. repeat.

(a business manual for generation why)

by mike edmonds

with ronnie duncan

WILEY

hello, i'm rachel

I was standing in a long queue at a rental car booth late one night. You know the place. One of those little huts tucked away in an airport car park. A few flights had just arrived and there were six or seven of us waiting in a line that went out the door.

Inside, there was only one customer-service agent. She wore an expression of blank despondency and a tag with the words, 'Hello, I'm Rachel'.

As I waited for Hello, I'm Rachel to print out each person's contract on the 1980s dot matrix printer that rental car companies seem to be keen on preserving, I noticed a little laminated sign stuck on the wall next to me.

It was titled 'Our Purpose' and it stated:

Dear Valued Customers. Our Purpose is to Drive the World Forward™. That means providing you with the latest models of today's popular auto brands and giving you the very best in customer service excellence.

I looked at Hello, I'm Rachel as she asked the next tired traveller for their licence and credit card without making eye contact. I looked at the water cooler with no cups. And the one chair. And the old magazines.

Only by anticipating your every need can we help you get to your important business meeting or family reunion faster and easier. Our Super-Server Team™ is ready to ... blah blah blah.

I looked at the people around me swiping their smartphones or staring at the floor as poor Hello, I'm Rachel recited the same insurance upsell monologue we'd all overheard a number of times now.

I sighed and thought what everybody else on the planet thinks when a company makes a promise these days.

Yeah.

Right.

I bet that at some point in the previous 12 months Rachel had sat in an auditorium somewhere with a few hundred other employees as their new confident'n'captivating CEO delivered an important PowerPoint presentation. About her rental car company's amazing New Purpose. Full of words like 'excellence' and 'innovation' and 'demographics'. With a snazzy video of happy car rental customers edited to the tune of whatever song was currently number 3 on iTunes. And ending with the big reveal that we're now 'the car rental company with Car-isma!™'

And like the dedicated employee that she is, Rachel would have sat there trying to remember the new list of five corporate values and trying to set aside her cynicism at having heard all this before at their last big company rah-rah, when the last confident'n'captivating CEO revealed that they were now 'the Happy Car Rental Company™'.

Rachel would collect her brown paper showbag with the Car-isma™ sticker on it and the Car-isma™ mug and mouse pad and the great little Car-isma™ Spirit Book that looked so well designed and professionally printed. And she would go back to her little airport booth and give it a good shot. She would genuinely try to put her cynicism aside and understand how Car-isma!™ might influence how she did her job. And she would contribute her ideas for better customer service on the Car-isma™ intranet.

But when management refused to add another person to the roster so Rachel could spend more time with each customer — and when they failed to renovate her tired little booth so that people might actually enjoy going in there, and when they didn't listen to her ideas about matching shifts with flight arrivals — she would eventually realise that all this New Purpose stuff is just pretend. It's not real. So she won't be either.

And she would gradually evolve into that blank, coldly efficient humanoid I saw at the airport that night.

This book is dedicated to all the Rachels.

First published in 2018 by John Wiley & Sons Australia, Ltd

42 McDougall St, Milton Qld 4064

Office also in Melbourne

Typeset in 10.5 pt/16 Utopia Std

© John Wiley & Sons Australia, Ltd 2018

The moral rights of the author have been asserted

Cover and internal design by Meerkats

Printed in Singapore by C.O.S. Printers Pte Ltd

10 9 8 7 6 5 4 3 2 1

Disclaimer

contents

introduction

Do you believe that telling the truth and having respect for others is more important than manipulating people for financial gain?

Good news. Your time has come.

The age-old tension that has existed for eons between the Seller and the Buyer is finally coming to a head. That fundamental distrust about what a Seller claims is their motive and what their subsequent behaviour reveals their motive actually is.

From snake oil salesmen in the 1800s declaring their interest was entirely in the health and wellbeing of their customers, to modern-day banks promising that people's happiness is their primary concern, the Seller's pitch to the Buyer has always been the same: we want what you want, we feel how you feel, we empathise with your needs.

Generations of consumers soon learned that this was ... well ... bull manure. Because of what happened after the money was handed over.

Gosh, darn it, that snake oil I purchased was worthless. I believe that salesman knew precisely what to enquire of me in order that I should furnish him with my money.

Ergh, my bank charges me a higher monthly fee than they offer new customers and kept me on hold for 23 minutes when I called to ask about it. I think they just research what a working stiff like me wants from a bank and then pretend that's who they are in their ads.

Have you ever felt like that? It's like we've all been playing a giant board game called Caveat Emptor, an ancient Latin phrase meaning *buyer beware.* In this game, Buyers kind of know they can't trust Sellers but they tolerate them, and Sellers kind of know that Buyers don't believe them but still pretend to be driven by what Buyers want.

In recent times the game has become increasingly sophisticated as imaginative brand communications driven by advanced research and big data follow us into every new medium on every new device. But the result is the same: consumer cynicism about companies' motives and a growing distrust about capitalism in general.

What a huge shame! The concept of capitalism is actually a terrific idea. Seriously. Throughout history it has been shown that an open market drives innovation and creates jobs, which helps people house and feed themselves and live longer, healthier lives. It leads to lower infant mortality rates, higher levels of literacy and fairer welfare systems.

Capitalism may have mutated during the 20th century into the shadowy spectre of greed many people see it as today, but at its core the theory of an economy being free is a good one. It brings out the creativity and industriousness in us humans and gives us choices about how we want to apply our talents and make a living.

Thankfully, the game of Caveat Emptor is changing. With a mere swipe of their index finger the Buyer can now share the truth about how the Seller is behaving. Instantly and globally. As a result, the Seller is suddenly finding that the TV spot they shot with that hot new French director has been made worthless two days into a six-month media schedule by a one-star product rating from a little old lady in Arkansas.

This new world of transparency is rewarding companies that are honest with consumers. Companies whose motive is to offer real value and genuine usefulness. Because they want to. Not just because that's how you attract customers.

At the same time, the savvier, connected consumer is punishing companies that under-deliver on their promises and hide behind brand image and PR spin.

In effect, capitalism has begun a new era. One in which the best way to guarantee a sustainable business is to tell the truth. Honesty is no longer just a fluffy credo your mum urged you to follow so you could get into heaven; it is rapidly becoming the only way to run a profitable business.

This book has been written to help the people who are fuelling this new era. A new generation of business owner. The car mechanic who believes the big auto-servicing firms aren't being entirely honest about what goes on in their workshops. The two friends from university who believe there's a more fulfilling way to help corporations recruit new employees. The housewife who believes her online store will be more helpful for new mums than the big brands at the mall.

This is the 'Generation Why' I refer to on the cover. Any person of any age with a yearning to start a business designed not just to make money, but to make a stand. For truth. And value. People with honourable motives who want to put their Why at the core of everything they do in business.

If you'd include yourself in that group the question becomes: What is your truth? What is authentically motivating you — and the staff you have or will have — to deliver something of real significance and worth to your customer? Without exaggeration, without spin, without preying on people's self-doubt and vulnerability. What is your True Purpose: that higher ideal that will align your consumer promise with your actual behaviour?

This book explains what True Purpose is and why you need to know yours in order to survive in this always on, super-connected world we now live in. It gives you proven tools to surface this truth; and it provides you with a system to implement it, to measure its success and to keep growing, improving and succeeding.

I have worked in the marketing industry for close to 40 years. In 2004 I co-founded a new kind of branding company, Meerkats. One that doesn't just give companies a cool image, but helps business owners unleash the commercial viability of what truly motivates them. For over a decade we have been applying the methods shared in this book to such great effect that we felt compelled to share it with business owners everywhere. Especially the ones who might not be able to afford a professional consultancy like ours.

My aim is to give you a jargon-free instruction manual on how to do what you love, make it commercially viable and maybe, just maybe, help change the misconceptions about capitalism as an idea to advance humankind.

how to use this book

If you're like me, the way you read business books is a little different from the way you read a novel. At the start, you study every word like an eager student. But after a chapter or two you begin to skip the bits that bore you. Or maybe you fast-forward to the next chapter the moment you think you've grasped the author's meaning on a particular theory. Or you jump to a whole other section with that eye-catching title you spotted in the Contents.

Hey, I empathise. We're all smart, busy people. We live in a world of snack-sized information: the two-minute YouTube video, the 20-word Tweet; even the Harvard Business Review includes a summary panel at the end of its longer articles.

This particular book, though, is not so much a collection of theoretical points, but a step-by-step 'how-to' guide to doing what you love, earning a good living from it and making a difference to the lives of others. Perhaps many, many others.

read it like a workshop manual

There are three main parts to this book. And I humbly ask you to read the first part first. It really is in your best interests. If the content of the first part doesn't resonate with you, then the second part won't work and you may not even need the third part. Let me give you a snapshot of these parts and see if you agree:

- Part One explains what True Purpose is, how The Circle of True Purpose works and why I believe it is such a potent system for anyone wanting to grow a purpose-driven business in this transparent world we all now live in.

  It essentially establishes the context for the self-help work in part II: what is going on in the world that we believe demands an evolution of the way capitalism works.

  You know how diet and exercise books start by asking, 'Sick and tired of being sick and tired? Feel listless all the time? Do you want to run and play with your kids? Is there a healthier, more vibrant person inside you just busting to come out?'

  In this case I'm asking, 'Sick and tired of compromising your integrity at work? Feel like companies aren't telling you the truth? Is there a True Purpose inside you that could trigger an amazing business? Want to make money *and* a difference in your life?'

  By sharing the things I think conventional business is getting wrong, and what I believe are the solutions, I hope to light a new fire inside you. A fire that's fuelled by truth. I want you to get to the end of part One and not just say, 'Uh huh, I understand'. I want you to be smiling to yourself and saying, 'Yes! This is so true. This is exactly how I feel. This is the itch I've been feeling but couldn't explain!'

I figure that unless you're a little stirred up about all this, you may not have the drive to properly tackle the purpose exercises in Part Two.

- Part Two is a personal workshop to help you surface your True Purpose and apply it to either an existing business that you're already running, or a new business you want to start.

A common myth in business is that a company owner can come to a branding expert like me and 'get' a brand purpose. They think we just pick them off a shelf and package them up for our clients. 'Hey, Jeep has an Explorer brand meaning — gimme one of those.' Or 'How about that cool brand purpose Harley Davidson has — the Rebel — yeah, gimme a Rebel'. 'No wait, Google is the Sage, maybe that's what our customers want.'

The truth is we don't create purpose for our clients, we surface it. We believe there is only one brand purpose that will work for you: the one that lies inside you. The truth about what motivates you.

The way we do that professionally at our purpose-driven ad agency, Meerkats, takes a considerable amount of time and money. So I've condensed the key parts of this process into five exercises that you can do yourself.

Part Two explains these exercises, gives you examples of other business owners who have successfully used them and then guides you through the process.

- Part Three gives you important advice on implementing the True Purpose that you have hopefully uncovered for yourself. Including how to recognise the scale of the task ahead, how to prioritise your actions, how The Circle can be used as a kind of strategic compass during your journey and a bunch of street-smart tips that I've gathered from decades of helping others do exactly this.

The final chapters contain some background information that I felt compelled to share with you but didn't want to put at the front. I'd much rather you get stuck straight into the meaty part of the book and begin your journey of self-discovery. I figure if you find that enlightening and useful, you might want to then read about my company and me. But not before. This final section also includes some terrific books to read that have inspired and guided us.

when you see the word 'business'

This book is for anyone who wants to be their own boss, to build their own little empire in the sun. Because you want to make a living doing what you love. What you feel strongly about. Whether that's a tech startup, a shop, an online service, a consultancy — you name it.

But the methods in this book will also help those who want to run a social enterprise or charity. That is, anyone who wants to gather a group of likeminded people around a powerful idea with the sole aim of making the world a fairer, better place for all, with no thought of wealth creation at all.

Truth. Growth. Repeat. can help you achieve any of these dreams because the thinking is equally potent for all types of organisations. For the sake of simplicity, however, I have consistently used the word 'business' when referring to whatever organisation you want to run.

Apart from not having to write 'company/startup/social enterprise/ charity/etc.' 6000 times, I chose the word 'business' to represent every shape of purpose-driven organisation for a very specific reason. The thing I fear the most is that truth in business will be misunderstood as being just another soft, fluffy idea. Well-meaning but ultimately unprofitable. Created by goody-goodies who want to make everyone happy but not wealthy.

I reject that notion. In fact, I'm writing this book largely as a rebuff to all those traditionalist business thinkers who believe that money is the only god to serve. I want you and me to show them that the future of capitalism as a sustainable concept to advance humankind is all about telling the truth. That the desire to not just line your pockets but to help make the world a better place is not a 'soft value' that belongs on a dog-eared poster in the staff canteen. That in fact, in a transparent world inhabited by smart consumers, truth is becoming one of the most powerful generators of enduring financial return.

So while I absolutely want to help anyone with a dream of running any type of organisation, it is the world of business where the most righteous change is needed. That's why I have chosen to use the word 'business' as the generic term for all organisational types.

you don't need to be a boss

You don't need to already be running a business to get the most from this book. You can be on someone else's payroll and simply be planning to start your own company one day. You may be in your final year of university and aiming to launch a startup the day you finish. You may be a mother whose kids have grown up and you've decided now's the time to pursue that cool business idea. It doesn't matter. The principles still apply. The exercises still work.

For the sake of simplicity, however, I use the generic situation of someone already running a business as my primary reader. For example, I might ask you, 'What is the core idea fuelling your business?' If you don't already own a business, just replace the word 'is' with 'could be'. As in, 'What could be the core idea fuelling my own business?'

Create your own envisioned future. You'll get exactly the same value from this book as anyone who's already running their own business.

there's no tax law in here

I occasionally use formal business terminology like 'strategic plan' and 'management hierarchy' and 'commercial viability', but this book is not intended to teach you the practical aspects of owning and running a business. In fact, it assumes that you already know — or are planning to learn — the mechanics of business ownership in your country. Things like writing a business plan, doing your market research, understanding pricing and distribution, knowing the laws governing company ownership, being aware of the fiduciary responsibilities of a company director, and so on.

These learnings are the minimum non-negotiables of running an organisation of any size. The stuff you just have to know if you want to be your own boss. But they're not what this book is about. Because while knowing the brilliant basics of business ownership may help you avoid immediate failure, they don't always help you enjoy enduring success.

To me, knowledge of the mechanics of free enterprise is the concrete foundation on which you can build something extraordinary, not the extraordinary thing itself. I believe what's inside *you* is the extraordinary thing. And that's what this book deals with: unleashing the commercial potential of authentically motivated humans. So expect plenty of discovery and inspiration in the next couple of hundred pages, but no tax law.

i'm not dr phil

There are thousands of self-help books on shelves and online that will get you in touch with your inner seven-year-old and help you understand yourself. Many of them are exceptionally good.

This just isn't one of them.

Yes, the process of surfacing your authentic purpose as a business owner will touch on some deep personal ideals and emotional drivers. But I have to be careful that I don't inadvertently over-promise you what is possible from following these methods.

This book is about business purpose. I am primarily concerned with helping people start businesses for the right reasons. That they don't fail because they figured 'one business is just like any other so what does it matter which one I start as long as I'm my own boss?'

My primary motivation is the deep personal sadness I feel when I walk past a shop with a For Lease sign draped across it. The failure rate of small businesses in the first 12 to 18 months hovers anywhere from one-half to two-thirds in most free-market economies (which, let's face it, is most of the world now). Many of these failures occurred because people didn't understand what genuinely motivates them. So they started a business without the skill to run it or the incentive to acquire that skill.

This is my goal: personal insight to drive a business idea that motivates you authentically. Personal salvation may occur as part of that journey, but it's not my field of expertise.

part one:
the circle of true purpose

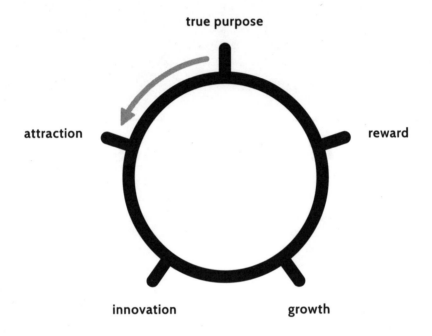

figure 1.1 - the circle of true purpose

(1) truth is a system

There are a lot of virtuous circles in business. They pop up with predictable regularity in PowerPoint presentations the world over. They're second in popularity only to Venn diagrams and maybe the two-way matrix.

Virtuous means righteous. Any circle described as virtuous infers the process being discussed is one with a cyclic effect: that after a certain sequence of behaviour you will end up back where you started but in a better situation. And each time you go around The Circle you're making that situation better and better. Each point along the way magnifies the effect of the next, and the benefits grow.

After more than 70 years combined in the field of brand strategy, my business partner and I have seen virtuous circles for shopping habits, manufacturing methods, environmental sustainability, financial modelling — you name it. But a decade ago we stumbled across a virtuous circle about management motivation that made us stop in our tracks.

It was in a book called *Authentic Leadership* by Bill George. The book's main theme is that the age-old mandate of capitalism — that you exist primarily to serve the interests of your shareholders — had led to a mutated form of free enterprise. One that was actually delivering less value.

George reasoned that the path to long-term shareholder value was through CEOs embracing their own authentic vision and values, not simply taking on the increasingly self-serving motives of corporate America. George believed this would motivate staff to create products and customer service that will better serve the customer's needs. Which will lead to better and sustained shareholder value.

We loved how George put the knock-on effects of authentic leadership into a simple, self-fulfilling sequence that anyone could apply to their business. It appealed to us as practitioners. You see, we work where the rubber of business theory hits the road: branding and marketing. Our clients expect that our thinking will make something happen for them out there in the real world, sometimes within one working day. So we're very good at spotting theoretical ideas that can be put to work.

The only problem was we felt this particular virtuous circle was somewhat hidden in a book largely aimed at the CEOs of major corporations. And accompanied by detailed information on the practicalities of running those corporations in the United States. As valuable as those lessons would unquestionably be to many people, we felt they could be made more accessible to a broader group of business owners. We thought it could be turned into a simple tool for anyone thinking of running their own business of any size. A map to a better future that could be drawn on a napkin and understood by anyone, anywhere.

So we drew up our own version, simplified the language and added the best examples from our own experiences that proved the thinking. After more than a decade of use it has evolved into The Circle of True Purpose that you'll see in these pages. It's the most commonsense, powerful, useful, game-changing virtuous circle I know of — a five-step plan to a better kind of business. One that I believe will inherit the future.

In our own business, Meerkats: The Brand Leadership Company, we've used The Circle of True Purpose to help companies change from being motivated by results to being motivated by a higher ideal. Companies in retail, banking, insurance, fast-moving consumer goods, telecommunications, education, healthcare, transport, leisure, entertainment, media and more. Every time, the new path they chose aligned with the five points on The Circle.

It's proven to be as potent a tool for startup entrepreneurs who are fully aware of their true motivations as it is for the boards of major corporations that may have forgotten theirs. And it seems just as relevant and powerful for social enterprises as it is for commercial ones.

We think this is so because it turns a philosophy into a system. The distinction between those two words — 'philosophy' and 'system' — is important. It's the difference between knitting a jumper to keep someone warm and making a pattern for the jumper that can be replicated by others anywhere in the world to keep millions of people warm. The Circle of True Purpose is a pattern of behaviour anyone can learn and benefit from.

In Part One of this book I take you through each of the five points on The Circle and then explain what happens when you travel either way around. What I'm effectively doing here is describing how I think the world works now. And seeing if you agree.

the roomful of mousetraps

I remember watching a video one day during science class at the Catholic boys' college I attended. It was one of those clunky old educational films our Jesuit teachers would play when they wanted to duck outside for a cigarette.

It began with a freckle-faced kid playing with a model submarine and looking up at the camera as a toffy announcer asked, 'Hey Jimmy. Ever wondered what makes that nuclear submarine go?'

They pretty much all started like that, whether the subject was photosynthesis, stomach acid or the dangers of skateboarding near traffic. But I remember this one had a very creative way of explaining how nuclear fission works. They covered the floor of a large room with mousetraps, hundreds of them, every one of them set and ready to snap. Then they stood in the doorway and threw a single ping-pong ball into the middle of the room.

In two seconds every single mousetrap had been set off. When the stunt was played back in slow motion you could see that when the ping-pong ball triggered the first mousetrap both the trap and the ball flipped up into the air and triggered two more, which flipped up and triggered four or five more, and so on.

This is a pretty cool metaphor for the importance of truth in business today. Your market is like that roomful of mousetraps. It's a new generation of smart consumers who understand how marketing works, who are extremely cynical about companies' motives, and who are set and ready to snap at the first sign of misleading corporate behaviour.

One false claim, one exaggerated benefit, one customer experience that doesn't match the promise and — bang! — their truth about you spreads around the world in seconds. A sarcastic meme that gets viewed 10 million times. A Facebook post that gets a million 'Likes'. An angry Tweet that gets picked up by the media.

The bottom line, folks, is that you have a choice: spend your working life in a roomful of mousetraps just dreading the day when somebody throws a ping-pong ball in your direction, or unset those traps — put them in a big box called Outdated Business Convention and tell the truth about why you're in the business you're in.

Then relax and enjoy it.

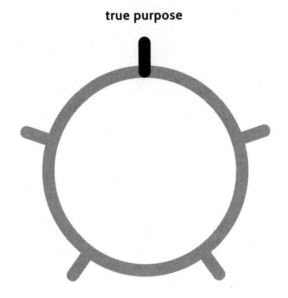

figure 2.1 - the starting point on the circle, true purpose

② true purpose

As a boy, I was taught to tell the truth.

I was told that it's a better way to live. A more honourable way to live. As I grew up I would read quotes and mantras saying that lies are fleeting but truth is forever and the truth will set me free.

A couple of hundred years ago Mark Twain said that if you tell the truth you don't have to remember anything.

A couple of thousand years ago Aesop advised us to not pretend to be anything we're not.

As a man in his 50s, I now know that these creeds are so abundant in history and literature because they work. Being honest with others about what genuinely motivates us and making sure that our behaviour towards them reflects this delivers fulfilment for us humans. It fills a hole inside us that nothing else can fill. Not money. Not popularity. Not material possessions.

In this way, telling the truth can actually be seen as a very primitive behaviour. An inherently natural human act. And after a long career in advertising — one of the most suspect industries for honesty — I firmly believe that the future of free enterprise as a sustainable idea to advance the lives of everyone on this planet depends on truth.

Which is why True Purpose is the starting point on The Circle. It's the sun that drives the solar system of your career, your company and your life. It's the nucleus of all that's to come.

Your True Purpose is the higher ideal that's authentically motivating you to do what you do for work, for a career, for a meaningful life. It's the end reward that's beyond money, or fame, or beating the CEO of your biggest competitor, or showing your dad that you do have potential after all.

Within all of us, but often most powerfully within those who are compelled to start a business, is a driving force for change, a desire to meet an unmet need, to right a wrong.

Understanding this motivation is critical if you're going to make the most of it. You need to surface it, enunciate it and then follow it like a guiding star.

It starts as an itch. A tiny tingle of possibility. An almost imperceptible hint of the thrill of doing something that may improve a sector of commerce, or a part of society, maybe even the world. Unfortunately for many people it will remain an itch that's never really scratched. Just a faint little voice way down inside of them, drowned out by the noise of our busy, complicated adult lives in a fast-paced world. For others, that little voice becomes a roar.

oh no, he's going to talk about steve jobs

Yes, I know. It's almost a cliché to use Apple as a case study. It's too easy, right? Pick the most successful, most inspiring brand on the planet and imply that you too can be a $100 billion company just by employing the methods described in this book.

Okay, fair call. But stay with me on this. The reason I cite Apple is because their story is still the fastest way to understand the concept of True Purpose. And I want you to grasp it quickly because we have lots of work to do to find yours.

So come with me (briefly) back to 1985. To a boardroom at Apple's head office in Cupertino, California. Steve Jobs, the wonder boy of the emerging home computer industry, is arguing with Apple's new CEO, John Scully.

Scully wants to continue manufacturing the Apple II personal computer because their sales data and consumer research shows it's the product people most want. He reasons that after years of being an unprofitable challenger brand Apple is finally making serious money and as CEO he wants to ensure a good return to Apple's stockholders.

Jobs, on the other hand, wants to move onto what's next. He's inspired by new microprocessing technology and wants to invent the next great application of it.

Jobs loses the argument with the company board and is fired from the company he started. Apple go ahead and focus on their big seller, the Apple II, and over the next couple of years their phenomenal year-on-year growth begins to slow. New competitors start bringing out computers that are just as good. And soon they're launching computers that are actually faster and better looking than the Apple II. Apple attempts to arrest the slide by rushing new products into the market (anyone remember the Newton?). Before you know it, people are predicting the end of Apple.

Long story short, in 1997 Jobs famously returns to Apple. Scully leaves and in the next decade Jobs takes his company from death's door to being the world's most valuable brand.

You know how he did it? By returning Apple to its True Purpose.

You see, Steve Jobs disagreed with John Scully that Apple's purpose was to make great personal computers. Jobs believed that making great personal computers was merely the first way that Apple implemented their actual purpose, which he described as 'to make a contribution to the world by making tools for the mind that advance humankind'.

Knowing that this higher ideal was the core objective that genuinely motivated Jobs and his team of smart young designers and electrical engineers, it's easier for us here in the present to understand why that computer company then built its massive global success on products that — on the whole — weren't computers: the iPod, the iPhone, the iPad, the Apple Watch.

Plus a whole universe of open source apps, the incredible music-sharing money-maker called iTunes, the Apple stores that reinvented retail design and service, and more.

In that defining showdown in 1985, Scully is reported to have said that the customer wants the Apple II. To which Steve Jobs is rumoured to have said that at Apple the customer doesn't get a vote!

I cite this story because that one statement is a real key to both the definition and the power of True Purpose. It starts with what *you* believe is important, not the customer.

Measuring the commercial viability of True Purpose comes after you've enunciated what you believe is possible with it: after you've explored the products and services that could be created when you unite a tribe of likeminded souls around this higher ideal.

Steve Jobs might have put it this way: If our True Purpose is limited by a fearful adherence to consumer research, we will just keep making slightly better and better personal computers. And gradually Apple will lose the visionary edge that led to the creation of a better personal computer in the first place. If, on the other hand, we understand the higher ideal that drove us to create that product — a desire to harness technology to advance humankind — and if we commit ourselves to it with bravery and optimism and self-belief, we can change the way the entire world works.

And they did just that.

That's True Purpose right there.

why motive matters

The fuel that powers True Purpose is authentic motive. It's the number-one most important business behaviour in the world today. And for a very simple reason: your customer is smart. In fact, your customer is you. Get used to that idea.

On average you're four IQ points smarter than your parents. You're more socially aware. And you're connected to the biggest knowledge-sharing network in history: the internet.

Critically, you've grown up with marketing. You know how it works.

You know that what a company says in its ads and press releases is not necessarily the truth. You know it because you've experienced it. Over and over.

Put simply, the corporate world has trained you to distrust it. To be cynical about the reliability of its stated motive. This is not a sudden occurrence.

For decades, we consumers have sat in our lounge rooms and watched jolly ads on TV for that friendly gas station on the corner of our street, only to read in the next day's newspaper that the gigantic oil corporation that owns that station is refusing to take responsibility for the environmental disaster they clearly caused. We've felt a tinge of connection with that sports-shoe brand when their cool ads about jogging somehow magically tapped into our minds and captured our desire to challenge ourselves physically, only to then watch them on the evening news admitting they've been using child labour in Asia.

And this is decades after our parents were viewing TV ads from cigarette companies promising that smoking wasn't harmful (many brands even used doctors in their ads), and watching the CEOs of car companies refusing to acknowledge that the big, old, heavy cars they kept making with poor brakes and sharp metal dashboards weren't dangerous.

After so much training, we all expect now that companies have ulterior motives to the ones they share with us. It's not just an occasional doubt anymore. It's the norm.

Which means that brand loyalty is largely fiction. Repeat custom is irregular. And all those billions of dollars the corporate world spends on increasingly sophisticated advertising techniques delivers a shamefully low return on investment.

True Purpose unlocks authentic motive. And in the eyes of your customer, authentic motive instantly makes your business one in a million. Maybe even a monopoly in your sector. And that's not just an honourable way to live. That's commercial advantage. By doing what you promise, you can achieve the same success as your competitors but with a lower advertising and PR spend and a lower cost per sale. You'll also have lower customer churn, better word of mouth, higher staff retention, and so much more.

Find what truly motivates you, shape your business around that and the world is yours.

In this first part of the book we look at what happens when business owners understand their genuine motivation and how the resulting series of knock-on effects form a pattern of behaviour. A pattern that becomes a system with the potential to not just ensure a happy, fulfilling life for you, but just maybe a better kind of capitalism for everyone.

Then, in the second and third parts of the book we help you surface your own True Purpose and implement it in your business or organisation to give you the rewarding, fulfilling life you want.

buzz word alert

Purpose is the business world's hot new trick to attract consumers. It used to be Brand Meaning. And before that Positioning. And before that Vision or Mission (take your pick — nobody ever really knew the difference). And before that it was your USP. And before that Enzyme X.

As such, many companies are spending a lot of money to get themselves one of them purpose things. They're paying for deep-dive focus groups in key markets, quantitative surveys nationwide, trends analyses, big data mining, and so on. Unfortunately, what this work usually ends up producing is nothing more than a neat epithet that's quickly cut out of plastic and stuck on the boardroom wall. So everyone can get back to business.

This is what I find sad and frustrating about so many companies these days. The humans inside them give up on their own potential so quickly for the comfort of conventional practice. They package everything up into neat credos and systems that are so locked down with ™ and ® and © symbols they ignore the basic truth: that we humans yearn to be liberated. Genuine motivation needs to be unleashed. Authentically enthused people given the freedom to explore can create commercial opportunities that fear-based managers only read about in books like this. Because the stimulus to be our best and achieve great things doesn't come from the logical part of our brain. It comes from our heart.

So if you want to attract great talent, grow your market share and build an inspiring business in this crazy, always-on, transparent world we now live in, remember this:

You don't need a purpose. You need your purpose.

The truth about why you're doing what you're doing. Your company's real, honest-to-goodness, cross-our-hearts, scout's-honour, truly-ruly reason for existing. Not some prefabricated, blindly optimistic blurb written for you by a researcher. Only the truth about why your company exists will genuinely encourage your employees to be their best. Because they'll want to, instead of just being told to.

Before we move on to the second point on The Circle there are a few important distinctions I need to share with you about what True Purpose is and what it isn't. The conversation around purpose is growing every day. Some business commentators are trying to package it up too clinically and control it. Some are claiming it can do way more for businesses in the short term than it actually can. And some are getting the definition completely wrong.

high horse optional

Many people in the business world have a dangerous misunderstanding of what organisational purpose is. CEOs hear the term 'conscious capitalism' and they think, 'Oh great, so now I've got to do good for the world. As if selling my products in an increasingly competitive, profit-starved market wasn't hard enough, now I've got to be some kind of semi-charity as well'.

The business media often supports this misunderstanding, along with a number of well-meaning but misguided bloggers and commentators.

Purpose is already in danger of becoming a commercial cure-all, the next must-have business accessory, and as such I fear it's being set up to fail.

I observed the same thing happening around the term 'brand meaning' in the 1980s and 1990s. Nike led the way when they stopped talking about the shoe and started talking about the thrill of pushing yourself physically.

Marketing departments the world over loved brand meaning and exaggerated its power. They admired how Nike owned an entire human emotion and conveniently ignored that organisation's enormous distribution network, their low manufacturing costs, their massive research divisions, and so on.

Boards, on the other hand, hated brand meaning and belittled its impact. They saw it as a soft power too far removed from the hard facts about why customers buy things. They believed it didn't deliver hard results.

Invariably, the eternal argument around how to allocate marketing funds came down to brand versus retail. As a creative director sitting in on these conversations, it never made sense to me. I saw that brand meaning — when executed well and in partnership with pricing, distribution, quality control, and so on — was a way of securing more sales over the long term.

What made it unlikely that brand meaning would ever be able to prove itself as a business asset was the fact it was bandied about as the next great antidote for any company's sales woes. The continuing success of brands like Nike and Volvo and Levi's would eventually wear down the board's doubt. Their eager marketing department had just too much seemingly solid data to support their case: brand awareness figures, predisposition to purchase scores, media spend reports, and so on.

So here we are in the 21st century with the business world abuzz with yet another magic pill that CEOs and boards are finding hard to swallow. And hey, if the definition of being a purpose-driven company was to find a charitable exploit and nail it to the side of your business strategy, I'd be agreeing with them. But that's not what it is at all.

Purpose doesn't always mean worthiness.

The word 'conscious' in the term 'conscious capitalism' doesn't mean being philanthropic. It means being mindful. It means making decisions knowingly, to a genuine motive. Which means, despite what many misinformed CEOs already believe, you can be a purpose-driven company and not have any altruistic intentions at all.

My company once helped a radio station surface their True Purpose and they went from number 7 in the ratings to number 1 within months. Make no mistake, this was a very commercial company. Sure, they occasionally ran charity drives on air and sponsored junior football, but the owners' primary motive was to increase the commercial value of their company so it would be more attractive to any media network looking to buy a radio station in this market.

What interested us though, was the fact that the owners were very purpose-driven. They believed they had a fantastic bunch of talented, passionate people on staff who really understood radio. They felt genuinely frustrated for their staff that all that ability and love for radio was being wasted, and frustrated for themselves that all that ability and love for radio wasn't delivering a financial return.

They wanted to find a single, unifying goal that would unleash their potential, for both the human benefits of pride and career fulfilment and for the commercial benefits of a more valuable company. They just weren't prepared to lie and deceive and manipulate people to get there. They knew that what authentically drove them should be good enough. It just had to be pointed in the right direction. Which is what my company did for them.

The bottom line is they didn't have to run a business *and* give 10 per cent of their profits to the poor just so they could call themselves a purpose-driven company. And neither do you. Helping the poor is a fantastic, honourable ambition. But if that's not what motivates you, it's okay. You can still run a purpose-driven company and help create a more honourable kind of capitalism.

Put simply, honesty is the only minimum non-negotiable folks. It's the price of entry to a purpose-driven world and you must embrace it. Altruism is optional and while it may have broader benefits for the world, it's a choice. Think of it as True Purpose having two levels of proficiency: basic and advanced.

the basic impact of true purpose

At its core, purpose-driven thinking is simply aligning your business practices with your actual motive. So you can tell the truth to your consumers. And your employees. And your investors. And their families. And society at large. So you can commercially benefit from the new generation of educated, connected consumers who are tired of being tricked. So you can sleep at night. So you can be proud when you tell your kids what you do for a living. So you can contribute to a better kind of capitalism.

Purpose-driven companies aim for respect for what they genuinely believe in, not some kind of fake sainthood for simulating what they've found out consumers want. In doing this, purpose-driven companies choose to stop pretending their product is any better than it actually is, they stop exaggerating service claims, they stop trying to bribe consumers to like them. Instead, they put all their energy into proving that an authentic motive delivers genuine benefits, true innovation and real value.

So that's where True Purpose begins: by telling the truth about why you're doing what you're doing. If you're telling everyone the truth about your genuine motivation for being in business, congratulations! You're a purpose-driven company.

Let me give you an extreme example. Imagine you're a used-car dealer. Pretend you know in your heart of hearts that you have no special interest in the car itself. And while you derive a small amount of gratification from helping people find exactly the right car for them, it's not your primary motivation. You started your car yard to make money and be your own boss. And yet for years you've pretended to every customer who walked in the door that you love cars, that you love the feeling of watching a customer drive out in a car that's just right for them. You did this because you learned, along with every other used-car dealer in the world, that this is what people want to hear.

Then one day while you're out in the yard turning back the clock on a beat-up Chevy, you get struck by lightning and decide to start telling people the truth about why you sell used cars. You change your slogan from 'I love cars and car buyers' to 'I love the money I make from selling cars'.

You may think this admission would instantly turn off potential buyers. But think about it. We all believe that most car dealers only pretend to like us. There's a reason they have an age-old global reputation for being fakes. So what do you think would happen if one used-car dealer — you — started telling the truth? If you came right out and said, 'Yes, you're right. No more pretending. The big secret that everyone knew anyway is finally out. I'm only in this for the money'.

But then you said, 'But you know what? This is actually good news for you, the car buyer. If I want to make as much money as I can every year until I retire, I need to make sure I sell you a good car at a fair price. So you'll come back again and again. My financial goals are dependent on you being happy. And telling your friends. If I wanted to make as much money as I can I'd be stupid to sell you a dodgy vehicle. Or rip you off on the price.

Or give you bad service. Or not take your complaints seriously. So come on down to Rich Pete's Car-o-rama and help me make money by looking after you better'.

While I may disagree with your ambition, I genuinely believe you would be contributing to a better kind of capitalism. There'd be none of the pretence that currently creates so much suspicion about used car companies' motives. There'd be no feeling among customers of being treated like gullible fools. And if every business owner followed suit there'd be no reason to be wary and cynical of the whole concept of free enterprise.

Eventually, though, I think you'd be sitting in your car yard enjoying the success that truth has given you, but asking yourself, 'Do I have a better truth?'

the ultimate impact of true purpose

The ultimate possibility of True Purpose is greater than just telling the truth. Once we realise that telling the truth has a beautifully counter-intuitive commercial appeal, a lot of us will eventually ask ourselves, 'Could I advance to a better truth? Is there a higher ideal I could be aiming for that would give me an even more fulfilling life than the one I get from being truthful?'

There are a lot of people out there thinking this right now. You may be one of them. I hope so. Because where purpose-driven thinking really starts to cook is when your genuine motivation for running a business has a broader win–win for society. When the truth about what motivates you and your business doesn't just benefit you and your customer, but has a knock-on benefit that contributes to society. That adds to our world, instead of only taking from it.

The TOMS brand is an extreme example of an organisation's entire business model being based on a triple-win: customer satisfaction, commercial success *and* societal good. For every product you buy from TOMS they give a comparable product for free to someone in need elsewhere in the world. Doing good is not just an honourable side effect, it's the company's entire reason for being (more on this incredible company later).

While I love case studies like TOMS, I'm wary that if only these 'perfect purpose stories' are spotlighted by the media, all those misguided CEOs out there will keep believing that purpose always means philanthropy. And they'll disregard it as an effective business tool. Perhaps at this point we need a more balanced example.

Let me quickly tell you about Zappos, the insanely successful online retailer. Here's a company that started with a motivation no nobler than to simply help people enjoy their jobs. They figured if their staff were enjoying their work, they would serve their customers better. In the category of online sales, where the customer is invisible and therefore easy to treat like a number, this seemed like a pretty good win–win. But what happened was a remarkable ripple effect that's resulted in hundreds of thousands of people challenging their distrust of corporations.

By throwing out those horrible stilted scripts most companies use in their phone sales department, Zappos staff were free to behave like humans. They were able to actually converse with their customers, listen to their needs and empathise with their problems. There were no time limits given for calls, no minimum numbers of customers to serve per hour, and every operator had the authority to spend up to $50 of the company's money if they felt the customer warranted compensation for a late delivery or the pain of having to return a product.

Zappos staff were also free to decorate their sales rooms and warehouses at Halloween and Christmas and Valentine's Day. They had a super-active social club organising all kinds of spontaneous, fun events. They had a management hierarchy that was inclusive and ego-free, where ideas could come from any employee and be considered as worthy as those from the owners. No-one had the big corner office. No-one had the good parking bay.

The impact of all this freedom went way beyond the job satisfaction of the staff members themselves. What Zappos found was that this approach had an amazing knock-on effect at home. Their employees were happier at the end of the day. They didn't go home grumpy, or kick the cat. This authentic business strategy actually encouraged a happier family life. Which in turn helped their employees sleep better and be more confident and want to keep fit. Which in turn made them more productive at work. You could even argue that Zappos helped reduce the incidence of alcohol and drug abuse in their employees' homes.

And of course, the icing on the cake was the fact that this approach was the perfect business strategy to drive terrific long-term sales in their category — online retail — a category notorious for terrible customer service and false promises. It also led to lower cost per acquisition, lower customer churn, higher staff retention, lower recruitment costs, higher quality control, and so on.

So you see, you can be purpose-driven by being a used-car dealer who simply tells the truth about what motivates them, with a limited knock-on effect out into society. And you can also be purpose-driven by embracing a higher ideal and aligning your organisation's behaviour to it, with a massive knock-on effect out into society.

It's your choice. Just don't be fooled into thinking that True Purpose means you have to be a saint.

i want my why!

Right about now you may be sitting there thinking, 'Yes! I love this way of thinking. But what's my True Purpose? I must know!' Trust me, you'll find out. The important thing right now is to learn the pattern of behaviour that occurs when people in business follow their True Purpose. And what happens when they don't.

We need to look at the theory of The Circle together and see if we agree (you and I) about how the world works now. We need to listen to the stories of other people first, before we look inside ourselves.

I felt this was the most useful way to structure the book to help people make real change in their lives. Not just give us all a quick thrill with some optimistic thinking, then watch as we drift back to the daily grind. I believe we humans have inside us enormous potential to bring something good into the world, and to make a good living from doing it. That potential often lays dormant inside us, tragically untapped by conventional business practice.

But finding that potential, naming it, describing it and then applying it is hard. It's fantastically exciting and rewarding, but it's hard. Intimidating even. You've got to be really honest with yourself about what you love, what you hate, what you find unfair in the world and what you find joyous. You've got to be brave about the implications on your current business or job. And you've got to be ready to sacrifice money or fame or comfort.

So, in order to build up the courage and confidence you're going to need to see this thing through, I felt it was best we sneak up on it. Let me set the context for you about why The Circle works so well in today's world. Let's see if you and I agree.

In fact, my hope is that during this first part, you'll not only be agreeing, you'll be feeling something rising inside you. An energy for change. A drive to find out what you were born for. And that's just what you'll need if you're going to complete the exercises in the second part, find your Why and then bring it to life.

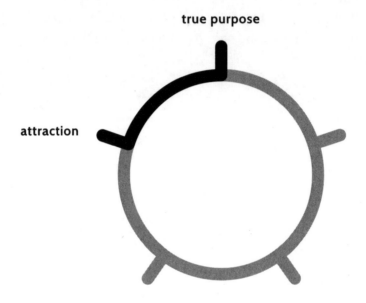

figure 3.1 - the second point on the circle, attraction

③ attraction

The first thing you notice when you know your True Purpose is its effect on other people. If you explain your purpose with passion and honesty — vulnerability even — a lot of people will 'catch' it.

What I mean by that is, instead of just nodding in agreement to signify a level of understanding, like people do when you're explaining a functional thought, it's as though something gets switched on behind their eyes. Like a narrow beam of light shining through a window that's opened just a little. I think the source of that light is that person's innermost authentic beliefs. It's faint because our core beliefs are often hidden away deep inside us. But that little light is actually a powerful fuel for a better kind of capitalism and it's incredibly exciting and rewarding when you spot it. Especially when it's your truth that makes it appear.

Sometimes I also notice a person's expression become slightly wistful, and they may smile. Sometimes they're not even aware of it. But I notice it and it happens a lot. Even in the most dour business person. In fact, these unconscious reactions have become one of my little tests as to whether or not I'm communicating a genuine True Purpose.

I think what's happening is that they're beginning to open up parts of their brain other than the logical bits (you can tell I'm no scientist, but stick with me on this). I think what I'm seeing is the authentic human coming forward, the primitive self that has an innate desire to serve an exciting higher ideal, with a broader benefit for them and their society.

I believe what I'm seeing in that moment is the thrill of possibility. They're already beginning to share your journey by instinctively considering some of the good things that might happen as a result of your True Purpose being enacted.

why does true purpose touch people?

Beyond the thrill of realising you can tell the truth in business and still succeed, I believe True Purpose connects with us at a deep level because we humans have a hole inside us that can only be filled by serving a formidable idea — an idea that creates something new and beneficial in the world. I think we acquire enormous satisfaction from being a part of something good, not just something necessary. Something that benefits humankind, not just ourselves or management or shareholders.

It seems to me that throughout our childhood and early adulthood we're often told by society that happiness comes from getting a good job, rising to a more senior position, or being able to buy certain things like an SUV and a house with three widescreen TVs. We're taught that this should fulfil us, but it often doesn't. Ask any 90 year old what a fulfilling life looks like and the answer usually isn't buying the right watch. Instead, it's what every young person already knows before they become mired in the complexities of adult life: that life is about being yourself, pursuing your inborn curiosity and making something happen in the world.

Let me provide some support for that point of view. My company once did some research among final-year university students. We asked them to write down in just one short sentence what they wanted when they left university and started the whole process of building a career.

The answers the students gave were incredibly consistent, even down to the wording: 'I want to make a difference'. And no, there was no collusion among the students; this was a confidential task, conducted in isolation and with each response sealed in an envelope.

Of course, each of those students may have had their own long-form definition for the word 'difference', but I think you can agree that their intent is clear. More and more, the coming generations of business owners, of civil leaders, of heads of social enterprises want to be the ones to cause a ripple effect of benefit in society that goes beyond simply 'making a living'.

I think that's why the light-behind-the-eyes effect I speak of happens so often, even with people who are seemingly conservative and set in their ways. And the more you can unfold the knock-on effects of your True Purpose beyond the basic structure of the business, the more people will catch it.

hiring on purpose

When you communicate your True Purpose to the world — and particularly when you share with the world what you believe is possible as a result, for your company, your industry and society as a whole — you'll attract business partners and employees who are inspired by that vision.

And just as importantly, you won't attract those who aren't.

Yes, I'm sorry to have to tell you this, but not everyone is going to get misty-eyed and evangelical when you explain your amazing purpose-driven business to them. One of the first things your True Purpose will do is polarise people. But that's a good thing. Seriously.

I told you earlier that pursuing a purpose-led life takes confidence, commitment, resilience and bravery. The polarised reaction to your True Purpose among the humans you'll need to start and grow a business will be the first major test of those qualities.

It's almost guaranteed that in your first rounds of explaining your True Purpose someone will poo-poo it. Maybe even someone you highly respect, or need.

This.

Is.

A.

Good.

Thing.

Why? Because your purpose will never be fully realised, and you will never gain ultimate fulfilment from your career and life, if you try and achieve it with people who don't get it.

It's absolutely critical that your core team gets it. That they sniff possibility in the air and chase it. Because implementing True Purpose takes enormous self-belief. You'll be forging a path into the unknown. You'll be venturing into territory that's counter to the current convention. All change begins this way.

no staff? no problem

For the sake of explaining how The Circle works, don't worry about whether or not you'll have employees, or how many, or when. Let's just explore what happens when people start a purpose-driven business. Because what we're actually exploring here is a better kind of capitalism: a process that delivers a win–win for everyone, not just the privileged few.

It's my belief that any purpose-driven business, when implemented properly, will grow. And will require staff. But it's not essential in this section of the book to buy into that. Just go with the process and see what you think.

explorers lead

It often helps to look at Attraction from the point of view of an explorer. Inviting potential partners and employees to better serve a certain category of business, or meet an unmet need, or go up against big companies in order to deliver better value to people is like a middle-ages explorer assembling the townsfolk on the beach and saying, 'I think there's a better place for us on the other side of that ocean. I can't see it, but I can sure explain it to you and I can paint you a picture of what life could be like there, and why that would be so much better than life here — with more freedom, fairer leadership, healthier food and a decent future for our families'.

Being disgruntled citizens struggling under the thumb of a feudal lord, they'll invariably cheer and applaud your vision. And as all the praise dies down and the assembled villagers look up at their inspiring leader with that light in their eyes, you'll explain that you're glad the people are so excited by this purpose — that they're so motivated to achieve that goal — because it's going to take some effort to achieve it. 'It won't be easy,' you'll say. 'We'll be going into uncharted waters. There'll be storms and sea creatures. We may run out of food or water. It would be far easier to stay in the current village, under the current system of abuse and inequality. But if you're motivated by the shared ambition, by the possibility, you'll join me in this worthy quest and we'll face the challenges together in a spirit of shared optimism and belief.'

All great explorers tended to lay the risks on the line like that. Right at the outset. To issue the invitation for something better as an unadorned challenge. Because they knew the last thing an explorer needed when leading people into the unknown is a lack of resilience. A subconscious quit clause born of doubt.

My favourite example is Ernest Shackleton. This is the wording of an ad he supposedly placed in the *London Times* to recruit the crew for his journey to the South Pole. (I write *supposedly* because nobody has ever actually been able to find such an ad in any newspaper of that era. But I love it all the same. And I'm happy to use it for effect here because I think you'll get what I get from it.)

MEN WANTED

For hazardous journey, small wages, bitter cold, long months of complete darkness, constant danger, safe return doubtful, honour and recognition in case of success.

As a more real-world example, if my business partner and I had written an ad for our purpose-driven ad agency right at the start, knowing what we know now, it would have read like this:

> ### *MEN & WOMEN WANTED*
>
> For hazardous journey into purpose-driven capitalism, no fancy offices, no company cars, awards unlikely in first few years, long days and late nights re-educating corporate Australia, constant ridicule from other ad agencies, a new future of trust and value for advertising industry in case of success.

I have a feeling we might have attracted our best staff a lot earlier. What would your 'Wanted' ad say?

people who want what you want

Let's say you've just started your purpose-driven company and you're delivering a keynote speech at an industry event and a lot of the people on your employee wish list are attending.

The truth you have to accept right now is that you might not attract the smartest lady in the room.

In order to truly innovate in your industry and deliver the new kinds of products and services that will solve that unmet need that's driving you, you're going to need staff who want this as much as you do. Averagely skilled humans who have a strong belief in your True Purpose will deliver far more category innovation than highly skilled staff with only a shallow business-like conviction to your purpose.

I say this because I've seen it happen time and time again. There's a unique power produced from the synergy of people engaged in a united mission. Especially a united mission against something they all believe, from the bottom of their hearts, is broken in the world. Even if that broken thing is simply the way people engage with a product.

learn from a nerd

My company once worked with a small internet provider. They were a feisty challenger brand going up against the two big phone companies that dominated the Australian market. Our client had a lot of smart people working for them but they had grown their internet brand in a small regional market. And small regional markets have shallow talent pools. They didn't have the endless suites of Harvard-qualified executives recruited from all over the world like the phone companies had. Nor did they have their nine-figure media budgets. Or the huge social media team. Or the massive sports sponsorships.

But guess what? That didn't really matter. Because when we dived inside this little internet brand to find out what was special and different about them, we found that everyone from the boardroom to the mailroom was united by two powerful forces:

- *A shared belief that the internet is the most incredible invention in human history.* That it's bigger than the Gutenberg printing press, which for centuries has been repeatedly named by historians as humankind's greatest invention. The passionate folk who worked for our client fervently believed that the internet would be the thing that made the entire world more equitable. That took the power of knowledge out of the hands of government leaders and media barons and put it into the hands of the people. And that the resulting explosion of creativity, self-expression and human connection would make for a better world.

- *A burning desire to liberate this incredible invention from the blinkered grasp of phone companies.* In our client's eyes phone companies were old-fashioned organisations that didn't fully understand the insane potential of this awesome invention. What's more, this small internet provider feared these old phone companies might seek to manipulate the internet's true potential for their own corporate ends. Our rebellious little internet crusaders believed that the big phone companies had been gifted control of selling the internet to Australians by default, and that people would not be served well because big phone companies didn't know how to give people a great experience of this new technology.

Everyone they recruited had to embody those two sentiments. For real. You couldn't just learn the company's mantra in order to get picked. You can't fake this stuff. You're either in or you ain't.

So even though this small challenger brand wanted desperately to grow and compete with the big guys, it didn't matter to them whether or not their new managers and staff had worked for other telcos, or whether they had MBA certificates on their wall, or whether they were the sharpest dresser or the snappiest presenter. All that seemingly important 'big-business stuff' didn't matter.

In fact, many of the people who ran this company were actually sceptical of those qualities because they feared that would lead them to become like those big phone companies (which is why I loved working with them).

So guess what happened when this super-passionate, super-united bunch of net nerds all got together around a crazy mission to liberate the internet from the blinkered grasp of two big old phone companies?

Yep. They created amazing innovations in product design and service delivery:

- They started building their own broadband network so they weren't beholden to the phone conglomerates who controlled most of the telephone exchanges that the broadband ran through.

- They created broadband packages that made sense to people; that didn't blind them with techno-babble or small print; that didn't hide any strings that might be attached to a tempting offer.

- They gave their products simple, friendly names that made the emerging technology more accessible to the average householder. Whereas a big phone company would try and impress people with a name like The Ultra Router 5000, these guys would call it JOE.

- They filled their call centres with passionate geeks and let them talk to customers in their own style. No scripts, no time limits, no pressure to 'always be closing'.

These very innovative, very human ideas were invariably harder to implement and delivered slightly less short-term business efficiency. But they were more commonsense and made things easier for people. They made for an enjoyable customer engagement, and critically, were all borne of a genuine desire to give people a better experience of the internet.

And what that recruitment strategy delivered was outstanding growth (the highest in the entire category), less customer churn (the lowest in the entire category), higher staff satisfaction, and more. They went from unknown challenger brand to the number-3 brand in the market in two years. Before those big old phone companies knew it, there was a cool, contemporary 'people's brand' nipping at their heels and stealing market share.

I feel I should point out that our client achieved a lot of their industry scale by acquiring other independent telcos along the way. They bought customers as much as won them from the big guys. But each time they absorbed another brand into theirs, they transformed the workforce with their True Purpose — they kept the likeminded souls and let the naysayers go.

The strength of their True Purpose to attract the right people and rally them around their mission in life was so consistent that their company remained a tribe of passionate, talented net nerds even as it grew from one regional base to a massive company with offices in five countries.

They even sent dedicated teams to every new overseas call centre to induct them into their purpose. Critically, this team almost always included their CEO, the ultimate holder of authentic organisational purpose in any company.

And hey, I want to make it clear, this wasn't about brainwashing anyone. This was about sharing a genuine desire to change the world and then drawing a line from that desire to the job of every employee in the company.

true purpose is contagious

True Purpose works because there's something going on below the surface. Something subtle and anthropological.

When a group of people we call a company find their True Purpose and pursue it with passion, it generates creativity and opportunity and optimism. Which generates a kind of commercial energy that people don't just observe and understand, they catch it. It gets inside them.

Not just owners and staff. True Purpose gets inside your customers too.

Because you're sharing a new quest with them that's built on honourable self-belief, that they see you pursue with rigour and bravery, and that they see has a win–win for them too. These are the same reasons people join clubs and societies and even cults — because these are collections of likeminded humans who have found a more attractive mutual benefit than the one-sided relationship we tend to have with commercial entities.

And because this unifying purpose is based on truth, you don't have to work so hard to communicate it. It springs so naturally from within you that it comes out in the way you look and behave, not just what you say. It's the sparkle in your eyes. The way your mouth turns up at the corners when you speak. That body language sends subtle, primitive cues to other humans.

This is what people around you first catch — before the rational support for it, before the left side of our brains puts logic and meaning to the feelings we're experiencing. I'm not an anthropologist or expert in semiotics (the study of subconscious messaging), but I've seen this time and again, sometimes in the most dour and resolute businessmen and women. And it's incredibly powerful. There's a momentum that comes from True Purpose that's hard to fathom.

true purpose powers progress in a time of change

It continues to be the buzzword of business the world over: change.

Our company needs to change.

Our industry is rapidly changing.

The whole world is changing.

If we don't change we're dead.

Change management is the key.

Yada.

Yada.

Yada.

The truth is, a tiny minority of humans like change. The rest like to talk about it. And they like to pretend to be open to it. But real change is scary. So most humans resist. And they resist in a very passive–aggressive manner. That is, what they say about change and how much they genuinely embrace it are two totally different things.

True Purpose removes that resistance to change. Because it triggers a primitive desire inside of us. A desire to move on, to make a difference, to contribute to something larger than ourselves. It's how we grow as humans.

So people will actually volunteer to do it. They don't have to be pushed kicking and screaming into that new world you know you have to lead them into. They'll race you for it.

what do you think so far?

How's your head? Is it nodding? Are you agreeing with these observations and stories? Maybe even feeling something rising inside you? The reason I ask is because I don't want this book to be only about imparting knowledge like a one-way flow of information from my laptop to your brain.

I want it to be about making something happen inside you. I want it to be about more than just new learning residing in your memory banks. I want it to unlock something inside you, to grab a belief about the world that you may be ignoring and bring it back to the surface, to awaken a dormant ambition.

This book is more about what you want than what I think. It's about finding the evidence for—and the words to describe—what you always knew deep down was right and true and honourable and important.

So I figure we're in this together. Me, the writer, and you, the reader.

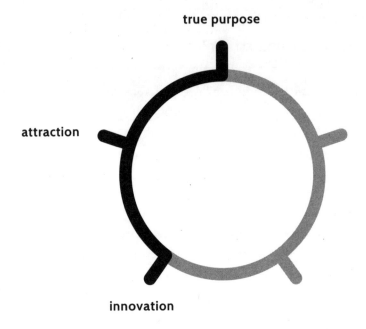

figure 4.1 – the third point on the circle, innovation

(4) innovation

So what happens when a bunch of likeminded people get together to form a company, motivated by a purpose that genuinely inspires them to achieve a higher ideal?

You get genuine innovation. When we humans are driven from the core of our being to change something in the world — to make something good happen — we can be extraordinarily innovative. We have the capacity to become brave creative thinkers with the tenacity and confidence to find new ways. We're driven not just by visions of money and fame and growth and success, but by the allure of changing the way the world works. For the better.

This is the key benefit of True Purpose. Authentic human motivation. Because only authentic motivation generates authentic innovation. And innovation is what drives business growth.

Let me give you a quick example. From an industry you're probably not expecting: motorbikes.

the incredible mr honda

In the years following the end of the Second World War (1945), Japan was getting back on its feet and consumer goods were beginning to boom. Its people were firmly rejecting the feudal, militaristic culture of the past and embracing capitalism and economic growth as a more honourable path to being a respected country in the world.

Hundreds of new companies in Japan began making Western-style products, especially in the areas of electronics. Most of them started by imitating the known brands from the United States and Europe. That's how they learned and evolved their own thinking. But they had a lot to learn and the early products were poor quality. The term 'Made in Japan' was a punch line right up until the late 1960s. I distinctly remember saying it as a child (it soon changed to 'Made in Hong Kong', but that's another story).

During this period there was a man who took a different approach. His name was Soichiro Honda. Unlike the dozens and dozens of motorcycle companies popping up, Mr Honda didn't want to just make copies of Moto Guzzi and Triumph. He was motivated by something else. He was motivated by the desire to help his fellow countrymen get back on their feet. And when he looked at the motorbikes being made by the known brands around the world — the ones that so many of his fellow company owners were desperately trying to copy — he saw that they were actually not very well suited to the Japanese market.

Their frames were too big, having been designed for the wide, open roads and spacious car parks of post-war Europe and America. Japan's roads were narrow and twisty and its cities crowded, even after they'd been rebuilt following extensive war damage. What's more, Western engines could afford to be big and thirsty as they came from countries where fuel was no longer rationed — unlike Japan, where fuel was still rare and expensive. Western mechanical components and electronics were also quite complex and required regular servicing by trained mechanics, whereas Japanese customers needed endless reliability and the ability to service their vehicles themselves.

All of which meant that millions of Japanese people could not afford to buy a motorcycle and so could not get around. They had to rely on rickety old bicycles. This was especially detrimental to small-business owners, who couldn't get enough of their farm produce to the markets, or couldn't deliver their goods to wholesalers or customers.

And so Mr Honda was driven to innovate. He bought up a big supply of tiny 50cc two-stroke engines that had once powered generators for military radios and re-engineered them so that people could attach them to their bicycles. This instantly increased the distance they could travel and the loads they could carry, boosting their productivity and therefore their ability to earn a living and grow their businesses.

This little engine was called the *bata bata* because of the sound it made. He sold thousands. When he ran out of those engines, Mr Honda and his growing team of likeminded engineers designed their own engines and fitted them to a stronger frame, so people could move up from a motorised bicycle to an actual motorcycle, again increasing the distance they could travel and the loads they could deliver.

That was in 1949. By 1964 Honda was the largest manufacturer of motorcycles in the world. And when Mr Honda entered the vehicle market, he was inspired to take exactly the same approach. His first four-wheel vehicle was a tiny pick-up truck powered by one of his motorcycle engines. The engine capacity qualified it to be sold in a much cheaper tax bracket, instantly allowing millions of small-business owners in Japan to compete with bigger companies and grow their businesses.

I can't help but think how exciting it would have been to work for Honda at this time. Imagine a young, talented engineer who wanted to be the best they could be and to use their skill and passion for mechanical engineering to not just make a profit for a company, but to make a difference for people. Can you imagine the level of inventiveness possible in such a company?

On top of the fulfilment that Mr Honda and his staff would have undoubtedly felt on a human level, this approach was tremendously commercial. Honda out-performed every other motorcycle brand in the country on sales, profit and eventually shareholder return. Today, Honda is the second-largest vehicle manufacturer in Japan, behind Toyota, and is still driven by an authentic desire to innovate, captured in its long-time slogan, The Power of Dreams.

This is a lesson you'll see repeated often in this book: following a True Purpose is not only a way to sleep better at night and be able to look your children in the eye and tell them their mum or dad is following their dream, it's a way to unleash incredible commercial viability. Almost always, as in the Honda story, this happens by having an authentic purpose that inspires others to be their best.

phoney motivation delivers phoney innovation

Before I started my own company I spent 20 years or so as a creative director in various ad agencies. I was asked countless times to stand in front of a company's staff and present a new, shiny brand promise that their bosses wanted them to be motivated by. It was hardly ever what they were genuinely motivated by ... y'know, as living, breathing humans with hearts as well as brains. It was hardly ever what the owners of their company were even motivated by. Rather, this new trademarked slogan I was presenting was invariably what some research company had recommended they be motivated by because they'd found out that's what their customers wanted.

I remember once standing beneath a colossal film screen on the stage of an indoor arena and telling a thousand insurance company employees that they needed to be happier. Like, 'Now, please'. Because the very expensive

TV campaign they were about to see, which was produced following a very expensive research study and was launching the next day with a very expensive media buy, was telling the general public that this insurance company was the happiest. And if those citizens call you up tomorrow and you're not actually happy, the whole thing will be a waste of money.

With the stage lights in my eyes I couldn't see anyone in the audience. But I swear I could feel the disconnect. The lack of authenticity hung in the air. Oh, they tried their best to go along with it. This is what you do when you're a loyal employee of a big brand. And it all made perfect sense: 'My bosses have spent millions of dollars to find out what our customers want and it's up to me to deliver on that, otherwise it won't work. Okay, let's go. I can pretend to be happy. Rah rah. Yay us'. Cue the big, expensive telly ad.

But standing on that stage that night, I knew my campaign was ultimately going to fail.

Because.

They.

Just.

Didn't.

Believe.

It.

I could tell they totally understood it. But did they believe it? Did they genuinely believe that this insurance company was founded on the principles of being happy? Was this insurance company's whole business model shaped around the notion of staff and customers living a happier life? Of course not. They were just like the other insurance companies. Their products, their corporate culture, everything this company made or did was motivated by financial return to shareholders.

Of course, as part of delivering that financial return, the company's owners would have very specific views on customer satisfaction and staff happiness. But was that the number-one driver of their entire business?

Nope. Otherwise, they wouldn't have kept callers on hold for 15 minutes. They wouldn't have offered new customers a discounted car insurance premium without first offering it to their existing customers. They wouldn't have given their staff a sad little lunchroom with a 1970s-era Coffee-Matic machine. I could go on.

As an employee, if you don't believe that the promise your company is making to the world is true, you can pretend to support it. For a while. But lack of authentic motive always comes out in the end. It's just too hard to keep up that pretence every hour of every working day. Especially in customer service. Why do you think we all experience so many moments of poor customer service, even from companies that are spending hundreds of millions of dollars on staff training and ad campaigns about serving people better? Because the whole thing is one big fake performance.

Much worse, though, if you feel as an employee that you're only acting out a consumer benefit, it's highly unlikely that you'll genuinely innovate in your category of industry. We humans have a huge capacity for inventiveness. But so much of what business calls innovation these days is simply a marginal improvement on the norm.

One suburban restaurant creates the first Pasta Tuesday and the next thing you know the whole category is innovating with Surf & Turf Fridays, $5 Pint Sundays, and so on. One car manufacturer brands one of their 4WDs an SUV and 10 years later every car brand on the planet has 'innovated' their way to the Mini SUV, the Super Urban Utility Vehicle, the Luxury Utility Vehicle, and so on.

When your motivation is entirely based on what others want, the level of product and service innovation you can generate will be limited.

Because the cognitive process will be, 'Well if that's what people want and if I was a company dedicated to that, then what I'd probably do is ...'

It's all surface. There's no heart. There's no vision.

Henry Ford is credited with saying, 'If I had asked people what they wanted when I started my company, they would have said faster horses'. Of course, he didn't ever ask them. Rather, he was driven by the need *he* saw in society. He saw every other car manufacturer looking at what Karl Benz had invented and trying to make it a bit better. Ford looked away from the car industry and into society. And what he saw was not only an unmet need for a simple, rugged, affordable car to help people get places, but also a tremendous commercial opportunity.

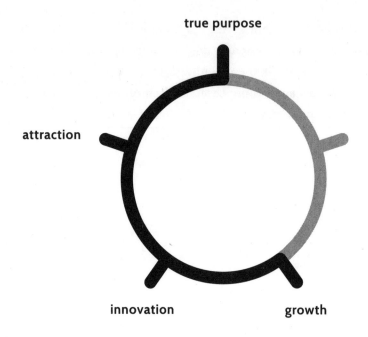

figure 5.1 - the fourth point on the circle, growth

(5) growth

When you're motivated to run a business with a higher ideal than just money, and that higher ideal attracts a dedicated tribe of people around you and inspires them to create imaginative new products and services, guess what happens?

Success.

Sales.

Market-making.

Growth.

The fourth point on The Circle is all about consumers. And whether or not they'll ultimately buy into your purpose. So, effectively, this chapter is all about the commercial viability of your purpose. The rubber hitting the road. The true test of whether you and your tribe are going to monetise all that truth and passion and build a financially viable business together, or whether you're just going to remain a kind of fun club of compatible souls — fulfilled, but broke.

The good news, right up front, is that I haven't yet seen a properly expressed True Purpose for a commercial business that didn't have great economic viability. The potential for authentically motivated people to attract likeminded people in the form of paying customers is extraordinary. Let me present to you one of my favourite purpose stories as Exhibit A.

the little dairy company story

One of the best case studies for demonstrating commercial success through embracing True Purpose is that of a dairy company in my home city. This little company defied the odds in a difficult consumer category and achieved something remarkable simply by committing to what authentically motivated them as humans first, and to the conventions of business second.

This case study is quite a bit longer than most of the stories in this book. But it's a real cracker, so dig in.

Let me set the scene (I'd like you to understand the context within which this particular purpose-driven change happened, because your own situation may well throw up similar barriers).

My branding agency is headquartered in a small regional market. The population base is just over two million. It's the kind of place the giant dairy brands like Fonterra and Parmalat would call a 'niche market'.

In this market lives a 100-year-old dairy company with a proud heritage for quality and innovation. It used to deliver fresh milk to just about every household every morning, with fresh milk sourced from dairy farms only an hour from the city.

It used to provide free milk to primary schools in cute little one-third pint bottles that the kids drank at recess. It used to pioneer innovative new products like chocolate-flavoured milks and individually portioned yoghurts way before these things became mainstream. It used to team up with a local ice-cream factory to create delicious new ice-cream varieties decades before Häagen Dazs and Ben & Jerry's. It even used to print its own recipe books showing people how to use milk, cream and cheese in interesting, healthy ways.

Key words: *used to.*

All that great stuff stopped about twenty years ago when this little dairy company was bought by a multinational dairy brand headquartered in another country. At the time, my home city was growing rapidly on the back of a mining boom. Along with housing prices and freeway traffic, retail sales in fast-moving consumer goods (FMCG) were booming. To the extent where some number-cruncher on the other side of the planet thought the commercial viability was good enough to expand their dairy empire into this area.

So a multinational conglomerate bought our little regional dairy. And the smart, passionate people who worked for it soon became just another little red dot on the map of somebody's global dairy domain.

If you're picking up on a hint of sarcasm, well spotted. I get a little tetchy with stories like these. I'm willing to bet that the global dairy company bought my favourite little regional dairy on numbers and numbers alone. Sales, cost per sale, margins, assets and liabilities, production estimates, farm contracts, potential for cost-saving via scaling that a multinational can bring to a regional market, and so on.

I'm willing to bet that nobody from that global company or the brokerage firm they hired to do the deal ever came and visited the homes of the managers and staff and asked them over a glass of cold milk what they thought about dairy's role in society, about the obligation they might feel to the mothers of this region, about their desire to deliver healthy products free of chemicals, borne of a love for this magical substance called milk, about their empathy for the hard work and values of local dairy farmers, and about the commercial potential of their passion and imagination.

Of course not. Conventional business goes the other way around The Circle. It starts at Reward and works from there (more on that later in the book).

Soon enough, someone at the global HQ looked at the numbers and told our passionate little dairy company to stop making cheese because they could ship cheese in cheaper from somewhere else; and stop making those frivolous ice creams because they're not very profitable; in fact, don't make ice cream anymore at all; we can get that shipped in too. You guys just concentrate on milk because that has to be fresh. Oh, and yoghurt and cream — but if they don't sell double the numbers by June we may pull those too. Oh, and by the way, we need lots more milk powder for the growing Asian market and our sums show that shipping it from your side of the continent is going to be cheaper for us, so be prepared to become a serious milk powder producer.

On the surface these may seem like reasonable business decisions. But this book is about potential. The potential to make a difference in the world by harnessing our authentic human motivation to do good. I saw the impact of these decisions on the humans inside that little dairy company. And it wasn't good.

The whole company slowly changed from a friendly, imaginative dairy-of-the-people into a boring milk factory. They stopped inventing clever new ice-cream and milk products. They pretty much stopped inventing anything. Which meant they didn't have as many of the cool ad campaigns coming out that they were known for. Which meant they effectively stopped conversing with the locals. They also stopped hosting hundreds of giddy children through their factory every week on school tours, which were once famous because the tours always ended with an ice cream picked fresh off the production line. None of these things made enough business sense to the suits sitting thousands of kilometres away.

what happened next

So, to cut a long story short — and I think you know where this is going —
brand awareness slipped. Brand meaning evaporated. Sales slowed. Staff
turnover increased. And slowly but surely the vibe of this remarkable little
company was anaesthetised.

I think it's fair to mention that at the same time this was happening, three
other key factors were influencing this company's results. The first was
that other multinational dairy brands were entering this growing market
and as they did, they were buying market share to get established. Some
had bought small local brands of their own. Others just ran big, flashy
campaigns telling the locals that finally they were getting the benefit of their
brand's amazing dairy products, which so many millions of people all over
the world already had the privilege of enjoying. Others offered two-for-ones
and special launch discounts. You get the picture.

The second factor was the rise of supermarkets' own brands. The two
gargantuan supermarket corporations that dominate my country's grocery
category were racing each other to replace many known grocery brands on
their shelves with their own in-house versions. The dairy aisle was still a sea
of different logos, branding and packaging devices, but a growing majority
of the fridge space was taken up by the supermarkets' own labels.

And finally, like many FMCG categories, dairy was also experiencing an
explosion of boutique brands, all promising natural-this and organic-that.
Their prices were stratospheric, but the public — tired of mass-produced
blandness — were turning to these brands and trialling their products in
big numbers.

So you could argue that this little dairy company's falling sales were
understandable given these unique market conditions. What we eventually
found, however, was that the commercial deterioration of this brand was
primarily due to the deterioration of passion and self-belief among the
humans in the company.

no pain, no change

We often say at my branding company that the best time to work with a client to effect real change is when they're in pain. Declining sales. Low brand awareness. Failing ad campaigns. Because when we humans are in pain we're more likely to roll up our sleeves, take a deep breath and try something new. It's like when you have a bad back or tennis elbow. It hurts so bad you'll do anything the physio tells you to get rid of that pain. But as soon as the pain goes, you're somehow just not as eager to get up early every day and do those stretches.

So the only good thing that happened in this phase of the story is that when this little dairy company's sales and brand scores hit rock bottom, they were sold. And the new holding company came to my agency and asked, 'What do we need to do to turn this around?'

Our advice was simple: Get back to your True Purpose. We helped them surface and enunciate what genuinely motivated them to create such a terrific company in the first place (many of the staff had worked there for more than 30 years and had lived through the changes).

It's important to note here that we didn't invent a purpose for them. Our skill is in helping people to uncover what's already inside them. It's often very difficult to see because it's covered in layers of conventional business practice, management mantras, self-doubt and fear of failure. But it's always there. We simply use our various techniques to help people rediscover it, enunciate it and point it towards an end goal that unites everyone around a common journey. For the betterment of them, their staff, their staff's families, their company, their category, and almost always, society as a whole.

It's like finding the key to a magic toolbox. Our role is to give businesses the key, but it's their job to open up the box, take out the tools and get to work.

For this dairy company, the key was to stop allowing field research to be the only trusted determinant for the product (consumer trends, sales data, shifts in competitor market share, and so on). This was leading to a reactive mindset at the company. Their original passion for making great dairy products had mutated into a fear-based response to whatever consumers thought they wanted or whatever new product or promotion their competitors launched.

Remember Steve Jobs' belief that the customer should not get a vote in what a company believes the world needs? The key was to get back to the human need. And not just the humans buying the product. I mean the humans working at the dairy company; the ones with strong opinions about what products a dairy company should be making and even stronger passions about making them happen. Interestingly, many of these passionate people at the dairy company were mothers. And many of them admitted they didn't feed their children their own company's products. Not only were they embarrassed to admit that, but they were also ashamed.

That's some pretty insane passion being bottled up there. Excuse the pun. Picture it: here was a group of talented, smart, inventive food scientists with tremendous passion for making great-tasting, healthy dairy products that mums everywhere could afford to buy and feed their family every day. As an alternative to the cheap supermarket blands (spelling intentional) and the boutique brands that were delicious but you could only afford to buy once a month.

These amazing people knew how to make tasty, healthy, fresh dairy products in mass volumes that people could afford. And other amazing people in that company who also believed in the same values knew how to package it and distribute it and sell it. We enunciated it as 'making better dairy together'.

truth = growth

Guess what happened when all that genuine human passion was allowed to be unleashed? Everything started changing.

For a start, sales rocketed. Not just increased: rocketed. They saw a 56 per cent sales increase in the first new product they launched under the new, purpose-driven regime: a line of new, chemical-free yoghurts, averagely priced and with real fruit. Let me tell you, that's an almost unheard-of leap in sales. This sector has massive competition. It's one of the most crowded product categories, with a dozen brands all fighting for the shoppers' attention. And each brand has dozens of varieties.

The yoghurt aisle at your average supermarket is a kaleidoscope of logos and six-packs and brand icons and cartoon characters. Choosing yoghurt is such an overwhelming and potentially time-consuming task that our observational research, backed by global studies, shows that the average shopper spends five to six seconds making their yoghurt choice. Five to six *seconds*!

That means they're probably not even making a conscious decision. They scan the chaos of colour and pick the one that lights up some recognition receptor in their brain. The one with the gold shield. Or the pink cow. Or The Wiggles.

The truth is the average shopper buys their yoghurt by habit, not by conscious choice. And of all the barriers to changing a consumer's brand preference, human habit is the hardest. It's why we all complain about the big banks but still stick with them.

So to achieve a 56 per cent increase in sales in *that* category is a real record-breaking result. They went from number 6 in the sector to number 2 in just a few weeks. Better yet, at the time of writing this book a year later, they've stayed there.

Following this product's success, there were all kinds of industry studies made of the campaign's strategy and results. It was big news here, with some of the senior people from the dairy company being invited to share the story at marketing and dairy industry symposiums around the country. The campaign has since won awards around the world. So there's been a lot of collating of causes and effects, and a lot of measurements and numbers and charts and the occasional two-way matrix.

But for me, what I saw in this case study was very simple: the power of truth.

The humans at the dairy company said the truth was they didn't like the products they were being asked to make. And they thought the reason they weren't selling was not because of increased competition, but because they weren't good enough. After years of having their passion compromised, it was like they finally stood up and declared: 'The truth is if we serve the idea of creating dairy products that taste great, are as free from unnatural ingredients as we can possibly make them *and* are affordable enough to buy regularly, we think that will not only contribute to a better life for people but will make our company more commercially successful. Our truth is we want a win for the consumer and a win for us.'

And the humans who saw the launch campaign on TV and the newspaper stories about 'the dairy mothers wanting better yoghurt for their kids too' sat back and thought, 'Hang on a minute. I think that commercial brand might just be telling the truth'.

mums know

The key to the potency of True Purpose was crystallised for me one night in a little room in the suburbs of my home city before any of this little dairy company's new commercial success occurred.

We'd done all the work inside their company to surface their True Purpose: all the workshops and interviews; researching their history and fact-finding about their founders; and global studies of dairy companies and product development. We'd enunciated their True Purpose for them in a one-line creed and in a longer, more narrative manifesto. And we'd brought to life their incredible potential for innovation and market-making with examples of new products and services.

We'd presented all this to the client's working team and we'd tested its veracity with key management and staff. And everyone agreed we'd nailed it; we'd totally captured their reason for being. They were fired up and ready to go.

Now it was time for the second most important part of True Purpose: finding out if all that truth and vision and passion had commercial viability. In short, would the dairy-buying public buy into it? We approached this task by first studying dairy-buying trends in our region and around the world, by exploring sales data from our client and their competition, and so on.

But the part of testing commercial viability that I love the most is the human part: the co-creation groups we run.

And so it was that I found myself sitting in a small, dark room looking through a two-way mirror at eight women sitting around a table chatting with my business partner Ronnie on what the average mother thought of our little dairy company's true reason for being.

This is intimidating stuff. By this stage in the process, Ronnie and I are usually totally vested in our client's truth. We *want* it to be awesome. We can't not make it happen. We're usually so in love with its potential for triggering good change in the world that we feel an obligation to make it work.

So we have to be extra-professional in our approach to consumer research, and even to the bulldust-and-buzzword-free, co-creation style that we employ. We can't just go into a roomful of cynical consumers weary from decades of advertising and try to convince them of a True Purpose's worth. Nor can we just explain it to them and ask if they like it (as a lot of research companies unfortunately still do).

Why? Because people are innately herding animals. They can't help but go with the flock. If a nice man in a suit gives you a glass of wine and a snack and uses your first name a lot and smiles and asks politely if you like this idea that he has obviously spent a lot of time on — an idea that the other people in this room have already said they like — well yes, you'll probably nod and say you kind of like it too.

On the other hand, if the first respondents have had a bad day and that slick guy gives them the creeps, they'll probably work a little harder than normal to find fault in his concept.

Either way, you can't ever just ask people what they think. Especially if what you're asking them about is new and different. The truth is, a lot of the time we don't really know what we think. There are plenty of books out there explaining why humans believe they're making a logical decision when in fact they're giving an emotional response.

So what my company does in these co-creation sessions is put into the room a series of what we call provocations. Not to aggravate in a negative way, but simply to trigger a more human conversation. Then we watch. Even more than just listen. We watch whether or not each provocation is engaged with in a shallow, rational manner, or in a more heated, emotional manner.

Even if the content of a heated discussion is a negative reaction to the thing we're testing, we find that far more valuable to us than a positive reaction without any emotional engagement. Because it shows us the first emotional human response, not the unrealistic rational response. So we watch for whether people lean in on their chairs, waiting for their turn to share a passionate opinion, or whether they sit back and say little, or pontificate a purely logical stance.

This is the key to understanding True Purpose and harnessing its power for a commercial viability that's a win–win for business and society. You must always seek the most primitive human cause and effect.

The main provocation we put into that room of eight women that night was this: 'The great aunty you never knew you had has passed away and you've inherited the dairy company she owned'. We called it Newco and described roughly its size and the kinds of things it made.

After the titters and nervous chat died down (they all seemed very happy that this session was already more interesting than the focus groups they sometimes attended), we briefly explored their attitudes to milk and yoghurt and kids and cows and health and motherhood. Just to warm them up to the idea and establish that when you think about it, we all have opinions about dairy and milk that we could easily bring to the role of boss of our own dairy company.

We then explained to them that in their first two weeks as CEO of their great aunty's dairy company, they meet and talk with the most senior people in the company: the people who are mainly responsible for the invention, manufacturing and sale of their company's products.

here's the awesome bit

We then presented them with some quotes from those fictional conversations to see what they thought of the people working for them. Did they seem smart and driven? Were they passionate about their craft? Did they come across as people who might be motivated to create great dairy products?

The head cheese-maker's quote talked about how he samples each and every 20-kilogram block of uncut cheddar to ensure no cheese leaves their dairy that isn't totally, utterly, completely perfect.

In the quote from the head of distribution she said how seriously she takes her role in society, because milk is such an important building block for little growing bodies.

The quote from a production-line worker expressed how much he likes the smell of strawberries in the air when he gets to work each morning: the real strawberries they put in their yoghurt.

The ladies cautiously all agreed that yes, this company they've inherited seems like it has some terrific people working for it — people with a genuine passion for dairy, people with interesting ideas for new products, people with integrity who seem prepared to work harder than the average Joe (or Joanne) to ensure the company turns out quality dairy with fewer chemicals, and so on.

I say *cautiously* because even though we had engaged their human side with an irresistible story, they still suspected that we were just another couple of ad execs wanting them to like something we'd created. They still had their guard up. And I dare say they still thought they were listening to a piece of fiction, the usual exaggerated world of marketing spin.

What they didn't know was that these quotes were in fact verbatim quotes from actual interviews we'd done with real employees of our dairy client.

Once we told them these quotes were real, that these people existed at a genuine dairy company right here in their home city, and that none of what we'd just read out had been tampered with by a copywriter or spin doctor, the mood of the room changed. Dramatically.

Slowly but surely, they all leaned in. They wanted to know more. They were — shock, horror — *interested.* Genuinely interested. Not because they were getting paid $100 for their time and felt an obligation. Not because a nice man in a suit had charmed them (trust me, Ronnie can be quite charming). But because there was a truth in the room that resonated with them. A truth that they saw as important and valuable.

Because of that, these hardened, defensive consumers softened and opened up their hearts a little. I could almost see the truth and transparency seeping into the room like laughing gas.

This effect *is* the commercial viability of True Purpose.

Not some false contract where The Adman says to The Consumer, 'If I demonstrate to you that we know what you like, will you tell my client that you'll buy their product?'

When you find the win–win that is True Purpose — that tiny overlap where the circle of all that you want to achieve in the world touches the circle of all that people want in their lives — the consumer leans in.

You don't have to exaggerate it. You don't have to change it to meet other people's expectations. You just present your truth, full strength. And capitalism happens. Good capitalism.

Let's go back into that room and wrap up what happened in the rest of that session.

The women leaned in, but they were still wary. Of course, they said, they would love it if a commercial dairy company was driven by these people and these values. If it was real. Of course, they said, they'd consider buying this company's products over the ones they robotically buy now. If it was real. Of course, they said, they would trust this company's marketing communications more than a global brand's. If it was real. Of course, they said, they'd love to engage with a company like this in order to co-create the new and better dairy products that they wanted for themselves and their families.

If it was real.

Seriously, such was their scepticism about being sucked in yet again by marketing spin, we had to figuratively swear on the Bible that all this was true. And during the whole 90 minutes, they pestered us ceaselessly to reveal the name of this magical dairy company. Finally, we laid out on the table the logo of every dairy company operating in this market and asked them to see if they could pick it.

The obvious choices for such as passionate company were the small boutique brands. Less likely were the big multinationals. And somewhere in between, as a long shot, was our client's company.

When we finally revealed the name of our client, the mums all sat back in shock. Their overwhelming perception of our client had become that of a big, old, boring milk producer. So we knew we had work to do to make the entire population aware of this truth.

In the end, the reaction of all 32 mums we eventually had this conversation with gave us a lot of heart. By the close of each session, their position was the same: 'This seems true; this seems to be actually possible; and if it is, holy cow (excuse the pun again), this could change everything!'

from resistance to resistance fighters

You know you've had a meaningful co-creation session with consumers when they don't want to leave. When I was working at other ad agencies as a creative director, I'd watch as people in focus groups would almost sprint out the door at the end. But the mums in our dairy groups stuck around; they wanted to know more about this idea of a 'people's dairy' and they wanted to share more of the ideas that were popping into their own heads around it. It was like they'd stumbled across something they never thought was possible and they wanted more of it.

What we see time and again when we test the commercial viability of a client's True Purpose is that when you present your true motivation full strength, and when you explore the knock-on benefits to consumers and to the general public, your potential customer will catch your True Purpose in a surprisingly similar way to your staff.

They don't simply understand it. They don't simply receive the information about your brand. They're engaged by it. It gets inside them and lodges somewhere more precious than where they put other brands. They become recruits to your cause. That, right there, is enormous commercial opportunity.

Can you see The Circle starting to work its magic?

When you serve a higher purpose than only money, the money comes. But it comes in a way that feeds your soul, not just your bank account. Because you're telling your customers the truth. There need be no exaggeration, no spin, no manipulation, no mind control. None of the sneaky tricks that have for decades been giving capitalism a bad name.

What you offer the world has genuine value and it needs no gloss. The truth of its value shines out naturally. And people respond.

the monopoly of you

One of the most valuable outcomes of following The Circle is that the relationship you build with your customer becomes almost impossible to be replicated by competitors.

Because while anyone can copy the practical design of a product or service method, they can't copy that almost subconscious feeling of authentic caring that customers get from company employees who are genuinely motivated.

I want to use an unusual example here. When Formula 1 racing car brand McLaren ventured into the production of luxury sports cars, they were genuinely motivated by a True Purpose: to bring F1 standards of technology and engineering perfection to road cars. Not because their research department had found a gap in the market. Not because they'd done quantitative research that showed the luxury car buyer craved this. They did it because they genuinely felt that much of what passed for advanced engineering in the luxury sports car market was below par. As mechanical perfectionists and believers in the potential of advanced motoring technology to change people's experience of the supercar, they were almost compelled to explore an entirely new market.

The car they created was the McLaren F1. At its launch in 1991 it was widely described in the motoring press as the most significant motorcar built in nearly a century. It used advanced new materials, engineering and technology. It was lighter, faster and looked more dramatic. It was a unique motorcar borne of hundreds of decisions guided by a True Purpose.

But I don't want to talk about the car; I want to talk about the car's owner's manual. This one item is a brilliant example of how True Purpose cannot easily be copied.

Up until the McLaren F1, even the most expensive luxury sports cars came with a fairly standard owner's manual in their glove boxes. Sure, they might have boasted a leather cover, but the role of the manual remained the same: to explain how all the car's features worked so the new owner could make full use of what they had bought.

The McLaren F1 owner's manual, however, was a work of art. It featured intricate hand-drawn pencil illustrations of the car's key parts, printed on separate pages using the thick art paper that you'd usually only find in the finest reference books. It shared stories and quotes from the engineers that went beyond the technical into the personal, and even the emotional.

The manual came bound in a hard cover like a valuable art book, with gold leaf printing on the cover.

Who would ever make a manual like that? Why would any car manufacturer devote such enormous manpower and expense to such a seemingly unimportant part of the luxury car buying process? Why would their board approve losing money on an owner's manual? What CEO would be happy explaining that counter-intuitive decision to investors at the AGM?

I'll tell you who: a company that could draw a line from that insanely beautiful owner's manual all the way back to the True Purpose that drives them forward as a company, that will help them make a difference in the industry they love.

The lesson here is that unless a company is genuinely motivated from the very core of its existence to produce something extraordinary like that, it will most likely fail at it. Extraordinary cannot be faked. Maybe once, as a fluke. But eventually the weak, simulated bravery that comes with pretence snaps. The replica resolve at board level to sacrifice short-term profit for long-term achievement disappears.

These are the smartphone companies that go up against Apple ... but their operating system just doesn't react quite the same on the tip of your finger.

These are the online retail companies that go up against Zappos ... but just can't seem to replicate, year after year, Zappos' insane levels of authentic human customer service.

These are the discount airlines that go up against Southwest in the United States ... but just can't match the buzz of their aircrew or the innovation of their products and promotions.

They can simulate 95 per cent of how a purpose-driven competitor shows up in the world, but that last 5 per cent is just too hard. Because that last 5 per cent is the human factor. That indefinable, uncopyable expression of human will that comes from deep within.

And it's that last 5 per cent that will make your purpose-driven company a new kind of monopoly. And anytime you have a monopoly in business, you're likely to have great potential for success. But this time, instead of monopoly meaning a company applying an unfair level of control or domination across a category of smaller competitors, it will mean a company that's so unique that it has created its own category within a category.

on the defeat of deficiency advertising

When business owners embrace a powerful truth so they don't have to lie or exaggerate to consumers, one of the most satisfying side effects for our company is the continued eradication of what we call 'deficiency advertising'. That's when a company promotes a product in a way designed to make the consumer feel deficient as a human if they don't have it.

It's a subtle distinction, but it's an important one to grasp. Advertising is one of the main voices of free enterprise and I believe deficiency advertising is one of the biggest contributors to people's distrust of capitalism.

It works like this:

Instead of a men's deodorant brand saying to consumers, 'You will feel more self-confident if you use our product,' they say, 'Girls won't like you unless you use our product'.

It seems like a small shift in emphasis, but it's actually designed to prey on our innermost primitive fears as humans. Sophisticated marketing research can uncover all our insecurities and pinpoint the exact occasions that trigger them (those pictures of consumers with electrical nodes attached to their heads are real, folks). And in many categories of consumer goods, fear is a better sales tool than self-confidence and hope.

You see it everywhere:

- You won't be a worthy mother unless you feed your family Snibbo margarine.

- You won't be a cool career woman unless you drive a Tornado XL.

- You won't be seen as rich and successful unless you wear a Bravo watch.

- Your girlfriend will think you're a loser unless you buy her a Spiffi diamond.

They're rarely expressed as overtly as that, but the takeaway message from that carefully scripted and cast TV ad, or from that meticulously staged photograph, is loud and clear: you are deficient and only by buying a certain product will you be fully realised as a human.

This may have worked in the 1950s and 1960s when the number of advertisements being thrust at people was way lower. And the creative techniques being employed were fresher.

There was a famous long-running campaign by Colgate for its scented soap brand, Palmolive. The slogan was 'Don't wait to be told, you need Palmolive Gold' and each TV ad showed a person being hugely embarrassed when someone — usually a loved one — confided in them that everyone is talking about their appalling body odour.

In those days, this was just how ads worked. It was almost innocent. And there were so few of them that we consumers just kind of tolerated their exaggerations. Fast-forward a few decades to a time when advertising infiltrates every part of our lives in increasingly sophisticated — that is, sinister and annoying — ways. Now add in the fact that we consumers are way more educated about branding and advertising. The outcome is that we now totally reject the rude insinuations by brands that we're somehow incomplete unless we buy their product.

We're tired of it. We see it as puerile, not powerful. We see it as insulting, not intelligent. Even when it's done with the cleverest simulated sincerity.

Just the other night I saw a TV commercial for a skin cream aimed at women with families. It opens with beautifully filmed shots of young mums going about their normal day in that just-a-bit-too-perfect way that ads do these days, and the voice-over says, 'Just because you're a mother doesn't mean you've stopped being a woman'.

The company behind that ad were probably very proud of that line. They probably spent a big chunk o'money on focus groups to find out that's exactly how women feel after they have children. They probably thought that their expensive ad would make women everywhere gaze at the TV with a tear in their eye and say, 'Wow. They really get me. I'll go out tomorrow and buy their product'.

I saw that ad while sitting on the couch with my wife and 28-year-old daughter. Their reaction was a little different. My wife simply murmured 'Oh pleeease'. Instantly, whatever money that company had spent on research and concepting and production and airtime was, for this one potential customer, totally wasted. Gone. Forget it. You tried to suck up to me and you failed. Bye bye brand. Come back when you've got something real to say.

My daughter went a step further. The ad actually made her angry. 'Oh my God. That's so pathetic. That's not one of yours, is it?' (That's the question I often dread being asked by this particular consumer.) After confirming with a hint of indignation that it wasn't, she asked me, 'Why do companies do that, Dad?'

I explained to her what I'm explaining to you. As a purpose-driven business owner, your deep understanding of what your customers want — whether through gut instinct or by sophisticated consumer research — should be used to test the commercial viability of what you believe they need. Not as a weapon against their frail self-image.

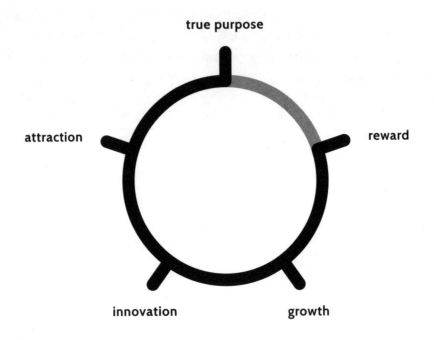

figure 6.1 - the final point on the circle, reward

(6) reward

For a majority of business owners today, Reward is the only starting point to consider in any model reflecting how free enterprise works. You set your targets for income and profit and work from there. It's overwhelmingly the standard choice. So much so that many of the business owners I meet can't conceive that there may be another way. Capitalism is all about the financial return. Full stop.

The fear of not making money, the constant pressure of shareholder return, the insane levels of modern-day competition, the squeezed profit margins, the transparency of corporate leadership: all of these conspire to embed this thought. Like an addiction.

purpose isn't anti-money

At this point I want to be absolutely clear with you on something: I don't think making money is wrong. Don't paint me as a bill-burning hippy because I'm most definitely not. I'm a genuine fan of capitalism. I just think having a money-first attitude in business is blinkered.

In a world where consumers are becoming smarter and smarter about how business and branding works, and about how companies research what our feelings and values are and then pretend that's what their feelings and values are too in order to sell us something, I think money-first is an increasingly short-sighted way to run a business. What's more, when you add our ability to share the truth with our fellow consumers instantly and globally, you could even argue that money-first is foolishly naive.

You see, I agree with the CEOs of the world that financial return is essential for a commercial entity to succeed. Of all the societal systems we humans have ever designed to advance the creativity and inventiveness of humankind, I believe capitalism is the best.

For the past 200 or so years — pretty much since the start of the Industrial Revolution in the late 1700s — almost every country adopting the principles of the open market economy has lowered infant mortality rates, raised literacy levels, raised life expectancy and raised the average household income.

It should have a terrific brand image. But somewhere between the heydays of the post-war economic boom and today, capitalism has become the new c-word. Millions of people distrust it. It has become a symbol for all that's wrong with the world. The word appears on protest banners, like the words Vietnam War — and End Racism and Cure AIDS — once did.

Which is a shame because, at its core, capitalism is simply a belief in the power of an authentically motivated human to make a difference in the world.

As I see it, there are two main problems with money being the place to start the journey towards commercial success:

- *It sidelines all that passion we spoke about in Attraction.* The passion of an authentically engaged workforce to create new pathways to commercial viability. Because it immediately sets in play a sequence of decisions where the demands of the humans buying the products become hugely more important than the hopes and dreams of the humans working for the company. And to me, that always leads to a sad waste of human potential. And true innovation. And societal growth.

- *It assumes that Reward means money.* And only money. Even when Reward is couched in a company's annual report as higher customer satisfaction scores, growth in brand awareness, industry awards, and so on. They're all valued in terms of how they'll contribute to a richer bottom line. And other rewards like employee happiness, emotional fulfilment, moral and ethical growth, the advancement of a fairer society, and so on are seen as soft measures. Companies motivated by the money-first mantra often consider these rewards as optional extras only to be properly embraced when consumer research shows that any of these things are beginning to influence the customers' decision-making process. Let me give you an example.

excuse me, your strategy is showing

In the 1980s the environmental movement began to enter the business world in a serious way. Dramatic stories of oil spills, deforestation and poisoned waterways led to the adoption of the Triple Bottom Line, where the measures of a company's worth were expanded from just financial to include ecological and social.

Companies all over the world started spruiking sustainability to prove they were worthy corporate citizens. And they duly added tree planting and carbon offset to their donations to junior football.

If any of them had said at the time, 'We're doing these commendable things because … um … we kind of have to. It's a subtle societal blackmail so we'll go along and do our bit, but it's not going to change the way we approach business. Our actions will still be primarily motivated by financial return. But while our customers are concerned by the environment, we'll acknowledge that,' I'd be a happy consumer. Seriously. At least they'd have been communicating with me truthfully. I could respect them for that.

But the big corporations didn't do that. They did what they always do: they pretended that what people wanted was what they wanted too. 'If you're worried about the environment, then dammit, so are we [suddenly].' They all ran big, expensive ad campaigns showing their office workers recycling paper and planting trees, usually with a U2 song playing along in the background.

One company in my country even went as far as putting environmental responsibility at the very core of their entire brand meaning. They ran a huge campaign claiming that being ecologically responsible was now the whole reason their business existed. They changed their logo, their slogan, their corporate identity, website, vehicles, advertising — everything.

I was sceptical because (I'm not kidding) they were a bank.

My thinking was this: why would a bank believe that their entire reason for existing was to help the environment? It didn't make sense. Their reason for being was to help people manage their finances, buy a home, build personal wealth. I researched their company history and nowhere was there any DNA of conservationism. None. They had some terrific truths about being my country's first bank, about being the best at supporting local business and giving the struggling worker a go. But ecological credentials? Zilch.

This was at a time when the banking industry globally was moving from paper-intensive passbooks and printed statements to ATMs and online banking, so it didn't even make sense from the point of view of doing more than other banks to save trees, because going paperless was quickly becoming the norm in the banking sector anyway.

I felt like calling up their board and saying, 'Fellas [they were always fellas in those days], calm down. Really, it's okay. We consumers aren't *so* wrapped up in this whole environmental movement that we want one of our favourite banks to sabotage their entire business just to make us happy'.

For the next four or five years this bank stuck to their script that this wasn't just a brand positioning. Ecology was now at the heart of everything they stood for as a company. Their commitment was so massive that my scepticism eventually made me a lone voice on the matter. My usual cohort of likeminded cynics began to think that hey, it kind of looks real this time.

And yes, I'll admit the bank committed to some very real, very expensive programs that were genuinely aimed at helping solve environmental issues. And all credit to them for doing that. But if environmental improvement was their *number-one* motivation, why did they feel the need to share with me, via expensive brand communications, every decision they made on this subject?

And why, when the environmental movement started to become mainstream and a minimum non-negotiable for businesses, did this bank begin to *not* communicate with me about it?

And why, years later, did this bank eventually decide, 'It turns out ecology wasn't what our bank was all about, deep down in the core of our founders' DNA. Ha. Sorry everyone. It turns out we stand for pride in our country'?

Which is what its slogan says now.

That's the problem I have with 'money-first' being the mantra on which to build a business: it leads to an addiction to giving customers what they most want, at the expense of what you most want. It sidelines authenticity and promotes falsehoods. And in today's smarter, always-on world those falsehoods are being found out. People can now put substance to their innate suspicion about corporate motives.

kneejerk commerce

Let me give you an example from a company one-thousandth the size of that bank. A man once came to one of the purpose workshops my company holds for small-business owners. He was a mechanic by trade and wanted to start his own car-servicing centre. I asked him why he wanted to start a business and he said, 'Y'know, to make my own money, be my own boss'.

I asked him what he'd say to a customer to attract them to his new servicing centre. He said, 'Ohh, y'know … I've got a lot of experience, I do good work, I'm quick, I've worked on all models of car, I offer competitive pricing …'

It was clear that he was reciting the things he thought he should be saying: things learned from reading *Attracting Customers For Dummies*, or he'd picked up over many beers with friends who all knew for sure how you get customers.

Just like all those other small-business owners who feel compelled to say:

No job too big or too small!

Obligation-free quote!

Competitive pricing!

Experienced staff!

Free coffee!

After chatting with him further, however, I found out that he had a very strong belief about an unmet need in the world (which is always one of the most powerful creators of effective organisational purpose).

I learned he was currently working for a large car-servicing company that ran a national chain of centres. This company dictated the exact amounts of time he and his fellow mechanics were allowed to spend servicing a car — how long they had to replace brakes, how long to do a wheel balance, and so on. It was all linked to this company's extensive research into competitive pricing.

He told me he and his fellow mechanics — the good ones at least — had a serious problem with this. They felt they weren't able to do their job properly within these time restrictions. That is, to the degree that they felt they were capable of ... the degree they felt was warranted by the task.

In one extreme example he gave, he found himself handing car keys to a woman after changing her brake pads. As she strapped her young children into the rear seats, he stood watching them with an uneasy feeling. He wasn't entirely sure he'd done a good enough job. A safe enough job. Not that the brakes would fail (modern cars are too good for that to be likely). But he felt that he'd let them down, that their car might not perform as well as it should because of the shortcuts he was forced to make.

As a proud career mechanic he felt he wasn't being honourable. He just needed another half an hour to test the brakes thoroughly; to double-check the bolts and fittings; to re-read the manufacturer's guidelines and tick them off. And so that's what he wanted to do in his own business. And that's what deep down he really wanted to tell people.

When I helped him surface how his new business's True Purpose might be expressed, he agreed it had completely transformed what he would say to a potential customer. To him, the fact that his own truths might be more persuasive than conventional promises was a revelation. And yet, as a marketing professional who's spent decades measuring the power of brand propositions, I knew his True Purpose had massive commercial viability the moment I heard it.

I believe that, empowered by his True Purpose, this honourable man is going to attract fellow-minded thinkers — better, more quality-conscious mechanics. And they're going to do a better job. And the quality of their work will become known by the right kind of customer — the kind of customer who appreciates that quality.

What's more, their drive to address the current injustice in the world of car servicing will drive customer innovation: they'll invent all kinds of new service guarantees and make a book of happy customers and build a website that shares stories and educates people about how modern cars work and what they need. And they'll become outspoken about the inferior — and perhaps even unsafe — practices of the big chains.

And they'll attract the right customer for life instead of just once ... and that will deliver better long-term financial results. They'll avoid the eternal bargain-hunting consumer who flip-flops between providers and is always trying to drag the price down ... and that will deliver better profit margins.

And yes, in the short term he might lose some sales to those big discount chains, but over the long term he'll be prouder and happier and more consistently profitable. And those things are all linked.

So let's look at a more complete list of rewards that are possible when companies put True Purpose first.

money (yes, money)

Earlier in this book I wrote that many business people believe True Purpose is a soft power and that it doesn't deliver serious company growth. Not compared with the hard-nosed, sales-first approach of a CEO on a big bonus to raise the company's share price.

That's hogwash. Make no mistake, when you put True Purpose first the money comes. It just comes in a different way. It takes a little longer to fully deliver, but when the numbers arrive they tend to stay. As opposed to the transient nature of financial returns that arrive from a non-purpose-driven approach.

Think about it this way: a never-ending ride on a flimsy wooden rollercoaster versus a solid marble stairway to heaven.

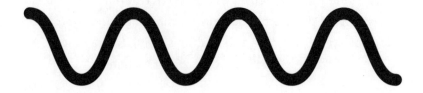

figure 6.2 - the false wins of a money-first mantra are like a rollercoaster

Starting at Reward and going the wrong way around The Circle often creates a reactionary cycle of false wins. That is, a sales increase resulting from the desire for a sales increase rather than an enduring increase in your customer base resulting from a genuine desire to provide genuine value.

At best, you launch a new product on the back of consumer research and it delivers a sales blip. After the launch hoopla dies down, two things happen to turn that curve back down again:

- *first:* your competitors copy you (which can happen remarkably quickly in this technological wonderland we now live in).

- *second:* people realise that the 'exciting new product' you told them about is really just an extension of what they had before, so they provide only average word of mouth about it and no repeat custom because they feel let down by your brand.

The combination of those two outcomes means your sales increase stops. Indeed, sales often revert back to previous levels because while you've been building shiny lures for new customers, your existing customers are leaving you for someone else's shiny lure.

Let's say you create a veiled bribe: an alluring prize to entice consumers to buy your product. The business world calls this a 'sales promotion' — and they're very popular. But let's be honest, beyond a genuine once-a-year stock clearance, sales promotions say to the world, 'We know you don't like our product enough to buy it on its own merits so how about if we sweeten the deal by making it cheaper for a bit, or by giving you a one-in-a-thousand chance to win a trip to Disneyland, or a car, or <insert whatever the research company told you bored consumers now gravitate towards>?'

The eventual downturn that arrives from these kinds of sales-first actions is often the exact same percentage of market share as the rise. Because the people buying your product are doing so for even more fleeting, self-serving reasons than your existing customers. So they'll leave you just as quickly as they came. What's more, your faithful existing customers — whom you've been disappointing for a while now because you're channelling so much money into sales and marketing — start shopping around, often in large numbers, because they see their existing brand giving new customers incentives they can't get themselves.

The insidious evil of the forced sales blip is that it becomes addictive. The initial successes are hailed internally as proof that market share can be bought. The CMO stands up in the board meeting and takes a round of applause and says, 'yes, we are cleverer than our competition, we have better consumer intelligence, our big data is bigger than their big data, our ad agency is more creative than their ad agency,' and so on.

They claim ownership of the new growth. It was all their doing. But when the marketing stops and the sales slow down again, they don't claim responsibility for that. Oh no. Sales decline is all about market forces, or aggressive competition, or the weather (seriously, I've heard that used as an excuse many times). So they think, 'Bugger. Oh well. We'll have to do it again'.

And again.

And again.

Each time a bit bigger and costing a bit more. Because everyone else in the category is doing the same thing. Before you know it, your cycle of sales blips and declines are happening more quickly. And then more often. Your rollercoaster ride is scary and out of control.

Then you wake up one morning and realise you all work in the discount rug industry. A world where nobody pays full price, every customer is a shrewd dealmaker who'll squeeze your margins to zero, and all your staff are tired and disillusioned. And you lament the decline of your industry as if you had no part in it. Pretty dismal, huh?

Okay, well it's not all gloom and doom on the rollercoaster. The truth is, you can keep doing this and still be seen by the business world as successful. I'm not one-eyed about my own theories. I can see that some industries are actually maintaining a kind of weird equilibrium by running their businesses in this way. Like fast food chains, for example.

But it's still a wild ride. You'd better be prepared to keep spending more and more on marketing. And hiring more and more clever people to drive consumer insight, mine data, monitor social media, create new media channels, deliver branded content in movies and TV, create the best consumer experience, sponsor the hottest events, and so on.

Because an addiction to sales growth through false innovation and promotion is like any real addiction: the normal amount soon only delivers normalcy. To create something more, you have to put in more. This is why the whole world has become a cacophony of branded messaging. This is why your average fuel pump now carries more stickers promoting two-for-one energy-drink deals than safety warnings. This is why your YouTube video starts with an ad for the latest insurance deal instead of the video itself. This is why your sports team's stadium carries the name of a bank instead of the name of your team.

The bottom line is, while it *is* possible to ride this crazy rollercoaster of buying consumer love over and over, I don't recommend it. Not just because it's expensive and exhausting, but because in the end it's just a bad way to live. It promotes inward self-interest over outward mutual benefit. It rewards desire over value. It teaches our children that a fulfilling life is not about what you believe the world needs next, but what other people think they need now.

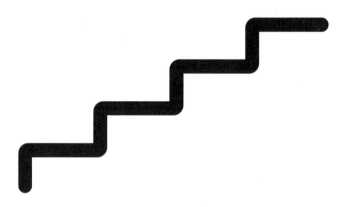

figure 6.3 - the cumulative rewards of being purpose-driven are like a staircase

When you're purpose-driven, the financial rewards can come in the shape of a staircase. You can build your income step by step, in a way that builds on itself. You're delivering genuine value so each customer you win rarely comes at the expense of losing a customer. Your company growth can be cumulative and dependable. Instead of haphazard and vulnerable.

This staircase will be made of the strongest substance known to man: the truth. Think of it as marble. Very hard for competitors to chip away at. So as your staircase grows higher it remains just as strong. Before long, that slow growth that initially worried you now makes you the smartest person in the room.

You see, initially the rewards for a purpose-driven company can be smaller. After all, you're giving up the dubious-but-proven, short-term financial returns of sucking up to your consumer, running a bribe disguised as a sales promotion or launching a faux innovation.

In the first year of my purpose-driven advertising agency, for example, we gave up the easy money that came with accepting million-dollar clients who weren't a philosophical fit for us. Our houses were on the line and we had to start earning. But if we chose clients who wouldn't allow us to apply the thinking we'd started the agency to prove, what point was the money? What point was giving up good, salaried positions at a big, traditional agency to go out on our own? We knew what was down that path: the rollercoaster.

Instead, we accepted a slower growth. The kinds of clients that were attracted by our theories on truth and purpose tended to be the owners of smaller companies and startups. The challenger brands that couldn't outspend the big guys so they had to out-think them. The kinds of companies that were still in touch with their original purpose.

Our income grew more modestly as a result. But it grew in a whole new way: instead of each burst of new billings being a transitory moment before a cyclic fall, we saw that it grew like a staircase. Each step up in our client billings came on top of what we were already doing; each new client that came to us for the genuine value we were authentically motivated to deliver added to the existing clients getting that genuine value already. So while our returns grew more slowly, they grew more cumulatively than any ad agency I'd ever worked at. And they grew on a far more solid platform: the truth.

To us, moving from the conventional business practices of our industry to a different model of our own creation was like stepping off a rollercoaster that we thought was taking us higher but actually just kept going up and down and around and around, and stepping onto a staircase. Far less exciting, but incredibly reassuring. Because the staircase was solid. And it grew. We added step after step and before long we had a view back down to the rollercoaster far below us. And we knew we'd made the right choice.

This metaphor can be used by purpose-driven business owners about market share, customer loyalty or industry reputation. Instead of riding a haphazard sine wave of luck, you're building a platform for enduring success. And *you* are in control.

you're the captain

I see a lot of people in business acting as if they're at the whim of unseen forces. I see it in frontline staff, middle management, even CEOs and boards. There's a sad lack of self-confidence in their decision making. And I think the outcome is self-fulfilling. If you choose, consciously or not, to put your own truths aside and be driven by factors outside of you — the shape of the market, the fickleness of customers, the latest strategy of a major competitor — you'll feel out of control. Because you are. You gave it up.

Being purpose-driven means standing up for something. Leading a charge. Planting a flag in the ground and rallying people around it. In this frame of mind, outside factors are less likely to control you. Your purpose controls you. And it feels good.

Like the last two stanzas of my favourite poem, 'Invictus' by William Ernest Henley:

Beyond this place of wrath and tears
Looms but the Horror of the shade,

> *And yet the menace of the years*
> *Finds and shall find me unafraid.*
> *It matters not how strait the gate,*
> *How charged with punishments the scroll,*
> *I am the master of my fate*
> *I am the captain of my soul.*
>
> I think those words capture the spirit of True Purpose. No matter what barriers you come up against, don't give in. This is your life. These are your values. Live them.

Simply put, following The Circle drives healthy long-term income because throughout the history of free enterprise we've seen time and again that when smart, passionate humans are authentically motivated by a higher ideal, they're more likely to create genuinely innovative products and services. And when that happens, this happens:

- higher *consistent* sales over the long term

- the ability to command premium prices that customers are happy to pay

- lower customer churn and an end to the cycle of having to top up your customer base because customers leave, disappointed that what you delivered was not what you'd promised

- lower cost per acquisition (because genuine value creates its own advertising)

- no more constant need to be on sale all the time, or desperately trying to bring that next piece of false innovation to market on the back of expensive marketing and PR campaigns

- a rise in your company's value on the back of a semi-monopolistic positioning in your market that often arises from fully implementing a unique and special True Purpose

- your idea becomes a franchiseable concept that offers mum-and-dad business owners the chance to genuinely grow their own piece of capitalism, be their own boss, find their entrepreneurial spirit, and apply their passion and creativity.

commercial karma

Don't panic when you see the word 'karma'. I'm not some kind of hybrid capitalist-hippy. What I'm talking about is simple common sense. When you place truth above the temptations of status and money you very quickly prove to the world that you can be trusted. And trust begets respect. And in business, respect brings commercial opportunity.

Again, it's all about giving up a perceived short-term benefit that requires you to be disingenuous, for a longer term benefit that comes from being true to yourself. In my experience, the reward for this bravery is that the long-term returns are way bigger and more enduring than the short-term ones.

My company once had a client that was a large private health insurer. For years they sponsored the biggest fun run in my home city of Perth. It was a classic example of what the business world calls sponsorship, but what I call paying to be liked: 'Hey, we're a health brand. Let's spend a lot of money to be associated with a big health event. So people will like us'.

This annual run, however, had existed long before our client paid for the naming rights, so everyone knew it wasn't their event. Everyone knew this health brand simply paid a lot of money to have their name on the start and finish banners. Like the bank brand before that. And the internet brand before that.

Sure, there was a little begrudging respect in there from consumers, because okay, maybe this health insurer's money helped keep the event alive and well organised. But they knew it was a commercial deal. So the result was never the tsunami of love our client secretly hoped for.

What's interesting is what happened after we surfaced this organisation's True Purpose: a dedication to immediate and individually relevant healthcare for us and our loved ones instead of the impersonality and delays of the public health system. As we began realigning their products and services to prove that promise, it became clear they needed their own public health event. The existing fun run — with its emphasis on winning and personal best times — simply didn't embody the same values that this company now realised was driving them: health, and love and caring for ourselves, our loved ones and our community.

So they gave up the short-term strategy of 'Please like us because we're paying for this event that you seem to enjoy' and replaced it with a far longer-term strategy of 'We're going to create our own run where the goal is not just physical achievement but the satisfaction of honouring someone or something in your life that really matters to you and raising money to help. Because that's a better reflection of the values our organisation is truly motivated by'.

We gave it a name that reflected each participant's personal reason for running, and although the budget to promote it was smaller, and the name unknown, it was 1000 per cent more true to the organisation's purpose. So guess what happened? Yep, within a couple of years it attracted the same numbers of competitors as the existing fun run. And gained the same levels of attention on the nightly news. More in fact.

What's more, on the back of its success, the health insurer created free training sessions for any of their customers who entered, which also appealed to the customers of their competitors, which drove customer growth. And with the event's growing success came a palpable sense of renewed optimism and confidence among their staff. And because of the event's rising competitor numbers and media coverage, other major brands wanted to partner our client on it, giving rise to new promotional opportunities.

Today, this run draws the same number of participants as the London Marathon and the majority are ordinary citizens embracing the idea of leading a healthier life and helping others. Which makes it way more fulfilling for this organisation because it reaffirms all their values about the human spirit. It is also delivering way more PR opportunities than our client ever achieved as a mere sponsor of the other event. What's more, every runner's story is a genuine reflection of this brand's authentic purpose, so every news article magnifies the growing truth about this brand.

This is what I mean by 'commercial karma'. If you give up the glittering lure of 'I want to be liked for giving you what you want' for the grittier reality of 'I want to be respected for giving you what I think you need', what you give up eventually comes back to you. In spades.

It's like the classic scene in many a movie where a bunch of Yes Men are sitting around a boardroom table agreeing with The Cranky Boss. The Naive Newbie who doesn't know the rules disagrees with The Cranky Boss. Everyone gasps and waits for the inevitable tirade, but instead The Cranky Boss laughs and says something like, 'I like the cut of your jib, son' and promotes him to Vice President.

brand value

In the old days, having a cool company name and a well-designed logo meant little to the broader business world if you were just a small, regional player. Until you'd worked hard for years to establish your customer base and then secured it and then built on it and then maybe grown your geographical footprint and become either a large brand or an incredibly profitable small one, nobody placed much value in you. You were just another small fish.

That sequence of logic has changed in the past couple of decades. Twice.

First, the rapid advancement of commercial technology, married to the speed of global communication via the internet, meant that you could be a known brand within days of starting. Call yourself Pango!, add a TM to your logo, hint at a stunning piece of new tech or software that will attract millions of users, use the words 'the next iPod' in your press release and you could attract the interest of investors, joint venturers, the media and ambitious CEOs looking to acquire innovative young companies (and the people who lead them).

The trouble was, a lot of this was brand image, not brand value. Many smart business people who should have known better bought into the idea of the brand, not the commercial reality behind it. Which, to be honest, was often non-existent. This unrealistic swelling of a company's image began with the infamous dotcom bubble of the late 1990s and continued into the (rapidly becoming infamous) startup boom of the 2000s. But thankfully, Wall Street's strange naivety around startups also seems to be waning.

Which brings me to the second change. And this is good news for all of us truth-seekers. Today, a growing number of those investors, joint venturers and media channels I mentioned above are just as turned on by visionary ideas and people, but now they want proof of commercial viability. They want to know the hard substance of markets and money behind the soft words of change and vision. And the really smart ones want to be convinced that your ambition is authentic. That you haven't just found a cool new way to look attractive. They know that the only way to guarantee long-term commercial success is to have a group of innovative thinkers authentically motivated to change something in the world, and preferably something that has a commercial upside.

In short, they'll want to see your planned path around The Circle.

So let's summarise: in this fast-paced world we live in, you can establish a visionary, purpose-driven brand and communicate its higher ideal very quickly. Align that with a solid business plan and you have a brand that's already more valuable to the modern investor than anyone in your sector who has merely started a company to make money.

company culture

Have you ever heard of 'Greek fire'? It's an ancient pyrotechnic weapon: a highly flammable gel that the Greeks could fire long distances, typically onto an enemy's wooden boats. The flaming goo would not just stick to the wood and burn quickly, but it was supposedly impossible to put out. In fact, water made the flames spread faster.

When it comes to building a great company culture, True Purpose is like Greek fire. It burns bright and strong and is almost impossible to extinguish once ignited because it fuels everything you do.

How does this happen? Well, purpose-driven companies embrace honesty and equality. They know that conventional business shortcomings like director perks, executive ego, staff cliques, Chinese whispers, lack of open communication and the like can't be allowed to thrive. Yes, they'll often occur naturally, as they do in any group of humans over time, but they must be identified and quashed. They're barriers to truth, change and progress.

So purpose-driven companies build open environments where truth trumps job title, where the agreed worthy objective beats the old established process, where the dumb question is praised not ridiculed, where common sense is prized over acquired wisdom, and so on.

All of these techniques to remove the falsehoods and fabrications of a fear-based company culture result in the world's best employee-retention system. Good staff want to stay and great staff want to stay longer. Not only do they buy into an inspiring purpose that genuinely motivates them to be their best — to learn and improve and grow and succeed — but they also live each working day in an atmosphere of truth, sharing, respect and, often, ethics and morality.

Nail that kind of culture and you have your corporate Greek fire, making it incredibly hard for competitors to poach your best talent. Better yet, this culture fuels your commercial momentum as your people are authentically motivated to think, to innovate, to try new techniques, to create new processes, to overcome old obstacles with new solutions, to stay late, to come in early, to mentor, to teach and to speak out in industry forums.

This is a huge benefit for the modern business owner as more and more businesses compete for talent. It's becoming clear not just from opinion pieces in the *Harvard Business Review*, *Fortune* and *Fast Company*, but from research projects too, that the new generation of employee is seeking a different kind of incentive to do their best work for you. Money is dropping down the charts as the number-one driver of staff performance. Replacing it is a sense of mission, a feeling of making a difference — of having a clearly defined role in something that matters.

(Again, I reiterate that this doesn't necessarily mean you need to be doing something worthy for the world, but you do need to be doing something of value authentically, with aligned actions and behaviours all the way down the system from boardroom to shopfront.)

category improvement

Without innovation, purpose is just an image. People who are authentically motivated to change the world for the better must begin fixing whatever they believe is broken. And that requires genuine innovation. Something entirely new to break the paradigm and move your industry in a new direction.

Consider the little dairy company that believes people are stuck between cheap, nutritionally suspect supermarket dairy products and superior-but-expensive boutique dairy products. This effect is changing their beloved industry for the worse because it's either devaluing dairy as a key food source or turning it into a treat to be enjoyed only occasionally. Both of these outcomes are bad for the future of their region's dairy industry, as it will lead to lower milk prices for a majority of dairy farmers, eventually forcing many of them out of business and leading to less fresh milk, more imported milk powder, and so on.

So they innovate. They source new ingredients, create better products and the new manufacturing systems required to make them, invent new quality control methods, and conceive new brand names and packaging. The result is not just commercial success for themselves (and important validation of their dreams), but also a tangible advancement of their sector. The commercial success of their innovation will lead to competitors following suit. Consumers will raise their expectations and demand the new product features or service experience that the innovation has delivered for them. And those benefits will become the new norm.

Look at what Volvo did for car safety around the world. Look at the level of intuitive design Apple inspired in personal computers, music and communications devices. The commercial success of those purpose-driven companies convinced others in their categories to get on board and innovate too. In short, their True Purpose changed an entire industry.

And hey, it's not just the big, iconic brands. Every single client of ours and every single case study I've read about a purpose-driven company boldly standing up for what it genuinely believes needs to change — whether that be dairy, insurance, telecommunications, healthcare, banking, electricity or energy — has led to an advancement of their category. They just make it better. Or fairer. Or safer.

And that's a pretty cool reward, don't you think?

societal maturity

Okay, we're getting into some fairly optimistic territory now, so stay with me. See if you see what I see.

One of the most interesting outcomes I've observed of purpose-driven companies is the effect they have on the partners of employees, not just the employees themselves.

I first noticed this happening in our own company. I'd be at an industry ball or a company picnic and I'd speak with the wives and husbands and girlfriends and boyfriends of our own staff members. They would share with me the difference that working at our company has made in their loved one. Things like, 'Oh, she comes home a lot happier now' and 'This has been really good for him, thank you'.

What may seem like trivial party chatter was, to me, a revelation. Our purpose, and the environment we were creating around it, was affecting whole families. I saw that as the first tiny proof that True Purpose had the potential to make the world better.

It soon became apparent that our purpose-driven company, with its accompanying culture of honesty and equality and transparency, was not just a chance for people to advance their careers, it was a chance for them to be better people. To overcome their demons. To make a choice about whether or not they actually wanted to be their authentic selves, as opposed to that overly serious professional suit, or that ultra-driven award-chaser, or that loud-talking bully or that always-on comedian. Or any of those acts we adopt over time to survive and advance in this crazy, competitive business world we all stumbled into after school.

I believe what I was seeing there were the first ripple effects of True Purpose out into society. That is, beyond the boundaries of a company's particular commercial sector.

Call me a dreamer, but I can't help extrapolating on that effect: someone comes home from work feeling happy and inspired after a day of applying themselves fully to a worthy purpose that they value and that makes them feel valued. I think that would help them to be a better wife, husband, partner, father, mother. Here's my logic: when we feel good about ourselves — and let's face it, what we do for a living has a huge impact on that — we're more likely to let little niggles in a relationship slide, to open up a bit more and talk, to be patient and understanding and caring and nurturing. All those things tend to go out the window when we're feeling underappreciated, tired and frustrated.

So am I being naive in thinking that working for a purpose-driven company could help us to be better people? Or at the very least, help us to *want to* be better people? I don't think so.

And if you imagine the employees of thousands of companies all wanting to be better people because they feel more valued and fulfilled in their work, wouldn't that then lead to happier homes? And wouldn't more happier homes lead to fewer broken marriages and to more children getting a balanced education about life and love and maybe less depression and repression and anxiety? Who knows, maybe the broader benefits of True Purpose could ripple out to lower crime and alcoholism and drug use.

I'd like to think so.

I'm not arguing that a happy home is the cure to all of society's ills. I'm just saying that there would have to be a knock-on effect out into suburbia from more and more people loving their work. There's just something insanely gratifying about doing something that's not only earning you a living, but also helping make others happy and perhaps even changing the world.

Think about your home life as a kid. How did your dad and/or mum come home after work? And how did that affect the mood of the house?

the young learn better

There's a terrific social commentator I recommend you listen to called Professor Alan Watts. Search his name on YouTube and you'll find all kinds of interesting and inspiring audio recordings from his lectures and interviews. The fascinating thing is they're all from the 1960s. The media pigeonholed him at the time as being just another beatnik philosopher like Timothy Leary or Jack Kerouac. But I think his contemplations on society are extremely commonsense and still resonate today.

For example, he put into words what I believe is one of the ultimate rewards of being purpose-driven: giving our children a better life lesson than they're likely to get observing conventional business practice.

Professor Watts said:

... if you say that getting the money is the most important thing, you will spend your life completely wasting your time. You'll be doing things you don't like doing in order to go on living — that is, to go on doing things you don't like doing. Which is stupid ... and to teach our children to follow in the same track.

See what we are doing, is we're bringing up children and educating them to live the same way we're living. In order that they may justify themselves ... by bringing up their children to bring up their children, to do the same thing.

Following the five points around The Circle breaks this cycle. Instead of seeing their mum or dad come home dispirited and tired and empty, your children are more likely to see an inspired parent pursuing what they believe in, and turning it into a business that provides for them.

And as any parent knows, (eventually) children learn about life not from what you tell them to do in their life, but from what they see you do in your life. Your relationship with work teaches them everything they will ever know about what work is. How you come home at the end of the day. How you talk about your boss. The learnings that take the deepest roots come not from your words, but from your demeanour. The tone of your voice. Your body language. Children have an incredible internal radar for the truth. If your voice box is saying that you're happy in your job, but your face is miserable, they'll know.

So you can teach them that work is a tiresome, deflating necessity that makes you feel inadequate and powerless. Or you can teach them that work is amazing; it's a way to turn passion into prosperity; it's a way to make great change happen in the world; it's a rewarding and uplifting experience not just for ourselves, but for everyone around us.

Which lesson would you rather teach your children?

better capitalism, better world

The ultimate goal of adopting True Purpose as your business mantra and using The Circle as your guide is for you to help create a world where the concept of capitalism is reborn as an honourable idea. This is the definitive win–win for all of us. Like the ultimate Reward that we leave for our children to enjoy.

As I wrote earlier, throughout history, but particularly since the Industrial Revolution hit its straps in the late 18th century, the free market economy has proven itself to be the best system to advance humankind. And no, I don't mean in areas like science and engineering, but the important human factors of lower infant mortality, higher life expectancy, increased literacy, fairer laws and welfare programs.

In short, a system designed to allow open and equal competition has repeatedly neutered the strangling power of church, state, monarchy or military and helped ordinary people move from uneducated, unhealthy, controlled and manipulated worker bees to literate, self-motivated mums and dads who get to choose their jobs or businesses. They get to decide for themselves how they want to earn a living. And because humans are inherently creative and industrious this leads to growth and prosperity. Which means jobs; and safe, clean homes; and health programs; and good education; and lower crime; and longer lives, and so on.

This exact phenomenon is happening right now in dozens of countries in Africa and Asia as they move from their Third World ranking to First World with the rest of us.

And yes, you can absolutely argue, 'What about the horrendous greed and obscene imbalance of wealth and sordid government corruption that capitalism is now famous for?' I acknowledge all those things, but to me the downsides of capitalism are due to a distortion of the system, not the system itself. Most religions have the same problem: they start as a way of embracing 'do unto others', but over time fall victim to the destructive traits that occur whenever humans form tribes: defensiveness, fear, aggression, isolationism, prejudice, corruption of power at the top, and so on. The base religion itself is a fine and worthy dogma, but certain humans are mutating it.

This mutation of well-intentioned collective ideas has been a regrettable, but unfortunately natural, occurrence since humans first dropped out of the trees and started forming into groups. We're attracted to tribes but are innately self-serving.

Personally, I think it's time we humans slapped ourselves in the face and grew up. I think we're mature enough now to make a conscious choice about whether or not we let fear turn us into selfish creatures over and over again.

what is a company anyway?

Here's an interesting viewpoint that purpose-driven business owners often adopt: a company is not just a way for a group of people to make money.

In their best-selling book *Built to Last*, Jim Collins and Jerry Porras back that view: 'Visionary companies pursue a cluster of objectives, of which making money is only one (and not necessarily the primary one). Yes they seek profits, but they're equally guided by a core ideology — a sense of purpose beyond just making money. Paradoxically, it is these visionary companies that make more money than the purely profit-driven companies'.

The authors also quote David Packard, co-founder of Hewlett-Packard: 'Many people assume, wrongly, that a company exists simply to make money ... that a group of people get together and exist as an institution that we call a company so they are able to accomplish something collectively that they could not accomplish separately'. This is the guy, remember, who co-founded a company that invented the LED light, the programmable calculator, the inkjet printer, the laser printer, the human heart ultrasound, the data storage drive, the cordless mouse, the rewritable DVD, and more.

When you change the definition of what a company is, you're already taking a big step towards changing what capitalism is.

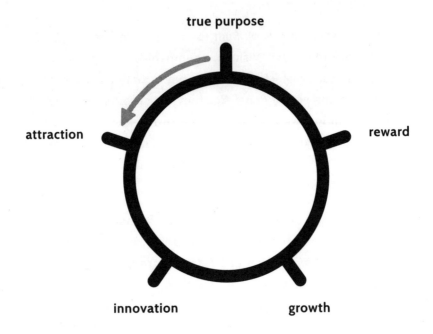

figure 7.1 - the right way around the circle

(7) the right way around the circle

In exploring the two directions you can choose to take your business around The Circle, I want to start with the right way. The true way. In my company, we made this the anti-clockwise direction because, even though it's our recommended course, it remains the unconventional way in business. Going the right way around The Circle is like being the rebel army, not the incumbent government. You've gotta get used to going against the grain.

In explaining how The Circle works in the previous chapter, we've already explored together the knock-on effects of being purpose-driven. We've seen how each point on The Circle magnifies the value of the previous point, creating an amazing momentum that can make markets, build businesses and (hopefully) change the world, one capitalist outpost at a time.

So I'm going to keep this chapter short and sharp. And rather than repeat myself, I want to summarise the cycle of good that happens by being purpose-driven and move quickly on to the long-term impact.

it starts and ends with the truth

True Purpose is the starting point for going the right way around The Circle. Which, I believe, is the right way to approach a job, a career, owning your own business and life in general.

Because it's all about telling the truth for the mutual benefit of all, as opposed to the one-sided pretence that's the modus operandi for most businesses.

Being motivated by a higher ideal allows us to bring out our very best skills; apply them full strength in order to create something of value; and have that value grow beyond only self-serving financial rewards to a greater good for ourselves, our partners, our family and friends, our staff, their family and friends, our communities and society in general.

Being driven by authenticity is also the path to making capitalism a trusted and valued concept again. In order for humankind to progress to a happier, fairer kind of society.

truth attracts the right people ...

This planet's next generation of employees put making a difference ahead of making money.

Purpose-driven companies are hugely appealing to them. Because the difference they can make is tangible, real and exciting.

That means purpose-driven companies have the chance to attract the very best minds coming out of our schools and universities. The smartest, the most imaginative, the bravest.

And rally them around an inspiring idea that genuinely motivates them.

This creates an awesome culture. A culture of shared belief with the power of a rebel army fighting against a huge but unjust incumbent government.

It creates an atmosphere of inventiveness and change that's fuelled not by management demands, but by a united desire.

This culture is self-fuelling. It doesn't need constant incentivising or whip-cracking. It becomes organic. It sustains itself.

... which drives true innovation ...

Not the shallow imitation masquerading as originality that we see so often when companies ignore the true potential of the people working for them and instead order them to merely satisfy customers' existing needs.

True innovation comes from genuine desire, not fear-based, acquired desire.

True innovation is meeting an unmet need with an original, inventive idea. Like Honda's first motorised bicycle. Like Apple's first iPod. Like Patagonia's first chemical-free wetsuit.

The people who are united around your inspiring higher ideal will be authentically motivated to pursue products and services that advance the world towards that worthy goal.

So true innovation is a joy, not a slog. Because people who have caught an owner's True Purpose are pulled towards it like a magnet, as opposed to pushing towards a money-based corporate goal, which can be like rolling a rock up a hill.

And when you have a group of smart, inventive humans emotionally and mentally vested in an exciting purpose, in a culture of curiosity and fun, amazing things can happen.

... which grows markets ...

Our testing has found that it's not only employees who can catch and fall in love with a well-defined, well-expressed True Purpose: your customers can too.

Customers are human. (Duh.) The same authentic benefits that register with you will often register with them.

Just not in the same way. We humans are way more guarded when we're consumers than when we're employees. Our trust has been betrayed so many times by companies promising us things that they then underdeliver on, that we all have strong defences.

But the truth is the truth. And in a world where a company's true behaviour — borne of their true motivation — will be found out and exposed, any company that's confident and brave and resilient enough to prove that they're genuinely motivated by authentic win–win ideals will be recognised by consumers and rewarded. First with their attention, and second with their custom.

And when they do, your growth will be hard for your competitors to copy. Anyone can copy an entrepreneur's new product, but it's almost impossible to copy an entrepreneur's authentic motive.

... which generates rewards ...

Purpose-driven companies prove to their customers that they're authentically motivated to deliver on the promises they make about their goods and services.

Today's super-savvy, super-connected consumers, tired of being manipulated and lied to, respect that authenticity and reward it with their custom.

The rewards are not just financial — in the form of sales, income, profits, dividends, and so on — but softer rewards like customer loyalty, staff retention and industry respect.

The feeling of creating something important in the world and leading it via an internal culture of honesty and respect is also highly valued by the owners of purpose-driven companies.

These soft rewards have the power to become some of your most valued outcomes.

Increasingly, they're also the values being looked at by fund managers seeking good long-term investments for their clients. Because they create a solid foundation for sustained growth and are hard to copy by competitors and so can contribute to an organisation being a good long-term investment.

Eventually, the rewards achieved by a purpose-driven company spiral outward into new consumer categories, new areas of society and sometimes the entire world.

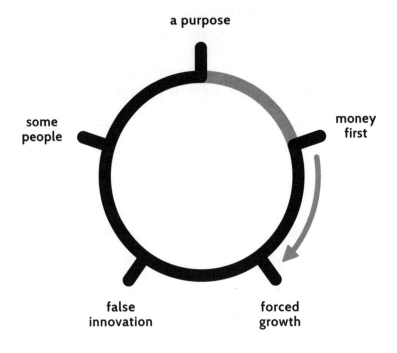

figure 8.1 - the wrong way around the circle

8 the wrong way around the circle

Maybe I should start calling this The Other Way. It's a big call to accuse 90 per cent of the world's businesses of doing the wrong thing. A lot of them are very successful.

But hey, I'm passionate about this stuff and I think people are pretty much nuts for going the other way around our precious Circle. There's nothing criminal about it; there's often nothing even unethical or selfish. A lot of business owners go this way and are still good, honourable citizens.

The reason I call it wrong is because of what it leads to in the medium to long term. And that's the seductive nature of going the wrong way: at no point will you ever feel like you're making a big mistake. Everything will feel reasoned and logical. Responsible even. But, bit by bit, the cumulative knock-on effects build up to a big mistake.

It's like pollution. Tipping the occasional barrel of industrial waste into the ocean doesn't seem that bad — 'cos hey, the ocean is huge. And nature is resilient. And we've been doing it for centuries and so far not much has happened. Until one day, someone points to a floating mass of dead fish and proves that it wasn't an act of God: they were starved of oxygen because of pollution. And then more studies are done and more people join the conversation. And before you know it the whole world is starting to realise it has to change its conventions because bit by unnoticeable bit it's led to something being very wrong.

I believe conventional business practices have been pouring waste into the idea of capitalism for a few generations now. It's been hard to notice because ... well ... it's the convention. And throughout the history of humankind, conventions have a habit of evolving from a shared technique to an impenetrable object. Especially when those conventions deliver financial returns to those practising them.

Only now are people starting to point to the money-first mantra of capitalism as being perhaps a tad short-sighted. The conventional motivation of business has been for almost 100 years now an undying responsibility to the shareholder. In the United States it's treated almost as a religion. So much so that if you dare challenge the basic premise of capitalism — to create financial returns for the greater good of free enterprise (and democracy) — you risk being labelled a communist or socialist.

Thankfully, the ever-improving educational levels of the global citizen, aided by the rise of the internet, have led to a kind of global emotional literacy on this subject. People are aware that capitalism has mutated from a sage-like entity that once guided humankind to a brighter future into a selfish beast that needs to be fed at almost any expense — and usually via a subtle deceit.

They're seeing that companies aren't being authentic with them about what their true motives are. They see the yawning crevasse that exists between what a company tells people it's driven by — in advertising, websites, Facebook, Twitter, instore displays, PR releases, and so on — and the actions of that company behind the scenes — in the CEO's office, in their boardroom, in their bank's boardroom, in the factories, on Wall Street.

And often not even behind the scenes, but to our very faces, in the form of poor customer service instore, long on-hold wait times on the phone, poor product quality, the difficulty we have in being able to speak to a human from the company once we've signed up, the way they bribe new customers with all kinds of discounts and deals they don't offer to their existing customers ... the examples are endless. I'd laugh if this barefaced hypocrisy wasn't so downright tragic.

Just today (at the time of writing) I saw a story on the morning news about an airline that had overbooked a flight. That's a good enough example right there. But this airline went even further: after failing to get anyone to volunteer to leave the flight, they had air marshals physically remove a passenger. This wasn't some terrorist suspect or even a drunk; this was a well-behaved paying customer! And initially the CEO didn't even apologise. He explained — with an air of logic that was ludicrously inappropriate for the context — about how the airline business model works.

Here's the point: all that reactive, self-serving behaviour wouldn't be viewed by the general public as so heinous if, all along, that airline had been telling us the truth about why they're in business. If they'd said quite honestly that 'this is the best we can do folks. The margins in the airline business are so tight we simply have to overbook flights and occasionally kick you off. And the benefit to you is lower fares and a smaller world'.

But they don't, do they? No. They run ad campaigns costing hundreds of millions of dollars telling us that they're the happy airline, the cool crew, the travel lovers. They ignore the truth and instead show smiling flight attendants and suave pilots and soaring jets and loved ones hugging. Because, guess what? They've done research that told them that's what we all want to see. It has very little to do with what that group of people called an airline company is actually motivated by.

I'm sure all those things are what the founders of that airline were motivated by. And I'm sure there would be many good people in that company who are still motivated by that. And I'm willing to even bet that some of the leaders of that airline genuinely want to believe that's still their main motivation. But I'm sorry guys, when it comes down to brass tacks, you have to agree that the only true judgement of someone's authentic motivation is how they behave towards you. Over and over. And the truth is, this airline put money before all of that feel-good stuff.

The sad thing is, companies like these also try to fool their own staff by asking them to buy into this untruth as well. They train them in how to behave to meet the researched and prioritised needs of their key target audiences, but just as we customers eventually see through this ridiculous pretence, so do staff. Only they do it more quickly because they're in the belly of the beast. So the truth comes out faster: 'Hey, check-in staff. We want you to be happy and chat to our customers. But you also have to process an average of 8.2 passengers per minute, otherwise we don't reach our cost-per-acquisition targets'.

The bitter-tasting but deliciously ironic icing on the cake in this particular story is that the airline in question has the slogan 'Fly the friendly skies'.

All this crazy fakery happens because companies go the wrong way around The Circle. They start at Reward and work backwards. Let's look at the knock-on effects of this misguided, but still conventional, approach.

rewards first

A good sports coach knows that you don't win simply by telling the players to get a big score. The big score comes after you motivate the team to be their best. So it is in business. Going the wrong way around The Circle begins with a company's owners focusing on the scoreboard: profit.

Instead of asking, 'How are we going to make this thing (your product, your category, your world) better?', you begin the whole process by asking, 'How are we going to make money?'

It's understandable. Putting your house on the line and becoming your own boss creates enormous instant boogie monsters about the possibility of financial ruin. I get it. I've been there too.

But when you start at Reward you immediately begin to put to one side what you love. You place the fear of not making enough money to survive ahead of all the benefits of pursuing your true motivator, which ironically include making good money.

When what you want is placed a distant second to what the customer wants, all the good stuff we explored in the previous chapter is compromised. The enormous potential of authentically motivated humans starts to be dramatically capped.

The fakery begins here. It's subtle, but the knock-on effects are enormous.

this is grey, folks

Like almost every system that genuinely works in this fickle world of contrary human behaviour, the principles of The Circle are coloured grey. A hazy, blurry, hard-to-define grey. Not black. Not white.

We humans love black and/or white. If someone says they're not funny, they must be serious. If someone says they don't like war, they must be pacifists. If a company says it has a culture of freethinking and sharing, they must be hippies.

The more fearful the society, the more black and white it is. In the United States, if you say you want to help poor people get access to free healthcare you must want to bring down the whole democratic state. If you say you want to make it a little harder for bad people to get guns, you must want to end all gun ownership, anywhere, forever.

We emotionally led humans find it hard to exist in that grey space where the black and the white meet. Instead, we behave like pendulums, swinging past that sweet spot to the extremes on either side. It's why people get divorced and wars start. It's like we all have a little terrified alarmist sitting on our shoulders who extrapolates the very worst (or best) of every new idea we hear and then shouts in our ear.

But the awkward truth is that most equitable solutions to the world's problems lie in that grey sweet spot between the two extremist viewpoints.

So when I recommend you don't *start* with money as your primary motivator, don't get sucked in by that little guy on your shoulder and think that I don't want you to make money.

Having people make money is the whole reason I'm writing this book. I see conventional business practices as being less and less the way to ensure long-term healthy profits.

I see capturing the power of authentically motivated humans to create business opportunities as the future of the whole idea of capitalism.

So let's do a deal: throughout this chapter I promise to do my best to clearly explain how The Circle helps you grow a great business and make money and pay off your mortgage and become financially independent, if you promise to keep an open mind when those words meet your eyes.

Deal? Great. Let's continue.

growth as pressure, not pleasure

When you start at Reward and move clockwise to Growth instead of being pulled towards a fulfilling, commercially viable higher purpose, you're pushing towards a clinical goal. It's triggered by a fear of failure and the addiction to logic that's so prevalent in conventional business. But it's wrong.

It's like you're saying, 'In order to make money, we must grow a customer base. In order to grow a customer base, we must provide them with products and services that they want. So what do customers want? Let's research it. Let's find out what people want and then we'll use our skill to give them that'.

It seems like the right thing to do. And yes, you're still accessing your passion and talent, but you're already pointing those powerful assets away from yourself. And the more you point your actions away from their true source of motivation, the more likely it is you'll be drawn into the conventional cycles of business — the cycles that lead to companies all looking and sounding the same in their desperate united quest to be the customer's best friend.

Have you ever met someone at a party and for some reason they latch onto you and want to be your buddy? They ask all about what you like and lean in too close or use your name a lot or compliment everything about you or laugh just a bit too loudly at your jokes?

This is how companies are perceived by the public when the people who run them put their own authentic thoughts and values second to what they've found out about the customer. It leads to that company being surrounded by a halo of desperation.

And that's a real turn-off. We humans much prefer making friends with people we respect; people who are likeminded but different; people we can learn from; people who complement us, not just compliment us.

When companies go the wrong way around The Circle, this is the vibe they're putting out into the world. They subjugate the things that would actually make us respect them (strong opinions, making a stand, ethics, values, transparency, vision).

My theory is that inside almost every human are those qualities, lying in wait, ready to come out and change the world. They just don't have enough faith in their value to overcome the fear of bringing them out. They don't see that conventional business wants it. So everyone keeps playing the same game of Money First = Customer First. And on they go the wrong way around The Circle, leaving their own beliefs and integrity lagging way behind. Today it's called 'customer-centricity'. But it's the same old backward behaviour.

There are two other key observations I want to make about attempting to attract customers when you start at Reward.

the temptation to manipulate

I want to briefly revisit a topic I shared with you earlier under the heading 'On the defeat of deficiency advertising' because it's acutely relevant here.

Going the wrong way around The Circle makes it much more likely that companies will be tempted to take advantage of consumers' insecurities. Research techniques and data algorithms are becoming so sophisticated that we can now find out the exact moment in time when people are not just predisposed to buying a certain product, but when they're experiencing low self-esteem, fear, hopelessness or vulnerability.

As a company owner wanting to advertise to such humans in order to meet their lofty sales targets, this inside knowledge often leads to a difficult choice.

Do you make use of a new understanding of people's emotional states to sell a product, even if it exacerbates them feeling bad about themselves? For example, a life insurance brand discovering that many middle-aged men feel guilty that they haven't created enough personal wealth for their family.

Or do you take the higher moral ground even if it means giving up potential sales?

Companies that decide, 'Yes those emotions are fair game' (all's fair in business and war after all), often defend their actions by saying that their product is helping to alleviate such feelings; that in fact, far from being a capitalist monster, they're the corporate white knights.

I don't buy it. And neither do a growing majority of educated, connected consumers.

We know when our emotions are being played with. We're hard-wired to detect phoney empathy. Like the car dealer who expresses concern about the base model of the car the young man and his pregnant wife are about to buy and instead recommends the fully optioned top model because 'it's safer for the kiddies'.

I'm not suggesting that everyone in business is exuding counterfeit sympathy. But I'm definitely suggesting that unless you're shaping your business model around a win–win for yourself and the consumer, you'll be tempted to use whatever consumer intelligence you uncover. Including the subtle manipulation that comes with preying on people's fears and insecurities. Because hey, everyone else is.

This is a massive problem for me personally. I think it's another cancer cell for capitalism, eating away at consumers' trust of the whole system of corporations and free enterprise. I think when companies prod you where it hurts, even while smiling and empathising, we consumers feel slighted. Maybe at a very subconscious level, but that's where societal trends begin: not as overt, conscious reality, but as subtle, primitive human feelings.

My theory is that over time, those thousands of hurtful little rebuffs build to a distrust of companies that resembles hatred. And hatred for the system that constantly delivers those feelings: capitalism.

The truth is, it's not capitalism's fault. It's the companies who know no better way to turn a consumer's attention to their product than to prey on their anxieties.

The single most startling — and desperately disappointing — recent example is Facebook. The one-time darling of free speech and humanity has, at the time of writing, been found to have created a computer algorithm so sophisticated it could report back to advertisers when its young users were feeling vulnerable. It could then target them with products that addressed youthful confidence. I'm presuming that would be acne creams, deodorants, tampons, energy drinks, fashion labels, and so on.

In a staggering betrayal of trust, Facebook was profiting from the anxiety of its own customers. When found out, they apologised and launched an investigation.

This is what happens when you go the wrong way around The Circle. Good, intelligent, sane humans subtly turn on each other. The tragic irony is that the people responsible for approving and creating that software would go home at the end of the day and somewhere between the front door of Facebook and the front door of their houses, they would turn back into humans again. They would sit down and watch TV and openly criticise any brand with the audacity to advertise to them in a clumsy way. It's like they leave the real world each day and enter an invisible bubble where the pressure of delivering results and elevating career status make common sense and compassion redundant. I refer to this as the Bubble of Bulls**t.

Going the wrong way around The Circle makes that bubble bigger, thicker and even more invisible.

bad customer service is a clue to a lack of purpose

Have you ever walked into a shop and instead of entering a world of warmth and authentic human contact, you have the feeling that the people who run that business don't actually ... um, *like* customers?

Sometimes it's just a vibe in the air. An invisible sense of coldness from the decor or the owner's body language. Sometimes it's blatant. The one I remember most is a fish 'n' chip shop I went into while staying in a coastal resort town.

Not only were there no smiles or hellos when I entered, I was immediately assailed by a sea of laminated signs:

No, we don't give tomato sauce for free!

Don't touch the vintage jukebox!

No eating of takeaway food on the premises!

And of course the globally used:

Don't ask for credit as refusal often offends!

Seriously, these pre-emptive strikes on me, the customer, took up more wall space than the menu board. Before I'd even made it to the counter, I got the clear and distinct impression that whoever owns this business hates it. Or at least, hates me. Which in a service industry is pretty much the same thing. Loving fish 'n' chips but hating the people who buy it is not a profitable business, it's a costly hobby.

I also once entered a bookshop that had signs on every shelf saying (I'm not kidding) *Don't read the books* and *This is a shop not a library* and my personal favourite *Soiled books will have to be paid for.* Yikes. Can you imagine a worse environment in which to browse for a book?

Whenever this happens to me, and it happens depressingly often, I don't think, 'You dicks'. Seriously. I think, 'Wow. You guys aren't being true to yourselves and you're going to fail'. Here are people who have started a business that doesn't suit them, that they don't love, that actually maybe even annoys them. All for the tiny reward of being their own boss.

It must be exhausting being those people with that mindset. Sales would be such a struggle. In order to bring in new customers to replace the ones they frightened off they'd have to start discounting and adding new product lines and trying those stupid gimmicky impulse buys that clutter up their counters ... you know, the ones that some visiting salesperson guaranteed would add $500 to their daily take. They'd start closing at 12 on Saturdays and not opening for late night trading. You see it all the time in failing cafés and newsagencies and delicatessens and gift stores. The whole store acquires a dismal air of defeat.

Now, I understand how a lot of small-business owners open a shop or buy a franchise because they're in their 50s and have few lucrative job prospects. I empathise with that. But why do it in a category of commerce that's going to make you unhappy?

Good customer service is hard. People can be annoying. They can leave a mark on that book they were just browsing through, meaning you probably can't sell it now. They can forget to put the sauce back in that perfectly good sauce rack you specially bought and put there for them.

My belief is that if you're not motivated by a higher purpose, these little annoyances can become huge, self-fulfilling barriers to success.

At their worst, non-purpose-driven companies can end up hating their customers. Which is a double whammy of unhappiness because you don't enjoy serving your customers and you find it insanely hard training anyone else to.

If the reason you started a business was to make money and earn a living because you'd heard that newsagencies or lunch bars or mowing franchises make good money, devoid of any measurement of your own fondness for that activity, you'll find it incredibly hard to provide long-term sustainable customer service. And if you can't enunciate to a young employee a genuine reason why you yourself enjoy being in the company of those annoying, fickle, contrary humans we call customers and clients, what makes you think they will?

The best you can hope for is to find ways to bribe them to serve well through sales incentives and staff awards. And they don't last. Because they create the illusion of good service, not the real deal.

I've met countless business owners who complain that it's so hard these days to train young people to properly serve their customers. In many of those cases I believe the cause was the owner's total lack of authentic motivation. They had very little genuine passion to pass on to their young staff. Let alone any bona fide end benefits that were true win–wins for their staff and their customers.

The only rationale they usually came up with to prompt better customer service from their staff was 'Because it's good business' and 'Because that's what I'm paying you for'. A sense of responsibility to the company only lasts so long in the minds and hearts of employees. Eventually, the contrary foibles of customers wear you down.

Bottom line: if you own a lawn mowing franchise and don't love being outdoors and making people's yards look awesome and seeing the smiles on their faces, choose something else.

innovation. now! hurry!

Do you know the old fable *The Emperor's New Clothes*?

It goes like this: one day in a far-off kingdom a pair of con artists hatched a plan to profit from the Emperor's famed vanity. They told him they were magical tailors and that they had made a royal robe that only the wisest people in the world can see. To everyone else it was invisible. They mimed holding up this incredible robe for the Emperor, turning it round for him to see the quality of the fabric and the stitching.

Of course the arrogant Emperor, fearful of not being seen as the wisest man in the kingdom, said the robe was wonderful. He put it on and asked his courtesans what they thought. Not wanting to be the ones to doubt the wisdom of their Emperor, each in turn said the robe was fabulous.

The tricksters duly sold the robe to the Emperor for a handsome sum and left the kingdom (in a hurry). The Emperor was so pleased with everyone's increasingly enthusiastic — if a little nervous — response to the robe that he decided he would wear it in the grand parade the following day. Word got out of the Emperor's unusual robe and all the citizens lined up along the main street and played along, applauding the Emperor, more out of fear for their lives than simply massaging their glorious leader's ego.

Then, a young boy stepped forward. As children do, he saw things as they are, not what they should be, and shouted, 'Look, Mummy, the Emperor is wearing no clothes!' Sure enough, underneath his magical robe the Emperor was wearing only his underpants and once the child had exposed the mass delusion, the bubble burst and everyone began to laugh. The whole silly façade crumbled and the Emperor scurried away in shame, exposed as being foolish and gullible, a victim of his own ego.

This is the effect that occurs in business with that magical driver of economic growth, innovation. Travelling the wrong way around The Circle creates a subtle air of desperation as every business seeks to please the consumer better than the other. This frantic search for newness leads to weak simulations of innovation. Products and promotions and service design that are neither original nor revolutionary. Because they weren't stimulated by genuine caring, authentic passion and bravery. And so while most companies think they're being innovative, it's really just the illusion of creativity. And like the Emperor's robe, the illusion is exposed when it leaves the boardroom and enters into society.

The group delusion usually begins while looking at an impressive PowerPoint slide:

- A research firm may be showing some white space they've found on a two-way matrix jampacked with competitor brands. 'If we shift the positioning of our product towards this part of that quadrant, it would be a very innovative move for this category.'

- A marketing strategist may be explaining how they can *own* a part of the consumer's emotional mindset that's currently unoccupied by the competition. 'This innovative strategy will give us new relevance and potency with our core market.'

- An R&D guy may be presenting a new product he's working on to combat a new entrant into his category. 'We have to innovate to fight the inroads they're making into our base product suite.'

Often what eventuates is merely an imaginative tweak to an existing norm. Which to me is not genuine innovation.

the three types of innovation

Let's take a quick pause here to put my last comment in context by exploring the three basic forms of innovation in business. I found this overview in an article titled 'The power of market creation: How innovation can spur development' by Bryan C Mezue, Clayton M. Christensen and Derek van Bever (January/February 2015 issue of *Foreign Affairs* magazine). I think you'll find it interesting too.

The authors define innovation as new thinking that generates economic growth, with 'economic growth' meaning primarily prosperity that creates new jobs.

I endorse the view that jobs should be the ultimate assessment of economic growth because job creation means the innovation is benefitting humans all the way down the commercial hierarchy. It is advancing humankind, not just the bank balances of a few CEOs and investors.

So let's look at the three types of innovation and the degree to which each of them is likely to drive job creation.

sustained innovation

The lowest form of innovation is where the thinking is merely improving an existing idea — for example, all the touchscreen smartphones that followed the iPhone. The various brands may call their products innovative because they have larger screens or better cameras, but really they're simply an advancement of an existing idea. To me, the first iPhone was hugely innovative. It created an entirely new market segment. All the versions following it do not.

Sustained innovation provides short-term prosperity, but in terms of job creation it triggers little overall growth because the result is more about customers moving from one brand to another.

Like the next rugged, sexy SUV. Or the next small, lightweight laser printer.

Yes, there is growth from new customers entering the market, but it's not because of an updated product. They were always going to enter the market anyway.

efficiency innovation

This is where someone has a new idea about a commercial process, usually manufacturing, that leads to a company making more money with less infrastructure.

For example, when a certain Mr Walton looked at the way department stores like Macy's and JC Penney structured their business, he found them to be hugely uneconomical and created Walmart instead. Efficiency innovation certainly elicits large economic returns, but it often leads to fewer jobs in society because one Walmart knocks out dozens of other retailers in that geographic area. What's more, in Walmart's case the entire business model is based on outsourcing the production of goods as that's the only way to undercut the competition.

Another good example of efficiency innovation creating the illusion of prosperity are the nations rich in oil and precious metals. Finding a rich vein of silver or a large subterranean oil reservoir activates big, headline-making economic growth. But to what end? The act of removing fossil fuels and minerals from the earth and turning them into money is incredibly cost-efficient. The numbers of staff required in relation to the money earned is among the lowest ratios in commerce. Add in advancements in robotics and self-drive vehicles and you get a kind of innovation that doesn't actually benefit broader society in the way those global mining brands would have you believe.

market-creating innovation

This is the kind of innovation that truly brings something new into the world. The personal computer. The scooter. The smartphone.

It creates a new market. Requiring new jobs. And these jobs are often permanent jobs that create enduring economic growth and prosperity in the region. Because this innovation is targeting non-consumption.

That is, market-creating innovation makes available to everyone what was previously only available to the elite. Whether that's using the power of computing, having your own personal transport or being able to make a phone call from anywhere. It usually requires someone to spot an unmet consumer need, or a wrong that needs to be righted.

A lot of the best market-creating innovations have turned the liabilities of an emerging nation into assets. A great example of this is Tata Motors in India.

Driven by an authentic desire to help their country grow and prosper, Tata's founders looked at the transport needs in their society that the current motoring brands weren't servicing. They didn't just look at what people were buying and improve on it. They saw what was not there: a need for a new kind of commercial vehicle. One that served those who were currently not in the commercial vehicle market at all: small manufacturers, tradesmen, farmers, and so on. They created a cheap, rugged delivery truck called the Telco (which stands for Tata Engineering and Locomotive Company). Its success was a double win for India as Tata then built manufacturing plants in Jamshedpur, Pantnagar, Lucknow, Sanand, Dharwad and Pune to produce them, employing thousands of locals.

Vespa did the same thing in Italy. Samsung did the same thing in South Korea. And right now, new purpose-driven entrepreneurs are market-creating in every emerging Third World country in Africa, South America and Asia.

Yes, the directors of Tata became rich in the process, but compare the knock-on effect of this kind of innovation to the ultimate benefactors of the Walmart approach to innovation: that one Walton family is worth more than $150 billion while employing fewer and fewer people per store to achieve the same profits. I wish them no ill. It's just not my choice of business philosophy. And if you've read this far into my book, I'm willing to bet it's not yours either.

innervation beats innovation

All three types of commercial advancement described above could be called innovation. And in any advancing society you'll have all three in play. So I'm not proposing we kill off the first two kinds. But I'm a firm believer that the only innovation that's going to fix capitalism as a concept is market-creating innovation. In my company we call it 'market-making' — it means the same thing but it rolls off the tongue better.

We also have another name for it: *inner*vation. It's a more powerful and enduring kind of innovation because it comes from within. And not just from within a company, but from deep within the minds of the humans working for that company who are authentically inspired.

By the way, you may be thinking that the word 'innervation' is just a clever play on 'inner' and 'innovation' but it's actually a real word. It means 'to stimulate a body part or organ through the nervous system'. I think that's a pretty darned cool analogy for a type of commercial innovation that comes from within inspired humans.

My key point here is that the occurrence of innervation is highly unlikely when you're going the wrong way around The Circle. Because you're more motivated by what the customer wants than by your own opinion about what the world needs.

wanted: some people

What kinds of employees does a company attract when it's going the wrong way around The Circle?

After spending several decades observing this process from the privileged vantage of marketing (where commercial intent meets reality), I think it attracts the same kind of people as those who are leading it: people who have learned that to succeed in business you have to find out what the customer wants and find a way to give it to them that's better than your competition. People who have learned that you must often subjugate your own beliefs — and sometimes values — to close the deal.

And no, I'm not implying that conventional businesses are always filled with hard-nosed salespeople who lie and cheat and do anything to get the sale. I simply mean they invariably become proficient in the customer-first, money-first mandate.

Hiring these likeminded people will therefore perpetuate that cycle. It creates a culture of hero worship for those who are best at it. Those who are at the top of the sales performance charts, conversion rates, cost-per-sale ratios. People who find a way — any way — to deliver better numbers for the company. And so that approach becomes the one that staff see as fully endorsed by management and is therefore the way to get ahead. So they pursue it. And eventually, nobody even considers there may be a better way.

and finally ... oh yeah, we need a purpose, i guess

Companies going the wrong way around The Circle skip over Purpose like it's Item 47b on the board agenda. They see it as important, but important like a catchy slogan is important. Or having an ad campaign that their friends compliment them on.

At best it's classified as a hygiene factor. 'We've got our business plan with the three horizons: our marketing strategy, our digital transaction policy and our cool Purpose statement.'

At worst, it's a bone they throw to their employees. 'Apparently we have to have a higher ideal these days, otherwise our millennial staff won't perform at their best for us. Get us one of those, will you Jenkins? Right, Item 47c ...'

Remember Hello, I'm Rachel? She was the victim of yet another company going the wrong way around The Circle, convincing themselves they had heart and worthiness because they had A Purpose.

I want to repeat some points I shared with you at the start of the book. Now that you've been around The Circle both ways, I hope they will make even more sense to you:

- Purpose is the latest cure-all in business branding. It used to be Brand Meaning. And before that Positioning. And before that it was your USP. And before that Enzyme X.

- Don't listen to any branding guru who offers to deliver you A Purpose. You don't need it. You need *Your* Purpose. Your organisation's true reason for existing.

- Adopting any old Purpose because having one is apparently today's smart business play won't work. Because Purpose is about aligning your behaviour out there in the real world with your genuine motive for being in business. Like, for real. What you sincerely, honestly, truly-ruly want to achieve from your business. You. The person reading this book.

- If your Purpose is not absolutely, unequivocally true, it will not survive the cynical eye of today's super-educated, super-connected consumers. Because today's consumers (remember, that's you and me and everyone around us) can see through corporate pretence better than any generation before. They will catch you out and expose your disingenuous motive instantly and globally.

- And remember, that super-savvy consumer is also your employee. So if you think a collection of pithy words cut out of plastic and stuck to a boardroom wall are going to fool the people you most need in order to grow a successful business, think again.

- Adorning your reception with the phrase 'Excellence in customer service' or any of the cliché words of inauthentic Purpose, such as trust and integrity and quality (at my company, we call them 'fat words') is becoming less of a reassuring promise and more of a red light to every cynical human who walks in your door, including investors, potential senior staff and industry media.

the more laps you do, the harder it gets

The truth is you can absolutely maintain a business going the wrong way around The Circle. Like I wrote earlier, it's not a black and white choice between success and failure. It's a conscious decision about how you want to live your life as you run your business.

Just know that going the wrong way means it gets harder and harder, not easier. More money to advertise your way out of having parity products. More research to find white space in the market. More temptation to pray on consumers' fears to make a sale. More ignoring the huge forces for innovation that authentic human motivation is. More R&D. More PR. More bulldust.

the story of the little radio station that went the wrong way ... then the right way—uh, then the wrong way again

(Stay with me; this is a great little story.)

I want to share with you a commercial tale to clarify the ramifications of each direction you can take around The Circle. It's about a radio station that was once a client of ours.

Radio stations are right up there as one of the worst business categories for going the wrong way around The Circle. Or should that be *the best*? Because they're exceptionally good at going the wrong way.

In the first decades of the 20th century, radio stations were the voice of the people, each with their own specific geographic catchment area, providing companionship, entertainment, news and community connection. Along with handy information about local businesses. In those days every new radio station had an impact on its broadcast area, like the internet has on us all today: sudden 24/7 connection with each other and the world.

It was a much-loved medium that enjoyed a very personal, trustworthy connection with its audience. And so radio stations were quite parental in nature, providing help and guidance and comfort and friendship. They took their role in society very seriously and were definitely of the opinion that they decided what people needed most.

Today, radio stations are owned by media conglomerates, the bosses of which most likely never visit the communities they serve. They are dots on a map driven by that money-first attitude. Audience numbers mean revenue and so audience numbers drive their every thought.

As such, they're addicted to consumer research. In decades of working with every conceivable type of business, I've never come across a category that researches company purpose like radio stations do. They take the Steve Jobs remark I mentioned previously and change it to 'The customer has the only vote!'

They ask people which songs they want to listen to, what kind of person they want to hear in the mornings and afternoons, when they'd like their news and weather and for how long, what kinds of traffic reports they like, and so on and so on. And I don't mean once or twice a year. Radio stations research these things every single week.

So is it any wonder that they all sound the same? With the same 40 minutes of ad-free music at the top of the hour, the same breakfast crews and zoos and teams with the same combo of two guys and one girl, who all laugh just a little too loudly at each other's jokes.

They're the ultimate cheesy guy at the party trying to be your buddy I wrote about earlier. Except that at the radio party there are dozens of them, all trying to suck up to you at the same time.

Our client stepped out of this muddle of desperate neediness and into our lobby looking for help. In a radio market of only nine stations they were number 7. The only stations with fewer listeners were community stations housed in universities. And even those were nipping at their heels.

'We've tried everything!' they said. 'The easy listening station, the rock station, the sports station, the talk station, the blokey station, the new age androgynous cool station. It's driving us crazy! We ask people what they want. We give it to them and they still don't listen to us!'

At my company, we love meeting a company in pain. Because pain forces change. Pain makes you braver. Rather than give them the advertising campaign they came to us for, we advised them to stop looking outside for solutions and to look inside: to rediscover their True Purpose. It meant giving up the short-term ratings blip that may occur with a really good ad campaign or promotion for the longer-term benefits of finding out their authentic place in the world.

It just so happens that this struggling radio station was the very first FM station in my city. They launched in 1980 and because they were the first radio station to play music in stereo they communicated a genuine appreciation for music. Real music. Heard the way it should be heard. In glorious stereo.

While every AM station at the time was a wall of cool cats and rocky jocks playing the platters that matter from the hit parade, this new FM station said to the world, 'We love music. We honour its role in our lives. And we're going to prove it'. By employing radio announcers who are knowledgeable about music (not cheesy DJs). By not talking over the beginning and end of songs (like the AM jocks do). By playing songs at 45rpm (not the 48rpm that the AM stations played them at because that gave them an extra three minutes for ads every hour). By speaking to their audience with intelligence and respect (as opposed to the tacky tones of many AM stations). Even by making the prizes in their on-air competitions about music (for example, a guitar signed by John Lennon versus the endless Asian holidays that research told the AM stations their listeners wanted).

So from the day it launched, every decision this new station made, from the boardroom to the studio, was driven by an authentic purpose to not only share good music with people, but to educate them about why it's good. This motive also affected the way their company earned its money. At AM stations the sales departments ruled the roost. They brought in the big money so they got anything they wanted: eight-minute ad breaks, outrageous promotions, news and weather and even songs sponsored by advertisers.

This new FM station, however, decided that commercials were an important part of their on-air sound, and therefore a part of their intelligent, authentic values. So they had a policy about the quality of ads they played. And they would reject ads that they deemed to be insulting or crass towards their audience.

Can you see that these guys were going the right way around The Circle, decades before anyone even named it that? They started from day 1 with a True Purpose: to foster a better understanding and appreciation for good music in our lives, for the betterment of not just their bottom line, but for the quality of life in society.

They gathered on-air staff and music programmers and promotions people and yes, even sales staff around this ideal. Motivated by their True Purpose, this group was inspired to create bold new ideas for their industry, ideas that served their higher ideal, not convention or ego.

Those innovations attracted an audience hungry for authenticity and passion and respect. Which grew their market and dominated the radio ratings for years and years. Which delivered great returns to the owners. Not just in income and profit, but in the personal fulfilment that comes from putting your soul on the line and finding out you were right: that people want what you love.

That station was the number-1 radio station throughout the 1980s and 1990s. And no, not just because they were the first in FM. They stayed at number 1 well beyond the introduction of many other FM stations.

Fast forward to today. After two decades in a media landscape upended by iPods and iTunes and Pandora and Spotify and thousands of digital stations, that same proud, authentically driven station was a research-addicted mess of self-doubt. They had been sold to networks a couple of times, had changed staff many times over and were now going the wrong way around The Circle in a desperate attempt to find their place in the world again.

And yet, just below the surface was the same DNA that started the station in the first place. It was still there in many of the people who ran the station: the music programmer, some of the announcers and the CEO. They still had a tangible love for good music and when we did workshops to tap into their authentic passions, out it all came again.

It was clear to us that this group of people had the same potential for innovation around good music as the founders did all those years ago. Better yet, we suspected that this was just what the current radio landscape was itching for, with all its similar-sounding stations.

We tested whether the original beliefs this station had about music could still be relevant to radio listeners today. Whether the same authentic principles about good music and respect for their audience that saw their station's founders create so much innovative on-air content in the 1980s would resonate with the media-savvy, always-on population of today.

To cut a long story short, yes it could. Humans are humans, no matter how much technology changes. They want guidance and leadership. They gravitate to entities with a unique opinion, even if it's counter culture. Like new TV shows, films, bands, and yes even brands.

We told this station to back themselves: to look inside their hearts and present their station to the world with a full-strength, authentic love for good music.

So instead of sitting back and running an ad campaign, these guys got to work inside their own product:

- They immediately changed the eclectic old decor of their offices and studios from 'any old radio station' with dog-eared posters of any old music artists that the record labels gave them, to a decor that clearly honoured good music, with framed portraits of rock greats and inspiring quotes from Lennon and Cohen and Bowie.

- They changed the wording and style of their promos from loud 'n' cheesy to calm 'n' smart.

- They let some of their cheesy DJs go and hired more knowledgeable announcers.

- They did a massive audit of their music playlists and started playing more album tracks and local artists.

It wasn't just a return to the old ways. It was a realisation that there was still a need for a radio station that authentically believed their role in the world was to keep real music alive. The purpose may have been old, but the application of it was entirely new, for a new audience.

And it worked. After just two ratings periods they went from number 7 to number 1, dislodging the top station for the first time in 100 surveys. It was such big news, the story appeared on the front page of our daily newspaper.

Seriously. Email me and I'll send you the clipping.

They were going the right way again.

In doing so, they remained either the number-1 or number-2 station for more than a year. And the really good thing is that not only was the company successful, and making money, the people inside that company were feeling awesome. They had backed their innermost passions and truths. They had resisted the urge to ask their customers what they wanted and instead held hands and jumped off a cliff called Real Music. And they were right. People came. And that's the best feeling in the world. Because it's authentically *you*. Not some fake simulation of you that you've found out you have to be in order to please others. The real you. This is the power of The Circle. To unleash the commercial value of what's genuinely driving *you*.

Unfortunately, this little fable has a sad ending.

Because of their newfound success, they attracted the eye of a national network that bought them and promptly absorbed them into their national, research-driven programming template. Out with real music and in with 'The Best of the '90s, Noughties & Now!' Out with the calm, knowledgeable announcers and in with The Afternoon Crew streamed from network HQ.

Yup, you guessed it. This poor little abused radio station started going the wrong way around The Circle again. And once again they dropped from number 1 to number 7.

I'm not kidding. They slipped back down the ratings ladder all the way to the bottom with those tiny community stations. They spent a fortune on advertising trying to bribe their way out of it, but they're still number 7 as I write this.

To be honest with you, I get a certain amount of *Schadenfreude* from this story (that's a German word that means the guilty pleasure we get from someone else's failure). My guilty pleasure from this tale is knowing that it proves the power of The Circle. When we met them they were going the wrong way around The Circle and were number 7.

When we showed them how to go the right way, they went to number 1. When they stopped and went the wrong way again, they dropped back to number 7. It's almost too perfect a case study to believe, but I swear to you, dear reader, this story is 100 per cent the truth. I hope they find their truth again soon.

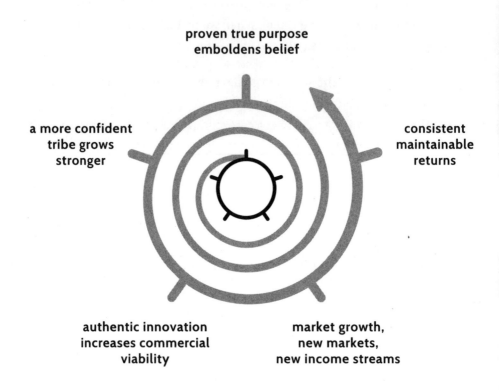

proven true purpose
emboldens belief

a more confident
tribe grows
stronger

consistent
maintainable
returns

authentic innovation
increases commercial
viability

market growth,
new markets,
new income streams

figure 9.1 - the ever-broadening benefits of going the right way
turn the circle into a galaxy

(9) when the circle becomes a galaxy

The enduring power of The Circle becomes more evident the more you go around it.

Once you've dedicated yourself to your True Purpose and seen its positive impact on people; and the inventive problem solving; and the commercial viability; and the rewards of income, pride and fulfilment, you'll want to go around again.

Like, *really* want to.

The second time around, however, is a little different. It's way more enjoyable. And exciting. Because this time you know it works. You've seen the potency of your authentic self. Doubt turns to confidence. Cautiousness turns to energy. You've jumped off a cliff and though you still may be flapping madly, you're flying. The possibility of being your own boss — doing what you love or believe is important for the world — *and* making money, is conceivable.

The common thought in the minds of business owners is, 'Holy crap, this stuff actually works'. So when you revisit your True Purpose on your second journey around The Circle, you love it even more. It emboldens you even more. Your emerging self-confidence strengthens your commitment to its potency for igniting good change, hardens your resolve to break down the barriers of bulldust in your industry and makes you even more resilient to turn around the doubters.

Gradually, this self-sustaining confidence grows the impact of your True Purpose. As more and more people take notice. As you grow and succeed and begin to influence people and things beyond your company. It's like The Circle has begun to spiral outwards, becoming a galaxy of growing impact and influence.

a galaxy of meerkats

My founding partner and I experienced this expanding circle effect ourselves at our branding company Meerkats. I remember it distinctly. It took about two years for our first journey around The Circle. It was a time of tenuous confidence in our idea: to use truth and transparency to transform the image of the advertising industry from distrusted Mad Men to valued business advisors. It was an uncommon purpose that went against many of our industry's conventional practices, like doing anything your client asked of you, recommending advertising solutions as often as possible because that was your primary source of income, and so on.

Using the metaphor of the explorer once more, we were stepping cautiously up a mountain. Every now and then we'd stop and look down at the traditionalists sitting in their comfy villages, around a warm fire, eating well while we ate meagre rations in the cold. And we'd have doubts. So we'd check our bearings and remind ourselves that this journey into the unknown was worth it ('We're doing the right thing, right? *Right?*'). But as soon as we got to the top of that first peak and saw what was on the other side ... well ... game over. You can keep your comfy villages; we saw something way better over the horizon.

Once we'd won our first few big clients — and taken them on this journey; and seen the remarkable impact it made on their culture, brand image, sales, recruitment, company's standing in industry and ability to re-invent their whole category and make markets — we sat back and actually said, 'Holy crap, this stuff actually works'.

We decided therefore to do our second lap around The Circle *full strength*. That is, with no hesitations, no doubts, no subtle softening of our stance because of how some owners of the companies we wanted as clients reacted to what are often counter-intuitive philosophies. We went for it without pause or apology.

We were wary of any righteous arrogance creeping in so we had the words 'Please leave your ego at the door' placed on the front door to our office. A message to ourselves, our clients and suppliers to give up the false gods of self-importance, management status, crisis heroism, and so on and, rather, to unite in an ego-free pursuit of good change.

And things just kept getting better. If we'd attracted one likeminded employee the first time around, we attracted half a dozen the second. And they were smarter and more senior, coming from established positions at our competitors' agencies.

If we'd toyed with ways of turning our philosophy into simple, sellable business tools the first time around, we created a neatly packaged suite the second time.

We scoured the world for every evidence of truth and purpose in business to back our views, especially if it came with concrete economic results. And we found it. And we made our case in the cafés and boardrooms of our city with more and more conviction.

Soon we noticed the commercial karma that I mentioned in chapter 6. All the decisions we'd made to give up the false appeal of the short-term win for the subtle building blocks that lead to sustained, long-term success generated a karmic effect as more and more clients and future employees — and even the media — were intrigued and attracted by our idea.

The more we thought, 'We don't care if we don't win this new client, or win this particular debate with an existing client, as long as we're telling our truth,' the more clients and debates we won. Yes, there were clients we tried to win and senior staff we tried to sign up who decided our thinking wasn't for them. They chose the comfy village of conventional practice instead of the barren mountainside of the explorer. But the ones who did come to us were right for us; they allowed us to prove that our True Purpose was potent. So overall, we kept moving up.

As business owners, our second time around The Circle was awesome. We realised that as we went, The Circle was growing: our True Purpose was fuelling a bigger impact at each of the five points. What's more, each of those points was magnifying the effect of the next. It was becoming like a little galaxy of influence.

Over the next decade our circle continued to spiral outwards. And the metaphoric growth from circle to galaxy reflected the real-life performance of our business as we grew in staff numbers, income, profit, products, reputation, pride and, most of all, potential.

Interestingly, we soon realised that each cycle aligned with our financial years because the moment we received our end-of-year results was usually the moment we sat down and revisited our purpose, who we were attracting with it, what products we were offering, and so on.

Every time we passed through our True Purpose again we would reset our hopes and expectations for what was possible. Every time we got back to the starting point, we were even more confident and brave because we had even more evidence that this thing was hugely potent.

Eventually we saw so much potential for good change in our True Purpose that we couldn't *not* pursue it. Full strength. It had become our obligation to serve this idea to the fullest.

I want to add a note of caution here. And honesty. I'm not implying that after a few scary laps around your Circle the clouds will part and everything will become sunny and happy and perfect forever and ever. Our little mob of Meerkats still made the occasional wrong step out of fear of financial loss, or loss of face. We'd pitch for a client that turned out to be a bad fit for us (and we kind of knew it going in) because they were a big brand or in a desirable category we really wanted to work in. Or we'd hire someone we kind of knew wasn't a good cultural fit because we needed their expertise.

These threats to your values are always insidious little things and almost never show up as clearly as they do in hindsight. So things weren't perfect in katland. But boy, they were way better than where we'd been before.

when truth becomes a movement

Once you've travelled around The Circle more than once, what started out as blind faith becomes informed confidence. And confidence, sufficiently fuelled by repeated evidence of success, becomes a movement. And movements are far more powerful inspirers of humans than companies.

When the group of people you've brought together sees itself more like a movement than a company, you'll have created something not only very powerful, but self-sustaining. Like that galaxy spiralling outwards, driven by huge unseen forces. People who feel part of a movement are more resilient to setbacks, more confident to challenge the status quo, more energised around objectives, less likely to be envious of competitors, and so on.

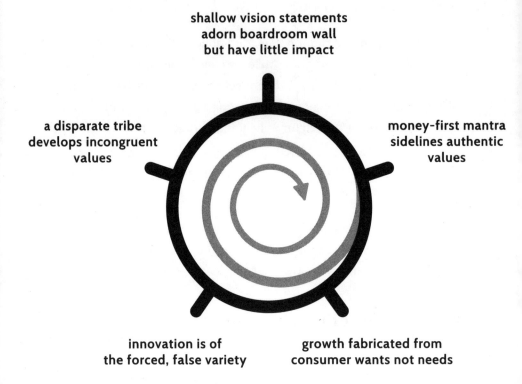

shallow vision statements
adorn boardroom wall
but have little impact

a disparate tribe
develops incongruent
values

money-first mantra
sidelines authentic
values

innovation is of
the forced, false variety

growth fabricated from
consumer wants not needs

figure 10.1 - the compounding negatives of going the wrong way
turn the circle into a black hole

(10) when the circle becomes a black hole

As a business owner, when I consider the conventional business behaviours that I believe are detrimental to the concept of good capitalism, it has always helped me to see them as behaving like gravity.

I mean behaviours like setting aside your personal values for a short-term financial gain, or using a consumer's low self-esteem as a way to sell them something, or promising service quality you know you can't really deliver just to try and beat the competition, and so on.

These actions never show up as clearly and dramatically as the way I've just described them. They're usually veiled and subtle. Just another little problem to overcome in the maelstrom of daily business.

But that's how they get you. Like gravity, they're an invisible force that's always there, ready to pull you down, bit by bit. Like a decaying satellite, money-first decisions pull you down from your original orbit. Slowly your dream begins to lose forward momentum — and you don't even feel it happening.

And that includes all those decisions that make perfect sense to a busy boss and are easy to explain to people as 'good business'. Like adding a product line that you kind of suspect is of a low quality, but is proving popular. Or hiring someone whose personality is likely to clash with your culture, but hey, you need a gun salesperson right now.

Add all these tiny gravitational pulls together and you get failure. Maybe not of the business itself. I've seen many businesses continue to behave in the ways described above and still hit sales targets, still make a profit, still grow.

But at what cost? In those same businesses I've seen the looks on people's faces. And it ain't fulfilment, folks. It's pressure. And angst. And hardship. And conflict. And fear. A lot of them don't even realise. They think that's what business actually is. It's tough and stressful and unyielding.

Eventually, being dragged down to earth by an unseen gravity becomes the way you work and live. There's no use fighting it, so everyone gives into it.

Do you know what happens when gravity keeps pulling inwards in this way, over and over? It gathers a momentum that's opposite to a galaxy. It's a black hole. It's a place you can't get out of. Because you stopped pushing against it when it was small and weak, you now can't get out of it.

That's my ultimate metaphor for going the wrong way around The Circle. Instead of creating a galaxy of goodness spiralling outwards to a whole new universe of possibility, it becomes a black hole of bleak inevitability.

And hey, I'm not just talking about the ultimate purveyors of bad capitalism such as Enron and WorldCom. Or the money-first devotees at Lehman Brothers and Goldman Sachs. I mean ordinary, innocent companies that succumbed to this effect — such as Blockbuster, Atari, Kodak, GM, Chrysler and a lot of banks and insurance companies.

push out, so you don't get sucked in

Like gravity, the lure of going the wrong way around The Circle is always there. It's a constant force in the business universe. It's invisible and hard to feel, but we all know it's there.

So the only way to know that you're not being subtly sucked in by it is to actively push against it. Every day. If you ever stop feeling like you're doing more than most business owners in order to stay on-purpose, you'll begin to fall.

It takes strength. And enormous resilience. And supreme confidence in the validity and value of your True Purpose.

Just know that it gets easier. It's as if going around The Circle a few times gives your True Purpose extra retro rockets so that even though you're still pushing against that gravity, it doesn't feel as hard.

part two:
finding your true purpose

(11) picture this ...

You're sitting in a rocking chair on the deck of that cute little house you've always imagined yourself retiring to. You know the one. Nestled on the shores of that beautiful alpine lake or sitting on a hillside overlooking a deserted beach.

Imagine yourself in that place right now, 90 years old and looking back over your life. This is the moment when you'll know for sure what really mattered in your life. Which decisions turned out to have the most influence on your happiness and which were inconsequential. Which problems were the right ones to focus on and which looked large and intimidating at the time but turned out to be merely trivial distractions.

Picture yourself sitting there, slowly shaking your head as the wisdom of age becomes apparent. Will that be a smile of contentment on your face, or a grimace of regret?

Will you be wondering why on earth you never took the risk of following your heart and doing that thing you always knew was inside you? That cool business idea or brave social enterprise you kept squashed down inside because of your mortgage, your two cars, your career status, that fear of failure, those doubts that you might not be very good at it so why try?

Or will you be remembering the day you decided to follow your True Purpose? That one scary day when everything changed. When you handed in your notice, or signed that office lease. Actions that seemed so foolhardy at the time, but in your final years of life will seem like the easiest, most obvious choices you could have made given the outcome.

I believe those of us lucky enough to live to an old age will have a moment like that. A moment of clarity about what makes a great life. So ask yourself right now: which 90 year old do you want to be? Because even though this book is about unleashing the commercial value of what authentically motivates you, at its core it's about you living a life that you're proud of. A life of not simply having more, but being more.

I strongly believe that this motivation is the key to a fairer, more sustainable kind of capitalism. The rebuilding of what was once a worthy notion will begin at the individual level. With individuals like you.

So let's begin. The following chapters are all about *you*. We're not interested anymore about what the world is doing or how business is changing or what the new age of connected consumers want. We're going to zoom out from your life and look down at you with new eyes. Then zoom in and explore your deepest inner motives.

A young entrepreneur once gave me some very insightful feedback on this work. He'd just completed one of the purpose workshops my company carried out to fine-tune the methods shared in this book. When I asked him what he found most useful, he said, 'Oh, the exercises and The Circle are all great, but the most valuable thing you guys did for me today was to ask some killer questions. Y'know, questions I'd never been asked before'.

The following chapters ask you those killer questions:

What is it about the business world that makes you angry?

What do you think is stopping your industry being better?

How will your business idea alleviate the anger you feel about why the world is broken?

Is your current business the ultimate expression of your True Purpose, or is it just the first way you found to implement a powerful motivator you didn't realise was driving you?

What ultimate destiny lies dormant inside you that will fire up the levels of courage and conviction you'll need to overcome the obstacles which will invariably spring up to stop you achieving something truly worthwhile in life?

Sure, these are all big emotional questions, but trust me, I'm no vague evangelist. I'm a practitioner. And a sceptical one at that. I'm not interested in warm, fuzzy philosophies that make you feel good but change nothing. Or smart academic theories that go nowhere. I'm writing this book because I've seen that the pragmatic workouts you're about to do make things actually happen in the real world. They drive real change in real people's lives. In tough retail markets. And complex service industries.

So don't be afraid to work with your feelings in this part. There's plenty of opportunity later in the book to apply those feelings to the cold, hard world of business. For now, relax and let your true self out for a play.

There are seven exercises to complete in order to surface your True Purpose. Some of them are traditional workouts for setting corporate missions and identifying personal values. Some are my company's own creations. But the key is the sequence I've put them in.

After more than a decade of helping organisations from one-woman startups to billion-dollar, stock market–listed corporations, my company has developed a specific sequence of workouts that we believe creates an effective pathway to not only surfacing your authentic motives but understanding how to then act on them.

So be patient, take your time and please work through the exercises one by one. They're like base camps up a mountain: it's risky to skip any if you want to make it all the way to the top.

(12) your first task: the before ad

This is a quick preliminary exercise before you begin the meaty stuff. It's paired with the final exercise, called ... wait for it ... the After Ad. But don't worry about that yet. Try not to second-guess what you might discover about yourself in the coming chapters and begin simply and honestly.

What I want you to do is write an ad for your business as it is right now. Just a headline capturing your biggest benefit to customers and then 50 to 100 words of copy to explain what you offer and the benefits of your business compared to the competition.

the little furniture shop example

A married couple, owners of a small furniture design and manufacturing business, came to one of my company's purpose workshops. Their designs were cool and contemporary and their build quality very high. But they were under increasing pressure by a growing number of competitors importing cheap items from Asia. They figured they couldn't beat these large retailers so they joined them and imported a few extra products to augment their own furniture creations.

Their Before Ad read like this:

TOP QUALITY FURNITURE AT AFFORDABLE PRICES!

Whatever your furniture needs, you'll find it in our showroom. We have our own designs, plus lots of affordable imported brands of lounge and dining suites, bedroom settings, home office furniture and more. Our knowledgeable staff will assist you in finding just the right item for your home. We offer a design service to amend any of the items in our range and we provide free delivery for orders over $1000. Call in today.

Once this couple had completed our purpose workshop they wrote a completely different After Ad, but you'll see that later. This is just a quick example of the kind of ad I'd like you to write for yourself now.

The key thing with this warm-up exercise is to not overthink your little ad; simply give yourself a good benchmark of how you currently talk about your business.

And hey, don't worry if it ends up sounding like one of those cheesy ads you see at your local cinema. The point is not to test your creativity at writing ads; it's to capture how you currently describe the appeal of your business.

what if i don't have a business idea?

In 'How to use this book' I explained that it's not essential to have an existing business to get value from this book. I think the concept of The Circle makes interesting reading whether you plan to start your own business or not.

But now that we're getting into the part where I can help you surface your True Purpose, it will really help to have some kind of idea for a business. Not necessarily *the* idea for *the* business. Just a notion of what category of business you feel you might want to get into: a retail store, a professional service, a certain type of social enterprise helping a certain section of the community?

Pick the commercial sector you want to be in and the physical shape. A shopfront in a mall or suburban street? An online retailer? A manufacturer? An app? A social enterprise? Draw the broad brushstrokes and as long as it's some kind of business or organisation that reflects your authentic desire to change something in the world, you'll be able to write your Before Ad and start surfacing your true motivations.

If you get stuck on this one point, email me about it: mike@ meerkats.com.au or post a comment at truthgrowthrepeat.com.

Some people need a little jolt from an unbiased observer to set out on their path.

worksheet: your before ad

Scenario: Write a functional newspaper ad for your business as it currently stands. Describe what you offer and the benefits of your business compared to the competition.

headline

Capture your key benefit in a headline. Just like the ads you see every day in the newspaper. You can make it as functional or as fun as you like. Write a few on a notepad and put your favourite one here.

_____

_____

_____

copy

Explain your products and/or services. Say why you think they meet the needs of your target audience. Don't worry about being clever. Just get the essential benefits down.

_____

_____

_____

_____

_____

_____

_____

_____

_____

_____

you can download this template at truthgrowthrepeat.com.

(13) exercise a: eulogy

Over the years I've come across many variations of workshop exercises that help you zoom out from your own life and see yourself and your business in the big picture. They're often hypothetical situations aimed at opening your mind, such as asking you to imagine travelling to Mars to start a colony and thinking about which inspirational public figures you would take with you (everyone says Elon Musk).

The first three exercises are described by David Taylor in his books *The Brand Gym* and *Brand Vision*. His aim is to help companies find their core brand meaning, but I found that with some tweaking, these exercises are also effective at starting to surface an authentic organisational purpose.

Okay, let's go. Smartphone off. Imagination on.

In Eulogy, I want you to pretend that your business has passed away. It's figuratively dead and is about to be farewelled with a formal funeral service. I want you to imagine you're standing in the chapel as the guests file in the door. Think about that scene and visualise it in your mind.

This hypothetical situation is a terrific way to start surfacing your True Purpose. And it will work for you even if you haven't started that awesome new business you have in mind. It just takes a little more imagination. All you need to do is pretend that this funeral is happening 10 years in the future, after your new company has launched and become a success. Imagine your business idea has worked out exactly the way you hoped it would: you attracted passionate employees, appealed to the right kind of customer, created bold new products that advanced your entire category, and so on. Imagine all that being in place for your future business, then picture its funeral as described above and answer the following questions.

who would come to the funeral?

If your business ceased to exist, who would be most affected? How big a hole would it leave in society? And to what degree? Take a look around the crowd in that chapel: who's crying, who's simply teary and who's already looking at their watch, ready to leave?

Think beyond the usual suspects. Sure, write down your family, your employees, your business partners and your most loyal customers. But think too about your company's suppliers, outside consultants and even your competitors.

Eulogy is an exercise for unlocking the impact your business is making in society beyond what it merely does to make money.

So consider all areas of society. Would anyone from the government or local council come? How about your employees' family members?

Does your business have a knock-on effect in the world somehow that would attract a broader list of attendees?

These prompts aren't suggesting there are mandatory inclusions. There are no good answers and no bad answers. Whatever is true for you is what will be most useful in helping you surface your True Purpose. So don't fake it. If nobody would come to your brand's funeral, write that. That's incredibly insightful.

funeral for a houseboat

When we did this exercise for the owner of a houseboat rental company, we were surprised at who he thought would attend the funeral.

Gathered around the casket weren't just his staff and customers, but the families of both, and *their* families. He said people would attend his company's funeral who never even rented a houseboat from him because he believed that, ultimately, a houseboat holiday is not just a way to relax, but a way for families to unite, to strengthen bonds, to repair old and broken connections, and to rediscover love and respect and friendship.

He explained that houseboat holidays had a terrific emotional knock-on effect that was unlike almost any other kind of holiday. He said it was because of a combination of factors that complemented each other: large family groups being confined to a small space (the houseboat) and experiencing something new and exciting (skippering your own watercraft — often for the first time — and sharing the duties) in an environment of calm and wonder (unspoilt waterways away from traffic and people and development).

He said the effect was to bring families and groups of friends closer and that when they go home their other family members and friends notice this. He admitted (sheepishly) that this was one of the main reasons he got into this line of work and that it directly influences the way he goes about his business — that is, the time he takes to brief his customers, how he strives to remove any causes of angst during their stay, and so on.

This one exercise opened up a floodgate of emotion and passion and truth in this man and led to us helping him surface a True Purpose for his business that went way beyond 'renting houseboats'. Indeed, he left with a head full of new service delivery ideas, web content and brand extensions.

what would they say about your brand?

The word 'eulogy' refers to that short speech people make at funerals. It's usually delivered by a close family member or friend, sometimes the priest, either at the church, at the gravesite or afterwards at the wake. It invariably commemorates the life of the deceased in a polite and hopefully moving way. So what would the eulogy be for your business?

If elegant prose isn't your thing, simply think about the conversations people might have as they stand around the gravesite, or what they'd whisper to each other over tea and canapés at your home, or perhaps what they'd write for the Obituaries column in the newspaper.

However it's worded, the key thing is to write down what you think people would say about your company at its funeral.

If they're sad, why are they sad? How will your business be missed?

Is it in the usual ways — 'I'll miss that coffee shop. They always gave me a good brew in the morning'? Or does it go further — 'I just don't know how our town is going to survive without the farm supplies store'?

Does your company's passing leave a hole in the world somehow? How big a hole? Who does it affect most?

Another effective way to do this part of the exercise is to imagine that all the mourners have asked one of their number to represent them with a moving eulogy. Who do they ask to step up to the pulpit and what do they say?

And hey, just for fun, what would the black hatters whisper? The ones who were dragged along to the funeral and who — to provide a balance to the overly worthy accolades being thrown about — offer to quietly point out your brand's faults?

a big-business example

My company once did this exercise for more than 100 managers and senior staff of a major health insurance company. We held several workshops over a number of weeks, and the answers we received were along a very clear theme: this organisation had an enormous impact on society. Way beyond just staff and customers.

For a start, they told us that the funeral would be packed out with thousands of current staff, past staff, customers, customers' wives, husbands, fathers, mothers, uncles, brothers, friends; plus doctors, nurses, surgeons, dentists, physiotherapists, chiropractors, paediatricians, pharmacists, ambulance drivers, midwives — even lawyers and politicians.

What's more, the comments they believed the guests would be making were of an emotional intensity I'd almost never heard for a commercial brand.

Things like, 'This is terrible. What will the hundreds of thousands of old people do now?' and 'I'm so worried about what's going to happen to all those new mums out there'.

We discovered very quickly that this organisation didn't just pay for people's healthcare, they helped huge chunks of society to function; and that the people who worked for them were driven by moral and ethical incentives, not just financial ones. It was a critical distinction in an era when commercial insurance companies driven by very self-serving needs such as delivering profits to shareholders were trying to convince people that they cared as much as this very old not-for-profit brand did.

It really is amazing what this exercise can bring up. So keep picturing that funeral service and answer the next critical question.

who wouldn't come?

Who's *not* at your business's funeral?

Your most fierce competitor is an obvious choice. But we're often surprised by business owners sheepishly admitting that other more likely attendees wouldn't actually show up.

One owner confessed that the service delivery of her current business was so poor she doubted that any but the most loyal of her customers would bother to show up.

Another owner felt that no-one outside of his staff and immediate family would find the time to attend.

The bottom line is, if you don't believe your business has an impact beyond the simple seller–buyer relationship, don't invent a ripple effect that's not there; write the truth no matter what.

It's all useful.

worksheet: eulogy

Scenario: Imagine your business has passed away and there's a funeral service for it. If your business is brand new or yet to start, imagine this funeral is happening 10 years after you've achieved everything you seek for it.

who would come to your business's funeral?

Think beyond your staff and customers. Who else does your business have a connection with in society?

_____

_____

_____

_____

_____

_____

_____

_____

who wouldn't come?

Who doesn't like you? Who likes you but just wouldn't be bothered?

_____

_____

_____

_____

_____

_____

_____

_____

what would the guests at this funeral say about your business?

How will you be missed? What did you contribute to their lives? How broad an impact did your business have on your community or society in general?

_____

_____

_____

_____

_____

_____

_____

_____

try to summarise all their comments into a short eulogy.

What would be said in that short speech before the coffin is lowered into the ground?

_____

_____

_____

_____

_____

_____

you can download this template at truthgrowthrepeat.com.

_____

(14) exercise b: protest

This is a simple exercise, but it can be incredibly powerful because it can help you bring to the surface the angry passion that's driving you deep down inside. You may think you started a business for logical reasons, like money and independence, but more often than not we humans start enterprises to make the world a better place.

Somehow.

Find that *somehow* and you'll find an almost inexhaustible fuel to power your dreams. You see, changing the world — or even one little part of it — requires us to go up against convention. And that's hard. Ask any of history's true change-makers, such as Mahatma Gandhi, or Martin Luther King Jnr, or for that matter Steve Jobs and Richard Branson. You need to find new reservoirs of energy and resilience and self-belief. And I believe we humans acquire those attributes more readily when we're spurred on by passions born of anger rather than joy.

In my experience, people who are driven by an anger about an injustice that's happening in an area of human endeavour that they relate to — that is, in their line of work, their particular category of social enterprise, and so on — seem to have more energy, be more action-oriented, be more resilient to setbacks and be less likely to procrastinate than those driven purely by optimism.

Don't get me wrong; I love optimists. I love people with a can-do attitude and an almost bulletproof relationship with failure. But I hate lazy positivity. I hate positivity that crawls towards its goal, or gives up and pretends things are better than they are. It seems to me that having a fire in your belly makes more things happen in the world than having a light in your heart does. Yes, you need both — but one leads the other.

Here's how the Protest exercise works: imagine you're going to go out into the street today and protest against something you feel very strongly about. Critically, you need to focus on things connected to your line of work. We all want to end hunger but if that's a million miles from why you started your business, it won't get you anywhere.

Try this: think about the reasons you started your own business in the first place. Think about where you were and what you were seeing when the idea first came into your head:

- Were you working for a large company that dominated an area of human need? Maybe this company just kept buying up all its competitors and so the whole category stopped innovating. (It's not uncommon.)

- Were you watching this from inside that company and becoming more and more frustrated?

- Did you have a love for a particular product in people's lives that you felt was being poorly understood by the brands who were currently making and selling it?

- Was it an injustice that made you feel people were being poorly serviced — or worse, taken advantage of?

- Was it a whole new area of commerce or social equality that every other brand or organisation was ignoring?

march of the geeks

My company once did this exercise for the internet provider I mentioned in the first part—that fantastically innovative bunch of net nerds, who when they first met us, had somehow convinced themselves that they had to put their passion second to being *smart business people.*

They had originally briefed our agency to launch their brand into a new market as the cool internet company that offered fast broadband. Cos, y'know, that's what they'd seen others do. After doing this exercise with their board, management and staff, it was clear to us that this wasn't just any old internet company; this was a fierce tribe united by a powerful anger about a huge injustice they saw in their category.

They passionately believed that the internet was the most amazing invention in the history of humankind — better even than the Gutenberg printing press, which in survey after survey of intellectuals and historians had been voted the number-one most influential invention of all time.

These guys felt that, just as the Gutenberg press had made knowledge accessible to the masses for the first time in human existence — thus taking away much of the power and bias of kings and popes and army generals who relied on misinformation to control the population — the internet could do that on steroids! Today's popes and kings are corporations, governments and the media. The internet can neuter their control of information and give people the power to control their own lives, to express themselves, and to share the truth with each other, instantly and globally.

And yet, in Australia at least, the internet was in the hands of the big, established phone companies. And in the words of our net nerd buddies, they were 'stuffing it up deluxe'. Phone companies didn't 'get the net' like they did: their sales pitches were full of technobabble, their product offerings conveniently ignored Skype and VoIP, their products assumed people knew what a router was and how to plug it in.

The unbusiness-like nerds at our client company were so driven to give people a better experience of the net that they worked harder to educate their customers, speak plain English to them, make technical products easier to understand, spend more time with customers on their help line, offer to send techies to their home to help fit stuff (this was way before Geek Squad), and make the phone sales team the same people as the help line team. More, they lobbied the government for faster national broadband speeds and spoke out against unjust behaviour by the big telcos and film studios.

We helped show them that this is exactly what they should be saying to Australia in their marketing. This core anger at the lack of creativity and equality in Australia's internet system was their true motive for being in business. Why hide it behind more traditional marketing messaging just because that's what everyone else was doing?

(Long story short: they ended up being the second biggest ISP in Australia.)

Okay, you get it now, right? Your anger may have enormous commercial potential. Good, so start thinking and writing. There are two sections to fill in.

what are you protesting against?

Write it down in long form first. Get it all down on paper. All your anger and frustration and disappointment and sadness (and maybe even guilt) about what's wrong with the industry your business is in. Anything and everything you can think of, even if it leads to sharing what you believe needs fixing in society, or the entire world.

Then read it all back and feel for the one that's most you. I mean, the protest that makes you involuntarily fist pump because it hits your hot button so hard.

Now write the two- or three-word headline that would go on your protest banner that captures that point. In our workshops we actually make little banners (A4 cards on sticks). When sharing their protests, delegates hold their signs aloft and shout out the message. It seems a bit gimmicky at first, but it really does bring out the innate passions lurking inside.

Let's say it's 1943 and you're Ingvar Kamprad, the founder of IKEA. Your protest banner might have been, 'The rich don't own good design!'

Or say it's 1984 and you're Richard Branson, the founder of Virgin Airlines. Your protest banner (the first of many in this guy's incredible career) might have said, 'The air is not fare!'

what are you protesting for?

Now switch it round. What's possible for the world if that thing you're protesting against is fixed? What could happen to people if you're successful in your fight against that thing?

This is a useful second exercise to do because while it's always best to start with what's wrong in our world, in order to clarify the task, it doesn't mean much if you don't *do* something about it. And doing something requires solutions. And solutions are positive things. They're the outcomes that come from our anger. They're the positive result of pointing our frustration *at* something.

Take our internet buddies. Their *protest against* was 'Big telcos are stuffing up the internet!', then their *protest for* was 'Free the net!' This objective-based version of their protest triggered their creation of innovative, customer-service ideas and products. It demanded that they pursue business objectives outside of short-term sales, such as lobbying the government for faster national broadband speeds and film studios to stop the forced disclosure of customer details in their pursuit of video piracy. Their positive protest statement helped clarify the True Purpose that had always been guiding them, but had been subjugated to the demands of business.

It's like you're saying to yourself, 'Okay, I make a good case. Everyone agrees with me. So what am I gonna do about it?'

It's worth spending time on this one. It's deceptively powerful. Try writing down some things, then taking a break. Go see your mum or best friend and ask them, 'Why did I start my company?' or 'What gets me worked up about my work?' They're often the best people to play back to us our own innermost drivers. The things that push us on the outside can often be buried inside our own head, and it sometimes takes people outside our head to see them clearly.

a social-enterprise example

My company once did this exercise with the CEO of a social enterprise. Their goal was to find employment for underprivileged youth and they had established an office and business skills training centre in an area with a high population of indigenous families.

They believed their purpose was to find gainful employment for those whom society had passed by; or to whom society (and broken family and dysfunctional friends) had taught were unworthy of anything of value in life. We loved their stated mission. They filled an important role in a society where even high levels of welfare still had large cracks that young people could fall through.

I've often found that the people who start the most inspiring social enterprises and charities are driven by a passion to help humans on a broader scale than the focus of their current organisation would have you believe.

So it was a pleasant surprise when the CEO of the job centre held up her protest banner and it said, 'Fix the education system!' I was intrigued. Where did that come from?

It turns out the reason this remarkable lady had started the job centre for underprivileged youth is because she'd been a teacher and seen how many young people get to the end of their schooling with no ambition, no hope, no sense of self-worth. It seemed to her that the system knew about this and turned a blind eye. It even sometimes actively worked to make it so: teachers would either hint to, or say directly to, some young people that the best they can hope for in life is unemployment benefits or lowly paid manual labour. Those young people would then go home and get the same messages from deeply unhappy parents whose own lives had not worked out as they'd planned.

The CEO wanted to give these people a reason to believe in themselves. She chose employment because that's one of the most powerful ways we humans get the evidence that we have some worth. She felt that society as a whole would benefit from more young people getting good jobs and following their passions to inspiring ends, rather than resigning to the inevitable disappointments and unhappiness of an unfair life. She felt that over time this would lead to a decrease in broken homes, alcoholism, drug addiction, crime, youth suicide, and lots more.

In short, a fairer, more caring society built on each individual's self-belief. After much discussion and soul-searching, and a fair bit of extra-curricular work after the workshop, it seemed clear to me that this lady's True Purpose wasn't to help underprivileged youth find work; that was simply a very honourable first application of her True Purpose. Her actual purpose was to help people feel valued in the world. The one thing that was fuelling all the passion and energy and resilience she required to establish and run the job centre was a burning desire to prove to every human that the world was better with them in it — that they had a role to play to provide something of worth.

This was something of a revelation to this CEO and her small team because all at once it not only clarified their role in the world — which instantly added power to their website content, their presentations to benefactors and their pitch to young people at risk — it opened up their entire strategy for the future. They now knew that their True Purpose had applications for single mothers, mothers whose kids had grown up and left home, men in their late 50s who'd been retrenched, old people who still had intellect and energy — in short, anyone to whom society was sending subtle signals that they had no real role in the world.

They started thinking about new training programs for startups, corporate-backed scholarships to university, workshops on franchises and small business, and centres not just in low socio-economic areas.

Can you see the potential of that organisation before and after? Can you see just how much the world is going to be made better over time simply by that CEO and her team understanding the difference between how they just happened to be currently implementing their True Purpose and their actual True Purpose?

That's how powerful this little exercise can be. For some reason, we humans often start an enterprise wanting to change the world, but slowly, over time, we suppress that core motivation — we push it sideways and let the more logical drivers of sales, strategy and profit take its place. In doing so we begin to look like everyone else in business. We succumb to the gravity I wrote about in the first part. The invisible force that draws us back down to earth — to sameness and boredom. Our rockets stop firing and we settle. Down.

I'm not saying you can't change the world by following convention. But I know for damn sure that it will take you a lot longer and you'll be way more exhausted along the way. Is that any way to live your life? Is that really sending the right messages to our kids?

another social-enterprise example (they're great protesters)

I did this exercise once for a community radio station. They represented the dominant indigenous tribe in my area and they were split over their True Purpose.

Half the station believed their ultimate objective was global equality and the other half believed it was equality for their tribe only. Like many first nations around the world, they had suffered so much at the hands of empire builders they were still rightfully seeking justice for themselves. And yet, beneath that desire, what was undeniably driving everyone at the station was a core belief in equality for all humans.

The Protest exercise helped clarify this standoff.

Two people had attended from the station, each one representing one side of the argument. They both stood up and took turns explaining their protest banners.

The message on one banner was 'We change the world!' and on the other 'Unity for our community!'

As I listened to the debate between them I saw a golden thread connecting the two banners. It occurred to me that one banner reflected a purpose while the other reflected a strategy for achieving that purpose.

I put it to them that perhaps their ultimate True Purpose was to change the world into a fairer, more equal place where the colour of your skin or the place of your birth did not determine your ranking in society: that everyone is equal and has value and deserves to be in this world. But that the only way to foster this sentiment was to unite their own peoples first: to overcome the anger from centuries of repression, to embrace the majesty of their culture and to be a proud, confident people. This would require education, celebration and motivation on a mass scale. And what better business model to adopt to achieve that than a radio station. And then maybe a TV station. And then an advanced social media network. And then publishing and events.

They had entertained all these options as brand extensions, but had allowed them to be stalled by the disagreement about their ultimate purpose.

It was an incredibly powerful moment because all at once the future came into sharp focus for this group. No longer would they give up a potent idea because 'that's not what a community radio station does'. They started to see themselves as global change agents who just happened to run a radio station. And their path to achieving their destiny was to unite their peoples.

I have to admit I shed a tear or two during that particular workshop. And it wasn't just sadness or joy. It was a powerful feeling welling up inside me about the possibilities on offer to the world now that these incredibly passionate people were all pointing the same way — as a collective.

I once wrote an article titled, 'The Agony of Potential' in which I described the clenched, knotted feeling I get in my stomach when I witness a group of people who have incredible potential to achieve great things for the world and are blocked. By fear. By an unimaginative board. By an egotistical CEO.

It's a kind of agony because so much good could be had. So much personal fulfilment and group pride and commercial prosperity. All sitting there just waiting to be snatched up and brought to life.

The feeling I get when I see a small business or startup or social enterprise embrace that potential is the exact opposite. I feel a joyous sense of impending liberation of the human spirit. Like the world just got a little better.

That feeling is why I'm writing this book.

worksheet: protest

Scenario: Imagine going out into the streets right now and marching against something your business objects to strongly. Think about the key thing you believe is broken in your industry that drove/is driving your desire to start your own business.

what three or four words would you put on your protest banner?

What snappy/clever/angry banner headline would get you on the nightly news? Write a few. Keep going 'til you nail it.

_____

_____

_____

_____

_____

_____

is there a positive version?

Once you've got your anger and frustration out, try flipping your banner headlines to the positive. What's possible if you end this bad thing? What's the ultimate benefit if it stops?

_____

_____

_____

_____

_____

_____

you can download this template at truthgrowthrepeat.com.

can't find the fire? write a letter

If you're finding it hard to pinpoint the source of your frustration or restlessness with the Protest sign technique, there are two other ways you can bring out the passionate restlessness inside you that could be the untapped fuel for your True Purpose. It's more of a stream-of-consciousness approach that has you writing a letter. Or two.

'for too long now ...'

This is one of my company's original exercises and a personal favourite. What you do here is describe in longhand a situation that's been going on for a while now — in an area of human endeavour that interests you — that you think is not ideal, or is unfair, or morally wrong or just plain stupid.

Describe that situation after the words, 'For too long now ...' and then describe your solution to this situation after the words, 'It's time that ...' The key here is to use your own language, the way you'd describe your feelings to a friend over a coffee. Don't worry about proper grammar or impressive adjectives — just write from your heart. Let it flow out.

Let me give you an example.

I once did a purpose workshop with a group of indigenous Australians. It was part of a two-week program to give 10 Aboriginal entrepreneurs the necessary commercial skills to start their own businesses. It was a terrific program offering rare assistance to an extremely motivated bunch of people, but each day was long and packed with learning. By the time I came in to do my session with them on day 3, their heads were already spinning with dozens of lessons on business planning, financial management, tax diligence, branding, marketing, consumer segmentation and so many Venn diagrams that the walls of the conference centre looked like polka-dot wallpaper.

Unsurprisingly, when I asked them why they wanted to start a business I was disappointed. What I heard was a collection of textbook responses about consumer demand and market opportunities, all cautiously delivered like they were trying their best to be business people. There was no mention of what they themselves wanted out of this. There was no fire, no passion, no humanity. This was hardly the galvanised group of fiery entrepreneurs the organisers told me I'd be presenting to.

I could tell they had spirit, but I felt it was already being neutralised by conventional business practices. So I sat them in a circle and said something like this:

'Listen. I don't want to hear about consumers and competitors and white space in the market. I want to hear about *you*. For the next hour, let's forget about what everyone else in the world wants. Let's only talk about what *you* want'.

The atmosphere in the room seemed to change. It might have just been my wishful thinking, but they appeared to relax a little. Some leaned forward. I then said:

'I want you to tell me just two things. One: what's broken in the world that your business idea is going to fix? Like, what are you angry about? What's fuelling your passion to choose this particular business idea, as opposed to just buying a Jim's Mowing franchise? Write that down after the words "For too long now ..." Two: how does your business idea fix this problem while at the same time giving customers something they'd be happy buying? Write "that after the words It's time that ..."'

The furious scribbling that followed warmed my heart. Here was truth and passion pouring out freely. Without fear of being wrong, without fear of being seen as naive or stupid. They might not have been able to describe their business idea, but they sure could describe what was going on in their part of the world that they didn't like.

At the end of the 15-minute time limit I asked them to read what they'd written. And I asked them to read it with fire and passion. I told them to have some fun. Be themselves. And boy, did we get some awesome rage.

Here were 10 business people who were so inexperienced they described themselves with words like 'naive' and 'innocent', and yet what I heard were 10 business ideas that would not only make society better for a lot of people, but would be absolutely commercially viable; for example:

- A middle-aged lady with a friendly smile and a fire in her eyes stood up. She said that 'for too long now' traditional funeral homes had completely misunderstood the Aboriginal culture around death and burial. What's more, they were notorious for hiding fees and running deceitful ads that exaggerated how cheap a funeral could be. So much so that it often took 10 weeks or more to bury a deceased Aboriginal person because their relatives had such a hard time finding the money. She said 'it's time that' someone created an Aboriginal funeral home that was affordable and honest, with truly transparent fees and a range of services that respected the cultural implications of their race. She said their entire community could benefit from not being made to feel like the losers of society. Especially at such a delicate time as the death of a loved one. Amazing, right?

- A shy, young man stood up. He was dressed in a hoodie that covered most of his face. He said that 'for too long now' the local government and the media had complained about the antics of young people loitering on the streets, holding Facebook parties that grew out of control and riding skateboards where they weren't allowed. The authorities were being hypocritical, he wrote, because they were so quick to criticise him and his friends for being lazy hoodlums, yet so slow to offer any solutions for their obvious boredom and pent-up youthful energy. He said 'it's time that' someone got together with the local government and created an entertainment venue that catered to young people with the full support and endorsement of the authorities. He wrote that it would be a great win–win for young people and society in general — that they could help each other see that they are really all alike.

- A soft-spoken young woman stood up and introduced herself as a single mother. She said that 'for too long now' the trend among young Aboriginal mothers was to dump their kids at grandma's house so they could go out and work, or worse, drink and laze about. It meant that the responsibility for raising children often fell to the grandmothers (often the grandfathers — like the mothers' husbands — were nowhere to be found) and that the balanced development and growth of their children was at risk. What's more, the conventional Western approach to childcare was shockingly similar: leave your kids at day care and let some bored part-time worker take care of them. She said 'it's time that' we changed the definition of the word 'care' in day care. It's time that we had day-care centres that not only looked after the children, but also the mothers, teaching them how to raise their children, coaching them on the importance of maternal love and affection, and so on.

One after the other these ordinary men and women stood up and spoke of a powerful commercial idea driven by a genuine, heartfelt motive. A motive that was clearly so potent it could inspire product and service innovations that could generate the sales and customer satisfaction to fuel a business. What's more, each concept had the potential to deliver a massive knock-on benefit to individual communities, entire societal groups and, who knows, maybe one day the whole world.

All made evident by tapping into what's wrong in the world first, and what could be right in the world second. I felt at the time that it was incredibly important for this group of future business owners to keep that original flame of True Purpose alive inside them. They were not about to just start a business; they were about to start a business as indigenous Australians.

That's doubly hard. They were going to need even more reservoirs of energy and resilience and self-belief in order to succeed.

'dear world ...'

This second letter-writing task was originally called 'Letter to a broken world' and appears in a book titled *Story Wars* by Jonah Sachs.

It's another way of bringing to the surface what you most want to see changed in the world and what you believe the benefits of that will be. It's a simple undertaking, but it has the ability to unlock deep-felt sentiments that you might have found hard to enunciate in the other exercises.

It's very much like 'For too long now ...' but with a more optimistic slant that really works for some people.

What you do is write a letter to the world that will be sealed away and only opened and read in 20 years' time. It begins with these words: 'Dear World, It is my sincerest hope that by now ...'

You write from your heart what you earnestly hope has happened as a result of you following your most authentic motivations to bring good change into the world. Imagine what might be possible to your industry if more and more people follow your example and pursue truth and genuine value in the way they do business. Visualise the possibilities for employees, their families, the customer and society as a whole. What ripple effects might eventuate if everyone started to behave the way you feel they should?

Write it for your industry as a whole. Imagine that this letter will be read out at an assembly of everyone working in your industry. And their families. And customers. And most importantly, the CEOs and board members and industry regulators.

I use the word 'World' as a generic thought starter. I recommend you insert the name of your category of business instead. Writing Dear Healthcare Organisation, or Dear Insurance Industry, or Dear Wall Street will be more likely to tap into your strongest feelings and most creative ideas.

Write it out in a stream of thoughts. Don't try to edit or perfect each sentence. Just spill your guts to a future generation about what you hope they're experiencing.

The best example of this exercise I can give you is one I had the honour of witnessing at a purpose workshop I ran in Thailand at Adfest, Asia's biggest annual advertising conference. I was trying to see if the current generation of young advertising professionals could employ their own beliefs and values to save the advertising industry. The workshop attracted 40 smart, young, creative people from Sri Lanka, India, Pakistan, China, Japan, the Philippines, Malaysia, Singapore and Thailand. Here was a collection of countries at hugely varying stages of maturity as free market economies. And yet within minutes the basic tenets of True Purpose bound everyone together in a common mission. It was a delight.

The high point for me was this exercise. I was only given a two-hour slot for the whole workshop so the delegates had just 10 minutes to complete this task: five minutes to think about their hopes for a better advertising industry and another five minutes to write down their key thoughts to share with the group.

When I asked them to put their pens down and for a first volunteer to share, a young man from an ad agency in the Philippines put up his hand. His name was Angelo Reyes and this was his letter:

Dear Advertising,

It is my sincerest hope that by now, you have come to the realisation of your potential and power. You have so much to offer the world, beyond the latest sale and newest phone plan. You can make things nobody else can imagine and you have the tenacity to see it happen. Your creativity can change cultures, behaviours, and futures. You. F * * * ing. Rock.

So it pains me to remember that you don't respect yourself as much. I hope that you finally stood up for yourself against all the bullies with money and their minions who don't know what they want. I hope you finally get the respect you deserve, you amazing industry you.

I have loved you and your work since the day we met and am still thinking of you during my dying hours. I hope the years that I have contributed to make you respect yourself more was worth it.

Cheers, advertising! You unnecessarily-insecure-yet-full-of-potential-industry you! Please be the amazing sexy creative beast you are meant to be.

I was blown away. Not only by his awesome passion and honesty, but by such beautiful prose. And in just a few minutes.

I told him to take that letter back to his agency, frame it and place it in reception. Or on his front door. And to make those words the first ones potential clients read on his website and LinkedIn profile. Because those words — that magnificent hopeful ambition — are the engine that will drive him towards his True Purpose. It will attract followers. It will generate innovative products and service delivery. It will appeal to a new age of clients who will pay them to bring those beliefs to life for them. It will catch the attention of today's cynical connected consumers and deliver extraordinary sales and growth for those companies. And it just might change his entire industry.

That's the power of this exercise: to say out loud to yourself what is actually at stake by pursuing your True Purpose. Why it will be worth overcoming the barriers to its success. Why you must uphold your belief in it. Why you must always remind yourself and your employees to stick at it when times get tough, when conventional business starts pressuring you to turn away from your True Purpose.

To that young man and his agency this wasn't just a fictional letter — it was their manifesto. And it could be yours too. Which makes it a pretty cool exercise. Ask someone to write a manifesto to express how they're going to change their industry for the better and they often freeze. Ask them to write a 'Dear World ...' letter and it all comes out.

So try one or both of these alternative versions of the Protest exercise for yourself. When you're done writing your letter, read it out to someone who knows you well and see what they think. Ask them if they think it reflects your true motivation. Ask them if they think it sounds like not just a good idea for a business, but whether it would be a good thing for the world to have a business like this in it.

And hey, if you really like your 'For too long now ...' or 'Dear World ...' letter, keep it somewhere handy. Frame it and place it right above your desk. Over the coming months and years of building your business, you can use its power to remind you of the passions you feel right now. You can use it to drive your decision making and to keep you resilient to the seemingly infinite hurdles that rise up before a purpose-driven business owner.

optional worksheet: 'for too long now ...'

Scenario: Imagine sitting down and writing a letter to your industry. A letter that will be read by everyone working in it, along with all the CEOs and boards and regulators and rule makers.

for too long now ...

_____

_____

_____

_____

_____

_____

_____

_____

it's time that ...

_____

_____

_____

_____

_____

_____

_____

_____

optional worksheet: 'dear world …'

Scenario: Imagine sitting down and writing a letter to everyone on the planet that will not be opened and read for 25 years. It's an expression of what you hope has happened in that time. Alternatively, you can write this letter only to the people in your specific industry.

dear world …

_____

_____

_____

_____

_____

_____

_____

_____

_____

_____

_____

_____

_____

Yours sincerely,

_____

you can download this template at truthgrowthrepeat.com.

(15) exercise c: headline

The Headline exercise is an ambition workout. It helps unlock the combined potential of you and all the talented people in your organisation. At the end of the day that's what a True Purpose really is: a way to surface the truth about what you and your team are capable of and then point it at an end benefit bigger than yourselves.

This exercise works exactly the same way if you're a startup with just you and a partner. If your True Purpose is as good as you think it is (and it almost always is), you'll eventually have a team of people around you. A team of people electrified around your idea; a team of people with talent and drive and determination and resilience — the qualities of a rebel army going up against an incumbent government. So all you have to do is ask yourself, 'What is this team of incredible humans capable of?'

This exercise starts to unlock those things. It plays with the question, 'What is possible if the hunches I have about the power of my True Purpose to genuinely help people are true?'

For this exercise to work fully, you have to free yourself from the constraints that may be clouding your mind right now. Y'know, all those day-to-day things that keep business owners up at night: income streams, profit margins, employment issues, aggressive competitors, and so on.

And so on.

And so on.

This is a chance for you to turn your mind from the problems that keep you up at night to the exciting sense of possibility that used to get you out of bed in the morning.

Come on. Just for a few minutes. You can do it.

Here's what you do:

- Pick a newspaper or magazine or website. Any title, printed or online, where stories are published.

- Write the headline to a story you'd love to see in five to ten years. That's far enough in the future for your purpose to have worked its magic on the world, but not so far that it becomes a distant fantasy.

I'll admit that this exercise requires a lot of imagination so I'm going to give you some tips:

- Ask yourself, 'What could my organisation truly achieve one day? If it stays true to its driving passions? If that unmet need or injustice I saw in the world is actually delivered? If the potential of all the smart people around me is truly harnessed?'

- Write down some simulated evidence that your True Purpose in life has been successful. Write it down as statements first; make them as long as you like. Then pick some publishing titles and try your hand at being a sub-editor (they're the people who read a journalist's story and create the short, sharp headline). Have fun with it.

- Start inside your category and work your way out into the broadest reaches of society.

the university example

My company once did this exercise for a university. At the start of the process, many of the senior staff doubted it was possible to have one uniting purpose for their organisation.

Their pessimism stemmed from a fundamental difference of opinion often found in universities that boast substantial research departments: the researchers believed that universities were primarily on the planet to advance humankind with new breakthroughs and therefore felt they should get the bulk of the organisation's support and funding; whereas the lecturing staff believed that educating the next generation of thinkers was most critical to the betterment of humankind, and so they too felt they should be number 1 on the funding list, and were usually disgruntled at how much attention and funding went to the researchers.

During a long, involved process over many months we had them see that both sides wanted the same thing: to make the world better. Further, they both agreed that the key to achieving that was having an open mind. We had them realise that no matter if you were a researcher or a lecturer, your driving passion was to foster an environment of free thinking in order to better solve the problems of the world today.

It was a revelation to both sides and the fresh sense of unity drove that organisation to new heights of internal harmony, peer respect, student intake and more.

A key moment in that process was this exercise. I remember it well. At first, we learned that even the most intellectual and creative thinkers can hold themselves back when it comes to truly exploring the potential of their beliefs.

Their first headlines were local newspapers and related to functional occurrences at the university itself, such as a state health institute being built on their campus, not at the other (then) more glamorous universities.

But after only a little nudging into broader territory, the excitement in the room was palpable. They were writing headlines in *TIME* magazine about their researchers finding a cure for HIV; in *The New York Times* about solving a major food problem in Africa; and somebody couched a terrific story in *Variety* magazine about making globally successful interactive movies in a new studio system built next to their media studies centre.

Their exploration of what was possible if they rallied the talent that already existed in their organisation and pointed it towards a unifying goal went from a bit of local PR to changing the world. And none of it was not possible. None of it was pie-in-the-sky. They all sat back at the end of the exercise when all the headlines were up on the walls around them and agreed that none of it was foolhardy or blindly optimistic.

Powerful stuff.

It's no coincidence that often when we do this exercise, the headlines stop being about the company and start being about the world. So the publications that people choose become broader and broader. And the full potential of that potent True Purpose lying dormant within their organisation starts to tug at their hearts, not just their heads.

By seeing how big an impact you can have on the world, your True Purpose starts to pull you towards something truly incredible. A benefit to so many people that you feel compelled to pursue it. As opposed to that feeling we business owners often have of pushing towards our destiny. Pushing anything is hard work. Being pulled, while sometimes scary, is a delight.

worksheet: headline

Scenario: Picture a magazine cover, newspaper front page or website heading in five years' time. It's about you and your company. What do you hope your business has achieved by then that will be newsworthy?

publications i would love to see my business appear in one day

Pick any publication that you admire or that inspires you, anywhere in the world.

_____

_____

_____

_____

_____

_____

_____

headlines for stories i would love to see written about my business in those publications

Have fun with this. Go crazy with ambition.

_____

_____

_____

_____

_____

_____

_____

my favourite story

Pick your favourite headline and write a summary of the story.

_____

_____

_____

_____

_____

_____

_____

_____

_____

_____

_____

(16) exercise d: why words

This is a powerful tool to use when applying your True Purpose. There is still some self-discovery in this exercise — as there is in Eulogy, Protest and Headline — but it also begins to point you somewhere. Somewhere exciting and real. And true.

You will begin to feel the guiding hand of an authentically motivating purpose. You will begin to feel pulled towards something that is clearly worthwhile, as opposed to pushing yourself to something that feels worthwhile but is vague to you.

It's called Why Words. It's my twist on the concept of brand archetypes.

a quick word on brand archetypes

In business, brand archetypes are a traditional method for clarifying what kind of personality you want your brand to have in the minds of consumers. And, if authentic, in the minds of your staff too. Knowing your brand archetype can help direct your brand behaviour in advertising and consumer engagement and can even influence product design and service delivery.

Some typical archetypes you'd recognise are Sage (Google), Explorer (Land Rover), Creator (Apple), Rebel (Harley Davidson) and Pragmatist (Volkswagen).

I find the thinking around brand archetypes to be valid in theory, but in practice I have one major problem: even the longest list of archetypes (and there are many lists out there now) tap out at 60. And they can often be as few as 12.

Here's my issue with that: the authors of these lists are basically saying that all the companies in the world can be divided into a few dozen types. That just doesn't make sense to me. So you have several hundred thousand businesses all behaving as ... what ... Rebels? You can see evidence of this theoretical drawback yourself: go buy an outdoor adventure magazine and see how many brands are trying to own the Explorer archetype.

That's not just a crazy way to try and differentiate yourself — I find it insanely inauthentic. It forces companies to mould themselves to a very specific and incredibly limited personality. Worse, I believe it encourages people to 'acquire personality traits' to reflect one of the few brand archetypes, as opposed to reflecting the infinite uniqueness of themselves.

You see the truth is, I've got a feeling that the people who own and run all those businesses adopting the same brand archetype have — deep inside them — a view of their category, a view of the world that's utterly exceptional. And that distinctiveness can be the thing that makes them more successful by being more authentic about their passions, to themselves, to their staff and to their customers.

Put simply, why settle for being just one of a dozen entities in the world when you can be *you*?

Why Words gives you a brand archetype that's yours — and yours alone. Nobody else will have it. This method unlocks millions of possible brand archetypes.

Okay, so here's how it works. This is fun. Go with it.

the annoying stereotype

Write down, using just one adjective and one noun, how someone who doesn't know you might describe a company in your industry. Their first knee-jerk reaction to hearing what you do for a living.

To kick off, try role-playing that classic barbecue conversation:

Stranger:	Hi there, I'm Fred.
You:	Hi Fred. I'm <your name>.
Stranger:	So what do you do?
You:	I'm in <your industry>.
Stranger:	Oh, okay. So you're one of those <adjective/noun>!

You (awkward smile): Ha. Yeah, I guess so.

It's amazing how often the conversation unfolds like this, where an entire industry is put into a sarcastic pigeon-hole. Let me give you a very personal example.

Even though my company, Meerkats, has spent more than a decade smashing all the old myths about ad agencies, we're still seen as Flashy Madmen by the general public. I also get Slick Adguy, Ponytailed Porsche-driver, Fast-talking Huckster and, if I'm lucky, Wacky Creative.

They're all clichéd and mildly insulting, but I understand how people get these one-eyed beliefs. They've seen the TV shows and movies and they're just trying to break the ice in that friendly, slightly belittling way that we Aussies seem to be so good at. And to be honest, watching the behaviour of many people in my industry I can totally empathise with this broad view.

Get the idea? Viewed from the outside, how would someone trying to jokingly disparage you describe your industry? Be Fred for a while and write them all down. Using the worksheet that follows will really help in this exercise.

the inspiring reality

Once you've exhausted all the cliché and/or mildly insulting ways strangers could classify your company, write down the descriptor that you *want.* Write down the adjective and noun that you'd love to hear come from one of your staff or customers.

Try this: pretend one of your most passionate employees, or loyal customers, is standing next to that guy Fred at that barbecue conversation and they interject to set Fred straight about you. How would they describe your company to counter Fred's one-eyed view?

And don't stop at just an accurate reflection of who you really are, or of who your team of amazing people are. Keep going until you find yourself with two words that move you ... that are inspiring.

Keep asking yourself, 'What's the ultimate benefit to people, to the world, if I'm genuine in my pursuit of this purpose? If I succeed?' Then write down how you need to behave, who you need to be in order to achieve that.

And hey, it has to be true, of course, so don't exaggerate!

I think the key is to get a little worked up about it. Tap into that frustration you feel when people totally misunderstand what you do for a living — that sense of injustice you feel when people constantly underestimate what's possible for the world in your line of work.

In my company's Find Your Why workshops, we've found that this fun little exercise can be challenging. People are either not self-deprecating enough in the first part of the exercise, or not visionary enough in the second. But it's insanely potent, no matter how big a business you are.

Here are two more examples, one for a billion-dollar land development company and one for an enormous government utility.

the urban developer

My company once worked with a land developer that's listed on the Australian Stock Exchange and holds land parcels all over Australia valued at more than one billion dollars.

They also build apartments, retail complexes and office parks. But their strength is in master planned residential communities — the ones you see advertised on TV with enticing house and land packages for first homebuyers.

Because of an explosion in land development in my part of Australia and the ensuing invasion of some pretty shonky developers, a slightly inebriated Fred (the guy at the barbecue) would say these people are Slimy Blockpeddlers or Bulldozing Fatcats.

In reality, most of the managers and staff we met were driven by a passion to find better and better ways for people to live in the modern urban environment. Their landscapers and designers worked harder than most to solve the problems that see too many large land estates end up as barren wastelands. They pushed for keeping more natural bushland in each estate. They figured in the walking distances from schools and shops and transport hubs. And they sought to maintain a relationship with homeowners long after the sale in order to foster community spirit. And lots, lots more.

So these amazing people who could, quite literally, change the world for the better, walked away from our workshop not as Greedy Landbarons but as Dedicated Lifemakers. They were the two Why Words we felt summed them up the best. Can you imagine the difference being called 'dedicated' rather than 'greedy' makes to the pride of being in that group; or the difference being known as a lifemaker rather than a landbaron makes to the quality of their work?

the energy company

The state-owned energy utility in my home state could arguably be called the biggest energy brand in the world. It's tasked with providing safe, reliable electricity to an area of more than 2 500 000 square kilometres. That's like one utility powering the United Kingdom, Ireland, France, Belgium, the Netherlands, Germany, Denmark, Switzerland, Spain, Portugal, Italy, Austria and Greece combined. With a similar diversity of terrain and even more extremes of temperature. An incredible feat of engineering and tenacious spirit.

But talk to the locals and they'd probably roll their eyes and describe them as being hopelessly inefficient and inept. You see, this massive electrical network still had hundreds of thousands of ageing wooden poles from the 1950s. And while the utility was fully engaged in replacing every single one, occasionally an old pole would fail and fall across a road or start a bushfire. Add in a long succession of increased charges and it didn't matter if they were providing power to the moon — their public image was woeful. Some of the managers confessed they felt like whipping boys for the news media.

So Fred would have a field day if he heard you worked for them. He'd imply you were basically just a lazy caretaker of an old electrical grid. The reality was that the people who ran this utility were miracle workers. Engineers from European energy companies would fly in to see how on earth they managed it. And in the front lines of energy supply, these incredible people were being lifted 30 or 40 metres into the air in 100-kilometre-per-hour winds and 45-degree temperatures, within inches of 50 000 volts, just so we could recharge our laptops.

So it was with some satisfaction that we helped this utility change its two-word descriptor from Lowly Janitors (of an ageing network) to Vigilant Defenders (of a critical product). The reaction when we presented this creed to the utility's staff was an outburst of pride and joy borne of pent-up injustice. Powerful stuff. Way more powerful than any reaction I've ever seen to a new marketing slogan.

it's about taking control of *you*

The first step in implementing your True Purpose is taking back control of how the world sees you in a way that encourages you to achieve great things. Those two words can help you do that by becoming a motivating mantra that's just as powerful as your True Purpose itself.

You can imagine the conversation around the boardroom table when that land developer has to decide how to brand a new estate. They will ask themselves, 'How would a Dedicated Lifemaker name and launch a new estate? To prove to the world that we're genuine about that role in society?' And, just as importantly, I imagine they would also ask themselves, 'Let's also explore how a Greedy Landbaron would do it so we know what not to do'.

Likewise, it's not hard to picture a discussion at that energy utility about, say, the type of content to put on their employment website. There's a massive difference between how you'd communicate Vigilant Defender in text, imagery and video as opposed to Lowly Janitor. The writing, the music, the storylines would all come from an entirely different mindset. They'd be right to take their cues from how the army and police portray themselves to prospective recruits. With talk of pride and accomplishment and filling a vital role in society. And the end result would be far more inspiring and appealing.

one final point

In this exercise, remember to be honest with, and about, yourself. This is not a case of whoever comes up with the wittiest descriptor wins. Your motivating two-word descriptor must stem from the truth — from how you really feel about your role in society; from what you genuinely believe is truly possible if your talent and vision is unleashed; from what you sincerely know could be the end benefit for the world if you're right about what you do.

worksheet: why words

Scenario: Change your two-word descriptor from one of stereotype to one of substance. Use an adjective (a descriptive word that explains your company's personality) and a noun (a factual word that captures your company's role in the world).

the stereotype

Pick two words that someone might use to describe your business if they thought you were just like every other business in your category. Imagine they're poking fun at your business or reflecting a well-accepted cynical view of companies in your area of business. Write as many two-word examples as you can.

_____

_____

_____

_____

_____

_____

the substance

Now write a few examples of two words that you'd love people to use to describe your business. Make them passionate, motivating and creative. Sometimes it helps to write lots of adjectives first (your style), then lots of nouns (your role).

_____

_____

_____

_____

_____

_____

best picks

Now take your favourite two words from each list and join them together to make a rallying cry for yourself and your staff. Try a couple, then pick your favourite.

We're not just _____.

We're actually _____!

We're not just _____.

We're actually _____!

We're not just _____.

We're actually _____!

We're not just _____.

We're actually _____!

you can download this template at truthgrowthrepeat.com.

(17) exercise e: purpose on a page

Okay, now that you've done the exercises, it's time to find the themes that tie them together. Actually, it's time to have a break and a strong coffee. But after that, ask yourself: 'What are my answers to those exercises telling me about the motives that are actually driving me? In my role as a business creator/owner … and in my career … and in my life overall?'

The next workout is to condense your responses to those exercises to just one key statement. That's not easy. You've just spent a few hours (or maybe days?) pouring out the unedited contents of your soul. But in order for this to work, it's essential that you now focus your passion.

What we're aiming for here is to complete a template called 'Purpose on a Page' — that is, a linear description of what authentically motivates you written on one side of one piece of paper. Let me help you edit down your responses to find the most powerful one for each exercise. Then we can fill in the template.

editing your soul

The first task is to go back through all the writing you did in each exercise in the previous chapters and decide on the key thought — the one response in each exercise that most resonates with you. This is always hard, but don't worry — I'm not asking you to throw away all that valuable soul-searching. You just need to focus. A bow on a ship needs to be pointy, otherwise it takes ages to get where you want to go.

So let's go through each exercise and see if we can refine your findings.

eulogy

The way to turn this rather unsettling hypothetical into a single useful sentence is to take all the things people would miss if your business wasn't here and prioritise them.

Or perhaps ask yourself, 'What's the *key* thing people would miss if my business wasn't here anymore?'

Ask yourself, 'Of all the things people would miss, which one resonates the most with me?'

What you're effectively doing here is establishing the cost of not pursuing your purpose. You need to verbalise the downside of not fulfilling your purpose so it acts as a motivator. Because it's going to be hard. You're going to confront bigger challenges than you would by following the status quo. That's how breakthroughs happen. That's how new things are brought into the world.

Following your True Purpose requires resilience and stamina and bravery and self-belief. You need to know not just the reward you'll get when it succeeds (a better world, a fairer society, personal wealth), but the downside of not persevering and making it work (unfair treatment of people, cynicism about an industry you love).

Remember the health fund that did this exercise and found out that they had a much broader impact on society than many of them appreciated? They realised that the cost of withdrawing into reactive behaviour to a radically changing marketplace was effectively letting down hundreds of thousands of people in need. That realisation tends to steel your resolve somewhat!

By the way, it doesn't matter if you don't get it *exactly* right. The ideal is to choose the thing that would leave the biggest gap in the world if you weren't here. But as long as that one thing at the top of your list has some kind of value that you appreciate, your Purpose on a Page is going to work.

protest

Of all the protest banners you wrote, which one do you love the most? Which one gets you most worked up?

Look for signs of anger and frustration inside you as you read through that list of unmet needs in the world. They're your most telling clues.

Remember, your most motivating protest may not be the most obvious one. We've found in our workshops that people often pick the protest banner that's closest to their current line of work — maybe because they're being too logical, or perhaps out of a sense of duty to their business. But watching them over the course of the whole exercise, especially during the group discussions, I've often noticed they were more alive when discussing a different one.

For example, the mechanic I wrote about in chapter 6 — the guy who wanted to start a more trustworthy car servicing centre — initially picked 'Let me do my job' as his number-1 protest headline. After a quick chat he revealed that 'Car servicing with honour!' moved him more but that it seemed too 'wishy-washy' for that industry. This happens a lot. People fear that their innermost sense of justice and morality have no real place in commerce. That it's somehow a weak behaviour. That in business we must all be steely and professional.

Can you see why so many corporations and brands feel so inhuman? Why so much marketing seems fake to us?

So go through your Protest lines and pick the biggest, fattest issue — the one that feels the most human.

And hey, if the positive expression of it moves you more than the negative, use that. I've found that, on the whole, rallying *against* something triggers more energy and emotion than rallying *for* something. But it's up to you. Just look for where the most energy is.

headline

This is a little easier to condense than Eulogy and Protest. All you need to do here is choose the most thrilling prize for following your True Purpose. Of all the possible outcomes you explored in this exercise, pick the one that inspires you the most. Pick the one that makes you say to yourself, 'Well hey, if *that* is what I can make happen in the world by implementing my True Purpose — for real — then let's go. Game on!'

Remember, though, to keep it within the bounds of possibility. Like, think big but not so big that you lose touch with reality. It's not very effective to choose a future outcome that you subconsciously doubt is possible from the get-go.

For example, the university folk I wrote about in this exercise did brilliantly at this task, writing some truly outlandish headlines for *TIME* magazine and *The New York Times*. But when it came to choosing the one that most motivated them they all agreed that while winning the Nobel Prize or curing AIDS was indeed possible, they felt those achievements lay too far in the future. So they chose a headline in *The Australian* about their university being chosen by UNESCO to lead a major food project in Africa. They felt while that was beyond their current ambition it was genuinely achievable if they all united around their True Purpose.

why words

Here, I'd recommend you cut yourself some slack and really go for it. Don't be logical and nice. Pick the boring, uninspiring descriptor of your organisation that's *really* boring and uninspiring. Then pick the braver, more energising descriptor that's truly brave and energising.

I recommend this because I've found that people really hold back on this one. For some reason, they can easily describe why their customers would be bawling their eyes out at their brand's funeral, they can stand up in a room full of strangers and shout out what's broken in the world and they can envisage a wonderful outcome in the future. But somehow, they can't put themselves in the shoes of someone belittling their industry, nor rise up and summon the anger and/or passion to boldly rebut that slur.

But boy is it fun when you do! It's a release.

Again, I'll use my own company for this example. I genuinely enjoy admitting that sometimes ad people like us are seen as Slick Madmen. I find it cathartic to admit that. It holds no fear for me.

But I also love standing on a soapbox, looking that imaginary person in the eyes and explaining why they're dead wrong about my team and me. I can picture myself bellowing — employing 19th-century English mannerisms, for some reason — 'Excuse me, sir! We are not, as you so ignorantly say, Slick Madmen. We are Ethical Market-makers!' [polite applause from the small crowd gathering]. 'In minds such as yours, polluted from prolonged exposure to the media, you could be forgiven for accepting the common view of people in my profession. But spend one day at my place of work, sir, and you will find not a coterie of egotistical, self-serving flim-flam artists, but a dedicated tribe of passionate truth-tellers — people with honour and morality who believe the only way for humankind to grow and prosper in an honourable and sustainable way is for companies to look inside their own hearts and understand what they have to offer the world that's truly good, and then going out bravely into society and proving that promise, without lies, without deceit, without manipulation. That, sir, is who we are!'

Wouldn't you love to do that for your business?

This is your chance. Go for it.

defining your true purpose (like ... in words)

Until now, you've been climbing the mountain to your True Purpose using ropes and ladders. Now that the summit is in sight, it's time to take a leap.

There's no easy way to quantify in a few words what your True Purpose is. Even if you've found it easy (and exciting) to select the one key thought from each exercise. Even if your two motivating Why Words just fell right off your lips as soon as you saw that exercise.

Defining your singular motivating True Purpose requires a leap of imagination. Sometimes self-confidence. Sometimes bravery. Because it's often not self-evident. It's like you've made a jigsaw with several pieces missing and now you have to look at the unfinished picture and understand what it is.

As your faithful Sherpa up this exciting-but-scary mountain, I can help you. Let's look at an example of someone else's Purpose on a Page first. I've chosen the little dairy company I wrote about in part I because I shared a lot of detail about their story. So I'm hoping you feel familiar with them now and it may be easier for you to spot how they ended up wording their True Purpose, based on their answers to the exercises you've just completed.

(Note: the key sentence that this exercise is helping you arrive at is underlined.)

purpose on a page for 'the little dairy company'

The key thing people would miss if our brand didn't exist is:

Being able to buy good quality milk, yoghurt and cheese that didn't cost a fortune.

The one thing we're most passionate about solving in the world is:

Helping people live long, healthy lives through the benefits of natural dairy products.

If we deliver on this promise, what's possible is:

Lower childhood obesity, healthier families and a new perception of corporations not as faceless evil empires, but as groups of honourable people wanting to make a difference.

So it seems clear that we're not just:

Boring Bottlers.

We're actually:

Honourable Artisans.

And the higher ideal we seek together could be described as:

Better dairy for everyone, every day, everywhere.

Which would be a win for us because:

That's not only a fulfilling way to live your life but it has huge commercial potential.

And a win for our customers because:

Mums can afford to feed their kids interesting and great-tasting dairy knowing that it's good for them.

They can also actively contribute to our product development, making a virtuous loop of trust and innovation.

And you know what, it would even be a win for society because:

Kids are too fat.

Too much food is crap.

Our purpose can help people live longer, healthier lives.

That has the potential to reduce heart disease, stroke and diabetes, just to name a few.

Which in turn could help make our country happier and more productive.

With more money spent on advancing humankind than fixing sick people.

————

Pretty powerful, huh? It seems so easy and commonsense when reading about someone else's True Purpose. But I'm fully aware that it's way harder doing it for yourself. So I've tried to make it easier by the way I've worded the key prompts.

You'll see, for example, that instead of writing, 'so our True Purpose could be described as', I've written, 'and the higher ideal we seek together could be described as'. This is to help you ease into the final wording of your True Purpose. All you're really doing here is describing the principle that is authentically driving you and your business. Beyond money and fame and success.

You're not etching a guru-like mantra into a stone plinth that will be on display for centuries to come. That kind of pressure would be paralysing.

You're simply expressing in one sentence what all the other answers on this page are pointing to.

Give it a shot and see what comes out. And again, if you're stuck on the wording, don't sweat it. The words aren't the most important bit. Or get in touch with me. I'm a writer. I can help.

'could be' versus 'is'

Why do I ask you to write that your higher ideal *could be* something instead of *is* something? Because it's not real yet. You need to work on it beyond this book, beyond this moment. You need to take your purpose out into the world and apply it, to see how it runs. I would consider it a personal failure if anyone felt that doing the work in this book is all you need to produce a bona fide, dead-set, guaranteed, foolproof True Purpose for life.

I can promise that this work will get you reeeaaalll close. Closer than any other process I've seen (that's why I wanted to turn it into a book — so I could reach more people with this thinking than I can at workshops or as clients of my company). But I can almost guarantee that you'll go on to evolve the wording of your True Purpose. Not the core truths behind it, but the way you describe it and the way you apply it.

It will invariably grow.

Let me give you another personal example. My business partner and I started our company, Meerkats, with a clearly defined purpose of using honesty to bring companies closer to today's consumers. Our core motivation was to smash the outdated-but-profitable myths that our industry had created about how marketing works. Things like 'Advertising can fix most business problems', 'Sales promotions are a worthy way to drive long-term sales', 'You need to own a consumer emotion', 'You can make new markets by finding white space in your category', and so on.

At the start, our purpose was to make a greater impact on society using our skills as truthful brand communicators, so as to gain a greater return for our clients' marketing budgets. Once we saw how well this worked, and in particular the incredible knock-on effect this thinking had on consumers' trust in our clients' companies and on the career fulfilment of the people who worked for those companies, the exact wording of our True Purpose evolved to reflect our broader desire to make the whole world better by creating a more honest, more sustainable form of capitalism.

In short, the True Purpose you write today will be powerful. It will motivate you. It will give you strength and resilience. But it will evolve.

So cut yourself some slack. You don't have to be struck by lightning and find *the answer* and chisel it in stone and keep it sacrosanct forever more. Find the truest, most motivating way to describe what you know, in your soul, your True Purpose could be right now.

worksheet: purpose on a page

Scenario: Use your most telling answer from each exercise to create a pathway to your True Purpose. This page is like a mini manifesto.

Okay, so if the thing people would miss most if our business no longer existed is:

_____

_____

(*Write the mourner's comment that most resonated with you from the Eulogy exercise.*)

And if the thing we're most passionate about solving in the world is:

_____

_____

(*Describe the enemy or unmet need you found most inspiring in the Protest exercise.*)

And if we succeed in solving this issue, then what's possible for us is:

_____

_____

(*Choose the future scenario that excites you the most from the Headline exercise.*)

Then it's pretty clear that we're not just:

_____

_____

(*Write your favourite uninspiring two words from the Why Words exercise.*)

We're actually:

_____

_____

(*Write your favourite motivating two words from the Why Words exercise.*)

And the higher ideal we seek together could be described as:

_____

_____

(*Considering all the above, what is the ultimate end goal of this business — this sentence is effectively your True Purpose.*)

That's a win for us because:

_____

_____

(*Write how your True Purpose fulfils you and your employees.*)

And a win for our customers because:

_____

_____

(*Write how your True Purpose meets the customers' needs in a better way than the competition.*)

And a win for the world because:

_____

_____

(*Write how your True Purpose makes the world a better place — this can be just your part of the world or the whole planet.*)

you can download this template at truthgrowthrepeat.com.

_____

testing for the presence of true purpose

There are three simple tests you can do to check both the authenticity and potency of your True Purpose.

you

If a little thrill of possibility doesn't rise up inside you when you're writing out your True Purpose statement, then you may not have cracked your True Purpose yet.

You'll know whether you've caught your own big ideal or not. You'll feel a physical reaction. It's like the first unconscious flush of love. You just feel a little buzz. Or a tingle. It's palpable.

I know, I know, it all sounds very fluffy and unbusiness-like, but I only write it that way because it's true. And I want you to look out for it. It's one of the real human tests of authentic value in a world of shallow promises. And hey, throughout the history of human advancement, truly powerful ideas once enunciated often deliver a physical tremble. You may not find yourself leaping out of the bath like Archimedes, but you should feel *something*.

It's important to embrace this because the thrilling potential of your True Purpose is going to become your fuel. It will power the long nights. It will feed the resilience you'll need to go up against a conventional competitor. It will provide the infectious spark to attract awesome people to your business and to motivate them to achieve extraordinary things.

Without that fire of truth, you'll find it hard to sustain the energy required to make a difference in the world. Or, as Steve Jobs put it, to make 'a dent in the universe'.

your family and friends

You shouldn't underestimate how important it is to feel validated by your family and friends. They may not have an actual role in your business, but they're often the first people to endorse your ideas and give you the confidence to pursue them.

And so I would invite you to make these guys the first test audience for your True Purpose. Run them through your purpose-driven business idea and see if that light goes on behind their eyes. Read them your Purpose on a Page and check the initial credibility rating.

The chances are good that you'll be validated in your thinking. Because often your family and friends know you well and can judge whether this idea of yours is authentically you. They can often ask telling questions that will help you peel away the layers of the onion to get to that innermost quality that drives you.

But leave your ego at the door when you do it. Don't be too hurt if Uncle Larry thinks you're crazy. Don't take it to heart if one of your best mates has doubts about the commercial viability. None of them are you.

total strangers

This is another Barbecue Test. And it's perhaps the most telling of all the ways you can test your prototype True Purpose. Here's how it works.

When you're next at one of those weekend barbecues where everyone stands around in somebody's backyard with a beer in their hand making idle chitchat, make sure you find someone you haven't met.

As these first encounters often go in our culture, within a matter of seconds you'll be asked what you do for a living. This is your moment.

Tell them the sector of business you're in. If they don't volunteer an opinion of your line of work, ask them what they think of companies in your industry.

If you live in Australia you'll get a fairly raw appraisal right off the bat. Usually in the form of a light-hearted roast like, 'Oh you're in law, eh? Why don't sharks attack lawyers? Professional courtesy'. Har har.

Whatever they say, tell them you're trying to do things a little differently. Then explain your True Purpose and maybe a little about how you're going to implement it.

Whatever happens next will be very useful to you. If they stop ribbing you, or better yet, start to ask questions about what you're describing, that's a pretty good sign that your True Purpose has credibility. Maybe even value.

Even if they just stop joking around and simply nod as you talk. That's a result. To me, it's often a sign that you're sharing something new.

You'll often be able to tell by their body language whether or not your True Purpose is hitting its mark, or at least starting to erode their entrenched beliefs.

If, on the other hand, you're met with a look of doubt — or worse, confusion — you may need to do some more work.

I love this test and have used it often in my own line of work. It's a purer assessment of not only the credibility of your True Purpose, but also of its accessibility — that is, how user-friendly you've been able to make it. Which is effectively what happens in modern consumer research techniques like observation and co-creation.

(18) your final task: the after ad

Remember the Before Ad you wrote at the start of this whole process?

This final exercise is the counterpoint to that. What I want you to do is write a new ad for your business, now that you have clearly expressed your True Purpose. Together we'll see what the differences are between that ad and the first one you wrote.

Here's what you do:

- Write a new ad for your business.

- This time, start with what you believe is wrong with your industry and/or the world. Or what could be so much better, if not for your idea.

- Then describe what's in it for your customer. What do they get out of that ideal themselves, for real, for their money?

- Then finish by completing this sentence: 'And if we both do that, then society gets a little better because …'

Once you've done that, get your original ad and compare them. Ask yourself these questions:

- Which one feels more human?

- If I was a customer reading these ads, which company would I feel is being more honest with me?

- Which company feels more unique — that is, which ad seems different from all those other ads I've read for companies in that industry?

- Which company seems more likely to innovate?

- If I was a talented employee in that field, which company would I prefer to work for?

- Which company appeals more to the new generation of smart investor, who knows the power of a competitive advantage in commerce and can see that in a world of product parity any brand with a unique point of view is going to earn bigger returns?

- Which company will be more attractive to those smart, successful brands you'd love to do co-promotions with in your field?

I'm going to give you three examples of Before Ads and After Ads so you get some thought-starters. Also because they demonstrate just how truly powerful this exercise really is.

the little furniture shop

Remember the husband-and-wife team who were feeling pressured to stock cheap imported furniture alongside their own designs, in order to compete?

This was their Before Ad:

TOP QUALITY FURNITURE AT AFFORDABLE PRICES!

Whatever your furniture needs, you'll find it in our showroom. We have our own designs, plus lots of affordable imported brands of lounge and dining suites, bedroom settings, home office furniture and more. Our knowledgeable staff will assist you in finding just the right item for your home. We offer a design service to amend any of the items in our range and we provide free delivery for orders over $1000. Call in today.

In order to be competitive with the big furniture chains they had decided to augment their own quality designs with cheap imported lines. Doing our workshop made them realise they were miserable with this compromise. They'd made that decision out of fear that staying true to the reason they'd started their own furniture business in the first place (their True Purpose) wouldn't make enough money.

The truth is, like so many small-business owners, they'd convinced themselves that if the customer didn't get what they thought they wanted, their business would fail. But the truth is, they'd never actually embraced their passion and told the world why they felt theirs was a better way. They'd never fully explored the benefits to the customers and the customers' children, or the knock-on effect to society as a whole. They'd never even explained it properly to their own staff.

Worst of all, they'd never fully explained it to themselves, so that when tough business decisions came up, they had no compass — no lighthouse — to show them the better way. They succumbed to fear and the myth of consumer demand and gave in. The stress and complexity of running a business weakened their authentic motivations from the get-go, and the fear of making money muted their purpose.

Can you see what they were heading for down that road? They might have survived as a business by selling cheap imported furniture, but it was making them miserable. They weren't just losing the great staff they'd attracted to help them design and make great furniture, they were losing their soul.

I think eventually their customers would pick up on that. I think eventually, as a customer, I would catch a vibe in that furniture store that these guys resented me a little. For keeping them from their dream. They'd be subconsciously blaming their customers and their competitors for making them into something they didn't like.

But the truth is they would have been doing it to themselves. It would have been their choice. Yes, you can say, 'Hey, I have no choice. I'm forced to sell cheap crap to survive. That's just the reality of my market'. But that's simply not true. A more honest statement would be, 'I'm choosing to go off-purpose because I can't find a way to stay on-purpose and make enough money'.

Now here's their After Ad:

FURNITURE BUILT FOR LIFE

We think the furniture industry is doing you a major disservice. We'd all like to believe that it's possible to buy cheap furniture that's also well made. And the big furniture retailers encourage this hopeful belief. They import cheap furniture made with cheap labour overseas and try and kid you that it's going to last. That it's going to survive your kids jumping all over it, or the constant moving and dragging that we do to our home furnishings as we move house or change our decor. But it doesn't. It can't. Cheap furniture has cheap wood, cheap glue, cheap stitching.

We design and make our furniture to be lived in, not just sold. When we say 'built for life' we mean two things: it can take the knocks of the average family lifestyle and it will last a lifetime. This makes us proud. We believe our world has become too disposable, too wasteful. And we're teaching our kids that. We're not just making furniture, we're making a stand.

So powerful. So inspiring. Compare the language with the Before Ad. As a gifted designer or woodworker, which company would you want to work for?

Doing this exercise reminds me of a sad truth: business owners often go off-purpose without really knowing it, without ever fully understanding what's driving them, and most tragically of all, without ever fully exploring the commercial viability of their passions — those innermost beliefs about people and the world that give them that purpose. It's a sad loss to the world because so many people have so much potential that goes untapped.

So many lives could be happier, so many children could learn to follow their dreams and be honest and hard working and have good things happen as a result. The whole misconception about capitalism being a harsh, unfair process could start to change. If only more of us pushed through the fear and pursued the benefits to others of what we passionately believe in.

Don't make the same mistake. Write your After Ad full strength. Think about the benefits to others that come from you pursuing fully what you believe in. Don't worry about whether it will make enough money to pay your mortgage. Do it ten-tenths. Just for now. We'll get onto your mortgage later.

the rural b&b

At one of our small-business workshops I met a lady from the country who wanted to turn some of her farm buildings into a B&B. Her kids had grown up, her husband managed the farm and she was bored. She loved the rural area they lived in and noticed that small accommodations were popping up.

This was her Before Ad:

> ### *GREAT VALUE WHEATBELT ACCOMMODATION*
>
> Come and stay in the heart of our picturesque wheatbelt region in a charming farm-based Bed & Breakfast. Your hosts will be only too happy to accommodate you and your every need. We have three comfortable units with modern facilities, tea & coffee making, colour TV, spa and more. Enjoy the down-home hospitality of this unique farming region. Affordable rates. Weekly discounts.

In this ad the wonderful, creative lady I met was writing only the things she thought (feared?) people would want to read. Because that's how she saw every other B&B wrote about themselves — on travel websites, in the classifieds, and so on. That ad was her version of the 'faster horses' that Henry Ford spoke about.

When the true nature of her purpose surfaced during one of our workshops, it became clear she had so much more to say. It turned out that her business offered paid hospitality training to local young people in areas such as cooking, cleaning and management. All she needed was a little confidence boost that the passion she felt for the youth training side of her B&B business was interesting to people, and different and ... well ... terrific!

Her After Ad:

REST YOUR HEAD, INSPIRE YOUR HEART

We run a great little B&B. It has everything you hope to find in a charming rural B&B — cute cottage-style rooms, comfy beds, nice hosts (even if we do say so ourselves!). But you know what? As our guests you'll help our community grow and prosper; not just with the money you'll spend in our town, but because our B&B gives hospitality training to young locals as chefs, cleaners, managers. We also pay them as they learn. Our dream is to keep more young people living in our town instead of moving to the city so it can prosper and provide them with a rewarding life. As our guest, you won't just feel good for helping our program, you'll really be looked after. We've found that our trainees deliver amazing service. They'll try harder than your average hotel staff to give you a great experience. We've also found that our guests enjoy chatting with our young staff about their hopes and dreams. It's an entirely new and very rewarding win—win. So if you're coming to the wheatbelt region for a holiday, or just passing through, we invite you to stay somewhere truly unique. Then travel home again with a rested body and a full heart.

I don't know about you, but I've never seen an ad for a B&B like that. I think it's fantastic. What's more, being an experienced marketer I just know there are several demographics of traveller who would find that concept hugely appealing. And the good news for our B&B lady is that a lot of these consumer segments are cashed up and looking for new experiences.

Naturally, in order to win over customers, her B&B still has to deliver comfortable, clean rooms and fair rates; provide knowledge of things to do in the area; and so on. What we call 'the minimum non-negotiables' of any business. But the added human story that guests become part of is a real attraction. Sure, there are people for whom this would mean little, but hey, they can go stay at the motel down the road.

I believe that this B&B could even charge a small premium for this idea because it's so unique. Not to take advantage of people's innate goodness, but to help make sure the idea is commercially viable, able to succeed financially and is a sustainable business concept.

---

truth needs more words

As you can see from these examples, writing your After Ad will often stretch the word count beyond that of your Before Ad. But that's okay. It's a far more involved story to tell, even when you're trying to be succinct.

You're not only explaining what it is you do, but why. And the benefits of that to you, your customer and the world. So try to be concise (people are busy) but never edit out the good bits, the true bits, the *you* bits.

Don't launch into a 10-page sermon on the mount, but don't sweat it if your After Ad is twice as long as your Before Ad.

---

the recruitment consultancy

Two smart, ambitious women were running a successful recruitment company serving the mining industry. But they had an itch that needed scratching. They felt the traditional recruitment methods did a lousy job of placing the right people in the right companies, from a values perspective.

Workers aren't workers, they figured. So they set about finding a way to offer a recruitment service that's purpose-driven.

Here's their Before Ad:

MINING POSITIONS FILLED FAST

Our recruitment service specialises in the mining industry. We know how to solve your manpower problems fast. With the minimum of downtime and fuss. We have access to huge databases of qualified people looking for positions in almost every area of the mining industry. Our rates are affordable and our service is friendly. So whatever staffing problem you have, why go to the big companies and be just a number when you can come to us and get fast, personal service?

And here's their After Ad:

THE RIGHT PEOPLE, RIGHT NOW

Tired of hiring people only to watch them leave six months later (whether on their own or because you wanted them gone)? Because they didn't fit your company? Because they didn't buy into what your company is trying to achieve? We think the recruitment industry is broken. Its method of interviewing potential people is the same as it was 50 years ago. Sure there are now all kinds of big data and algorithms. But most recruitment firms only want to fill a space with a person for a company. With little regard to cultural fit or shared ambition. We think our role is to find your space with your kind of person for your company. We believe that if you want to find people who will not only stay, but also contribute to your company achieving its vision, you need to recruit the way we recruit. By going beyond clinical qualifications and experience to the human aspects that make a great, long-term company-employee fit. We're talking about your people's personal purpose matching your company purpose, about their sense of justice matching yours, about even their personality matching your company's style.

If that sounds smarter than the last pitch you got from a recruitment firm, give us a try. You might just find we're a great match.

Reading that second ad gives me goose bumps. When you consider the potential of this business for making people's lives better, it's almost a crime *not* to pursue it. The world needs this.

Not only will more people be more fulfilled by their work because they're placed in companies that match their own career goals and values, the companies themselves will be more productive because more and more staff will be engaged in their purpose — being innovative not just because the boss told them to but because they believe in the mission.

I get another feeling when I work with people to surface their True Purpose and help them both enunciate it and clarify its commercial viability. It's a kind of 'parallel universe sadness' for what these people might have spent their lives doing if not for the courage to pursue their innermost drivers.

When I hear an idea that has the potential to not only earn people a good living, but to change the world a little, I can't help thinking, 'Oh my God, this is incredible!' and then in the very next instant, 'Shit! How many other people are out there currently squashing their True Purpose down deep inside themselves?' How many others are denying themselves and the world great new ideas that could, one by one, transform our view of capitalism?

How about you? Do you ever feel that when you're reading these stories? Does any of this resonate with thoughts you've had about your career, your life? I hope so.

worksheet: your after ad

Scenario: Write an inspired newspaper ad for your business through the lens of your newly surfaced True Purpose. Explain what genuinely motivates you and how that affects the products and/or services you offer. If you have room, add in any of the knock-on effects of your True Purpose in society.

heading

Don't worry about appealing overtly to the consumer's needs here. Write a rousing statement about what drives you and your business.

_____

_____

body copy

Explain the golden thread that ties your ultimate ambition to the delivery of a superior customer experience. Step us through the logic behind your authentic motive.

_____

_____

_____

_____

_____

_____

_____

_____

part three:
implementing your true purpose

⑲ i get it, but what do i *do* with it?

Of all the questions about True Purpose, this is the one I hear most often from CEOs under pressure to deliver profits in a fast-paced, always-changing world.

It will invariably be asked while I'm standing in a boardroom on the 47th floor of an office tower somewhere. The presentation is over. My business partner, Ronnie, and I have just delivered a True Purpose that captures the essence of our client's company — that inspires their staff in a way that's powerful and new but also human and real. Now the data projector is silent. All the backslapping and smiling is over and the VPs and CMOs and CFOs have all left the room.

That's when the CEO turns to us and says, 'Look guys, thanks, I love it and everything, but ...' and then the questions begin.

'How do I use this to motivate my staff to achieve better results? How does this help create the right brand extensions? How does this get us closer to our core demographic? How does this affect our marketing strategy?' and on it goes.

In our early years we learned quickly that as practitioners of purpose, not just researchers of it, we were obligated to build a bridge between the idealistic and the realistic. We had to create ways of applying the potency of the purposes we surfaced.

So our professional product suite for major brands now includes all manner of executive coaching, systems to ensure internal buy-in, customer journey mapping, product and service modelling, and so on.

For most of the readers of this book, however, it will be simpler. As the owner of a small business, social enterprise or startup — or as someone wanting to be that one day (soon I hope) — your primary focus will be to bring your True Purpose to life.

And I mean that literally. Take your True Purpose from words on a page to actions in the real world. Breathe life into it with what you now do. Every day.

This final section of the book lays out some key ways of doing that. It gives you practical advice on where to begin, how to prioritise your To Do list, how to gauge the commercial viability of your True Purpose without the benefit of large-scale consumer research, how to use The Circle as a strategic guide through this process and a bunch of street-smart tips for staying on track.

In some ways I feel this is the most important part of the entire book. Because this is what all that soul-searching and blue-skying you've just done is for. Unless you now roll up your sleeves and prove to the world that you sincerely believe in your True Purpose by fully aligning your company's behaviour to it, all the feelings of possibility and growth and success I hope you've felt while reading this book will remain just that — feelings. And as worthy as they are, feelings don't change the world. Actions do.

(20) measuring your truth gap

This chapter is about aligning the real-world behaviour of your business with your authentic motive as its owner.

I personally believe that as soon as you've defined a True Purpose, you're obligated to pursue it. You know in your heart of hearts that it's worthy, that it's valuable, that it will make a difference to the world. Yes, it's scary because just about every True Purpose I've seen involves breaking a number of business conventions. But if you don't set about implementing your True Purpose — for real — then all that good work you've just done will be wasted. You're effectively denying yourself and the world a better future.

So how do you do that? Where do you start?

In our workshops, we start with another one of those killer questions. We ask business owners to put themselves in the shoes of an unbiased consumer and ask themselves, 'If someone told me about a business with this stated purpose, how would I expect them to show up to me?'

It's an insanely powerful question. It's the clearest, most honest starting point I can give you to help you align your behaviour to your newly defined purpose.

What this question is doing is setting you a task: to review every way your business currently projects itself out into the world and see how well it aligns with your purpose. How you serve people, develop products, advertise, treat your staff, write your press releases, handle social media, and so on (and so on and so on!).

If most of these behaviours are not clear proofpoints that you're sincere about your True Purpose, then people will file your business in that folder in their minds labelled 'Corporate Bulldust'. Along with every other self-serving corporation they come across every day.

Take a deep breath. This is necessarily a complex project, as there are many ways the modern business connects with the world. But approach it methodically and you'll be okay. Let me help you through the steps.

step 1

Gather your existing materials — anything that currently expresses your company to the general public, to your customer, to your staff, to your investors, to yourself. Here's a guide to some of the most common items.

Brand:

- Name

- Logo

- Slogan (if you have one)

- Corporate design: company colours, typeface

- Language you use: copy

- Imagery you use: photography

Products and service:

- What your place of business looks like: storefront and internal fitout if it's a retail brand; website/app if it's an online brand; vehicle and uniform if you're a mobile tradesperson — even your reception and office space if it's a service firm

- How you pitch new business: PowerPoint, tender documents

- How you name your products and services

- Product packaging, point of sale display

- How you answer the phone (seriously, this matters)

Brand communications:

- Advertising

- Brochures, information leaflets, instruction manuals

- Website: design and content

- Social media activities: Twitter, Facebook page and posts, Instagram, Pinterest, Snapchat

- PR stories and publications

- Sponsorships or events

HR:

- Recruitment method and style

- Recruitment advertising: print/online (how you describe yourself)

- Interviews

- Inductions

- Employee communications

- Company intranet

Management:

- Business structure and goals

- Job titles

- Which clients you seek and which you don't

- Brand extensions (new business divisions)

- What you say to your competitors

- Industry memberships (which industries?)

Every single one of these behaviours will either be a reflection of your purpose, or evidence that you're not serious about your purpose.

step 2

Print the items from step 1 onto individual sheets of A4 paper. In colour if you can. Try to avoid double-ups or lots of pages on the same subject. For example, you probably don't have to print out every page of your website if four or five pages clearly communicates how the whole site looks and reads. For intangible things like job interviews, find a Google image that captures the vibe of how your business currently does it.

step 3

Find two walls somewhere in your office or at home. I know space is limited in a lot of small businesses, but it's totally cool to use, say, the walls behind people's desks, or in a meeting room that gets used a lot. It doesn't matter if people see your work in progress. In fact, it can often help make sure you're being completely honest with yourself.

Wherever these two walls are, however hard it is to find the space, trust me, it's invaluable to be able to see all the little threads that make up the tapestry of how your business is seen.

step 4

On the first wall, write or print out the words OUR REALITY and stick them at the top.

Underneath, stick up all those printouts of existing business behaviours. As many as you can fit. The idea is to make a collage of how your company currently shows up to people. We've found it helps to group them logically and give each page a clear title that you can easily read when you stand back and view the whole wall.

Now I want you to forget that wall completely. We'll come back to it. But for now, walk away from it and don't look back until I tell you to.

step 5

On the second wall, write or print out the words OUR POTENTIAL and stick them at the top.

Underneath, stick the True Purpose statement from your 'Purpose on a Page'. That's the sentence that begins, 'And the higher ideal we seek together could be described as ...' Write it in large enough letters to be read clearly when standing back from the wall. Just don't take up *too* much space with it. You're going to need plenty of space for what comes next.

step 6

Now for the fun bit. You're going to create an envisioned future. A model of what your True Purpose could make happen in the world.

Stand back, look at the words on the second wall and ask yourself, 'If I didn't know this company, but I was told that it stood for the purpose written up there, how would I expect it to show up to me? Y'know, if it genuinely believed in those awesome words. As opposed to just pretending to believe in them to win customers, like so many other businesses do'.

This is most effective when done with your business partners and/or senior staff. You're sure to come up with a lot of ideas. More importantly, you're going to *want* to. So clear your schedules for half a day and do it well.

step 7

The ideas will begin immediately. Write them down, draw pictures (stick figures are fine), find Google Images to suit.

When the initial outpouring of ideas starts to slow, try asking that same question from the point of view of a new employee. 'If I was working at one of our competitors and was told that there was this seriously cool company that believed in this purpose, what would I expect to see and hear when I rocked up to their office on my first day?' Then ask yourself:

- When I get out of the lift, what do I see?

- What's on the walls?

- How do the staff treat me?

- How do I notice the staff are treating each other?

- What is the attitude of the bosses?

- How is their office laid out?

step 8

Now step into the shoes of your customer and repeat the process with questions relevant to them.

- When I Google them what comes up?

- When I walk into their store/office, what do I see? How do I feel?

- When I meet someone from that company, what are they like?

- When I sit in my boardroom and watch their credentials presentation, what does it look like? How do they present?

- When I pick up their product and read the labelling, do I like the voice I'm hearing in my head?

- When I have a problem, what happens on the other end of the phone?

step 9

Draw the ideas that come from these provocations and stick them on the wall under the words OUR POTENTIAL.

Print out stock images that reflect your thoughts. Draw wireframes of website content. Do rough layouts of ads. Do a rough design of a different storefront. Print out side views of that cool new company vehicle and write different messages on the side. Sketch new products, write new signage and uniforms. Go crazy with possibility. You don't actually have to *do* it all — just envision it.

warning: ego at the door

It's hard enough putting your own ego aside during this exercise when you're the founder — when the original ideas you had for your company are being openly challenged or sometimes criticised. But when you have a whole team of people in the room who have all contributed to your company's current name, logo, website, product range, and so on, you can find that egos are being bruised very quickly.

Often, the power of a well-enunciated True Purpose unifies everyone in the spirit of newness and potential. Just as often, however, before the extraordinary potential of your purpose is fully grasped, people can think it's just shooting down all their hard work.

You have to shut down this defensive behaviour. Like, straight away. Before you even begin this envisioning task, ask everyone to leave their ego at the door. Seriously. Stand at the entrance to your brainstorming area and ask them to put their ego on the ground. Tell them it's okay. That this is a safe place. There is no bad idea. No dumb question. Hey, none of this is guaranteed to happen anyway so what's the risk? The exercise is to imagine a world where your company's True Purpose is fully realised and then see what you all think. See what's possible.

In our experience, the effect of opening minds to powerful possibility is 'Holy hell, this is awesome! This is going to kick butt! We can't *not* do this!' It just takes some people a while to catch on. So brief them well beforehand. Give them a safety net. Then have fun.

step 10

When the second wall is suitably plastered in all the inspiring ways a company could express itself if it was totally committed to its True Purpose, stand back and compare the two walls.

—

Voilà. Now you have your Purpose Gap: the difference between how you currently show up to the world and how you could show up if embracing your newly enunciated True Purpose.

If you're one of those rare entrepreneurs who's totally in touch with their innermost beliefs and values and has applied them all through the process of creating their business, this gap may be a small one. Congratulations.

In our experience, though, the distance between reality and potential is always big. In fact, it's usually not a gap, it's a gape. And it's suddenly so apparent to everyone. A lot of business owners look at, say, their existing website and ask themselves, 'Why were we so boring?' 'Why is this just all about what the customer wants?' 'Why did this end up looking just like our competitors?'

You should cut yourself some slack here. Running a business is hard. You make decisions you don't really want to make in order to survive and make money and keep people employed. But what you will probably be seeing now in the gap between these two walls is just how far off track that behaviour has taken you.

Seeing what's possible if you fully embrace your True Purpose helps turn it into an obligation that steels you to make tougher decisions — to make sacrifices to stay true to your True Purpose.

The next chapters will help you approach the task of turning your business into the one on the wall marked Our Potential.

(21) you don't have to be perfect, you just have to want to be.

Around about now you may be sitting back, looking at the gap that exists between how a business with your True Purpose should show up in the world, and how it actually is and thinking, 'Holy crap. I love my True Purpose, but I'm not sure I can deliver on it! It's starting to feel a bit idealistic. I'm a million miles from being able to claim this truth with any level of honesty'.

Relax. It's okay. The quality of a purpose-driven business owner is measured as much by the degree to which you're pursuing your True Purpose as by whether you've accomplished it yet.

This is an important point. Some company purposes are so worthy that trying to reach the endpoint too quickly can result in the owners feeling like failures and possibly giving up. The truth is, even if the progress towards your ultimate end goal is glacial, as long as you're moving towards it, you're purpose-driven. You'll be bringing into the world a new conversation; you'll be opening minds to your way of thinking. And all the good things that happen when you go the right way around The Circle will start to happen for you.

a less-than-perfect example

A decade ago Patagonia was just another name in the global explosion of outdoor brands. They made clothing and equipment for the growing hordes of adventurers who wanted to hike, climb, ski and cycle in the world's most beautiful unspoilt places. Because of the raw appeal of these pursuits, brands in this category had always projected a 'down home' authenticity in their image and communications. And Patagonia led the way, always trying to balance the commercialisation of outdoor pursuits with their genuine love for nature.

The trouble was, if you'd flicked through a bunch of adventure magazines back then, you would have quickly realised that big business was beginning to cotton on to this lucrative new market. All the ads had begun to look suspiciously similar, with photoshopped photos of ruggedly handsome men and toned Scandinavian women standing atop mountain peaks in the latest gear. And surprise, surprise, overt support for environmental issues was popping up more frequently alongside the bullet-pointed product benefits.

If you were a cynical observer (like me) you could have been forgiven for suspecting that a lot of focus groups were being conducted behind the scenes to find out what this growing tribe of cashed-up young consumers wanted in their outdoor brands. Findings that were then turned into appealing ads and on-point sponsored events that ticked all the boxes on this target audience's wish list.

It was around this time that Patagonia did something extraordinary. They began to acknowledge that some of their manufacturing practices were harmful to the environment.

Uh, come again?

That's right. Patagonia, known by outdoor adventurers around the world as an environmental crusader, was admitting that some of the materials they used were not recyclable. Sure, the plastic thread made their clothing more comfortable and longlasting, and the plastic coatings made their footwear and camping equipment more rugged and waterproof, but they couldn't be recycled and were therefore detrimental to the very environment Patagonia claimed in their marketing they loved so much.

Why did they admit to this? It sounds counter-intuitive, but it was because of their True Purpose, which was, and still is, 'Build the best product, cause no unnecessary harm, use business to inspire and implement solutions to the environmental crisis'.

The owners of Patagonia realised that in the increasingly competitive outdoor market they were at risk of veering off the path of their True Purpose in order to maintain sales. By conveniently ignoring the truth that they used some environmentally unfriendly materials in their products. By gradually turning their passion for nature into a shallow, disposable value.

So they did what any purpose-driven company does when faced with a business and/or moral dilemma: they told the truth. At a time when it seemed like a cardinal sin for any brand in the outdoor market to admit it was anything but environmentally virtuous, Patagonia developed a disarmingly honest new website. Beside each of their products was one panel that described what was good about the product (all the natural and recyclable materials used) followed by another panel that described what was bad about the product (any synthetic, non-recyclable materials used).

Pretty gutsy move, right? But here's the crunch: they then inserted a third panel that stated, 'What we're doing about it', with a description of how they were sourcing new materials that were environmentally friendly in order to solve this dilemma. And they weren't just buying time or whitewashing the issue. Everything they wrote in that third panel was genuine, endorsed by the company board. They showed the scientists and researchers who were experimenting with new fabrics and threads that were 100 per cent organic and recyclable, the farmers who were growing the plants and the companies that were processing these new materials.

They didn't exaggerate their progress either. They didn't make grandiose promises about when their clothing and gear would be completely synthetic-free. They simply shared what their True Purpose was urging them to look into. In short, they weren't scared about what the customer would think about them. The owners of Patagonia knew in their hearts that this was the best they could do in order to achieve the balance of environmental responsibility and commercial viability.

It's the kind of brave move that only the owners of purpose-driven companies seem to be able to make because it's based on the belief that if you do what you yourself know is right in the service of your higher ideal then your customers — your good customers, the ones who get you — will be cool with that.

And that's exactly what happened. Patagonia's sales increased. They gained enormous free advertising in the form of TV coverage, magazine interviews and online blogs. Their owners were invited to seminars and outdoor shows. The outdoor community praised them for their honesty and the business community wanted to know the secret to this audacious sales strategy.

(There's a funny thing about telling the truth. Business people who don't understand the joy of pursuing a greater outcome than just money are befuddled by it. They wonder how on earth anyone could be smart enough to pull off a genius, money-spinning strategy like that. It reminds me of an old joke in the ad industry: Making money in advertising is all about honesty now. Once you can fake that you've got it made!)

Patagonia's owners themselves were surprised by the positive impact. They were expecting a minor downturn in sales while they better aligned their production methods to their purpose. But they had unknowingly tapped into a consumer mindset that saw many outdoor clothing customers suspicious of any brand's claim to be totally environmentally friendly. It just didn't make sense to these educated, socially aware consumers that a company could make a jacket that was light, comfortable, good-looking and longlasting, and could protect you against freezing wind and rain and not use anything synthetic or non-recyclable.

In bringing to light the inconvenient truths about their own products, Patagonia opened up this conversation, thereby outing the possible corporate cover-up that customers had been suspecting all along. It wasn't that Patagonia had lied; they just hadn't overtly talked about it.

By staying true to their purpose, Patagonia sold more of their current products, which helped fund the research required to find and implement better materials in their future products. Their behaviour also sent an enormous message to all their staff: our True Purpose means something. We believe it, for real. From the boardroom to the stock room.

I tell you this story at this point in the book because the message here is: you don't have to be perfect in the pursuit of your True Purpose. You just have to be genuine about it.

The To Do list for having your business's behaviour align with your true motive may be a long one. But don't worry. As long as you *start* doing it, you'll make progress.

what if you're a manager, not an owner?

I've mentioned to you a few times now that our methods work for any kind of business, whether it currently exists or is just a gleam in an entrepreneur's eye. But I thought it was worth mentioning that you can be a manager in someone else's company and still embrace this thinking.

Let's say you're the head of a business unit. You may well be experiencing the kind of frustrations we've apportioned to business owners: a feeling that your team isn't performing to their potential, that they're not delivering enough real value to your customers, that they're being blocked by conventional business practice from embracing the truth and making a genuine difference in your category, and so on.

You can still surface a more authentically motivating True Purpose for your unit, and then use the five points on The Circle to drive a more effective business strategy. You may be constrained by an existing corporate brand identity and some protocols, but by and large we've found that independently managed business units can genuinely change the game in their category using these methods.

We once worked with a veterinary hospital that was a business unit of a university. It was run as both a teaching environment and a commercial business, giving the university's vet students real-world experience while also serving the local population of pet owners, horse stables, farmers, and so on.

The managers and senior vets recognised that they had been going the wrong way around The Circle. They proceeded to find their inner truth by doing our workshop exercises, and they eventually enunciated a more motivating purpose for their hospital that unlocked a multiple win scenario for themselves, the animals, the animals' owners, the university and even their competition, the neighbouring vet clinics.

And just like when it's applied to companies as a whole, True Purpose helped recharge this business unit's staff, rejuvenate their brand, reinvigorate their industry standing, revive their profits, and more. And for me, as always, it was a delight to watch this happen.

So if you've been reading and nodding along with the thinking in this book, but don't actually own the business you're in, keep an open mind about how you might still be able to apply it. And if in doubt, send me an email, post a comment on our website or get in touch via LinkedIn. I'd be happy to give you more clarity on this, related to your specific circumstances. You'll find contact details under 'Coaching and conversation' at the back of the book.

(22) commercial viability

After 'What do I *do* with it?' the question I get asked most often by business owners about True Purpose is, 'Will it work?' They'll confess to me, 'If I follow conventional business practices in my industry, I'm not happy. But if I try something new and risky like this, will it actually grow a business?'

The bottom line is you can never tell for sure. Nobody can. Consumers are contrary creatures. If humans were 100 per cent predictable, the owners of research companies would all be billionaires.

What I do know is that it will work if you believe it will work. The Circle is self-fulfilling. Even if the way you shape your purpose-driven offer to the market, as a product or service design, is a little bit out and it struggles, your desire to pursue your higher ideal will drive you to innovate. You'll solve those problems. You'll find a way. But only if you believe.

testing viability professionally

An important part of surfacing True Purpose as a professional service for the clients of my company is testing its commercial viability. You'll have already seen those two words appear many times in this book. It's a critical part of the entire philosophy of purpose-driven capitalism. Without commercial viability you won't have a business, you'll have a hobby.

Recapping briefly, commercial viability is the potential of your True Purpose to deliver a financial return. The authentic purpose that's motivating you and your team may deliver many rewards such as career fulfilment, improved quality in your particular industry, reputation, status, and more.

But will it sell? To people who've never heard of you. To people who are already defensive and cynical about corporate promises. To people who may only have a passing interest in the wrong that your True Purpose is righting? Or to people who love what you stand for, but see no reason to change their buying behaviour because of it?

Checking the cold, hard reality of free enterprise is something we take very seriously at Meerkats and we've spent years developing the right kinds of tools to test it. For real. Without bias. Without wishful thinking clouding the truth of just how appealing we think a company's True Purpose will be to outsiders.

Believe me, it's a slippery slope. After a couple of months of delving deep inside the history and psyche of a group of emotional humans we call a company, and finding something powerful that lights up their eyes and inspires a wonderful new unity and energy, all that passion and optimism can have an effect on your perspective. It can create a false view of the world similar to the Bubble of Bulls**t I described in chapter 8.

Over the years I'm sure you've had the occasional conversation with a friend or relative who has excitedly told you their brilliant idea for a new business. And while smiling and nodding eagerly all you could think was, 'I don't think this is gonna work'.

So at my company, in return for our professional fees — and the reputation of the CEO who is usually endorsing the project to the board — we do as much as we can to test the commercial appeal of the True Purpose we've just surfaced. This stage includes:

- reviewing research on purchasing behaviour in the category, from the region our clients are operating in at the time and globally as a benchmark

- studying buying trends in the category to get a sense of changing consumer habits and emerging needs

- interrogating our clients' own sales data and customer feedback, both past and current, in surveys and on social media platforms

- modelling consumer propositions, new products and new service design based on the True Purpose

- mapping out likely customer journeys from initial contact via advertising, point-of-sale or word-of-mouth, to instore experience, trial purchase, and so on.

My favourite, and the most insightful, part of this testing phase is the customer co-creation session. As I described in the story of the dairy company in the first part, this for me is where the rubber hits the road. Because I've found that it's actually not enough for consumers to simply understand a True Purpose. It's not even enough for them to like it. In order for a True Purpose to drive a company towards a higher ideal that delivers returns which are both financial and social, consumers have to have a little part of their hearts opened up by your truth.

That is, they need to catch the idea a little. They need to internalise it, not just understand it. They don't have to fully embrace a True Purpose to the degree that a company's management and staff do in order to fuel the energy and resilience they'll need to change conventions in their particular category. But consumers do need to be moved by a True Purpose. Just a little. Otherwise there's a risk that its appeal won't be enough to change their buying behaviour.

Because, let's be honest, we humans are a pretty lethargic lot when it comes to change. Especially on something as trivial as washing powder, or banks.

So we meet with them and explore this possibility in sessions designed to tease out their true feelings of a company's purpose. My company has spent a lot of time perfecting these moments so we get as close to the truth as we can. They're different from the global standard in consumer research known as focus groups.

People in focus groups are paid $50 to $100 and given some sandwiches and a drink in return for their opinions. So, by golly, they're going to give you their opinions. They go into the whole event with a very logical mindset.

And hey, I also personally believe that most humans are innately nice; they genuinely want to help us ad folk with our important new product or brand. And the nicer the hosting researcher is, the nicer they want to be.

The bottom line is, I never fully trusted what people said in conventional focus groups. 'Oh, that's a wonderful new corn-based cereal. Yes, I would definitely change to this brand.' I never felt they were lying — in that moment they probably genuinely believed what they said. But it was forced. It was simulated truth. And as such, was erroneous information upon which to base your business strategy.

So my partner and I changed the approach to this kind of research. We created a framework whereby the way people spoke was treated with more importance than what they actually said. We began placing more weight on body language and 'room vibe' than transcripts.

For example, it's amazing how often people in focus groups use the phrase 'I would', as in, 'If it does what you say, then yes I *would* buy that product'. The client hears 'I *will* buy that product', claps their hands and heads home thinking all their problems are over.

What I see in the consumer's body language, however, is, 'If it does what you say, then yes I would buy that product ... if I wasn't already so used to buying the other brand ... if I could be bothered even thinking about organic car wash the second I leave this building ... if I lived in some utopian *Truman Show* world where stuff like this even mattered to me compared to my mortgage and missing out on that promotion last month and my selfish teenage daughter who suddenly won't speak to me ...'

You get my point.

What we look for in our co-creation sessions with consumers is not convenient answers like 'Yes I would buy that', but signs of curiosity about the ambition of the company being tested. Any sign that something new and possibly important has entered their lives this night. And not just a new kind of energy drink, but something with a broader benefit. A new solution to something that's unfair or unchanged.

These signs are often visual— things that an anthropologist might spot but a researcher would miss. But they can also be a natural inquisitiveness that extends a conversation in the group beyond the standard question-and-answer format.

Here are some examples from the case studies I've already shared with you so far:

- *Ambition:* a little internet provider who wants to liberate the internet from the big phone companies.
  Valued response: 'Yeah, come to think of it, why *aren't* the big phone companies telling us about free phone calls over the internet?'

- *Ambition:* a company that will give a pair of shoes to the poor for every pair the customer buys.
  Valued response: 'That's interesting. Why *can't* businesses do good stuff too?'

- *Ambition:* an energy company seeking more respect for a role in society that's grown in importance.
  Valued response: 'Yeah, now that you mention it the people who keep the electricity flowing are *really* important these days'.

It's the kind of conversation that escalates without much prompting from the researcher. It becomes organic. Because it's true. And important. In fact, some of the most useful insights about True Purpose happen when the moderator leaves the room.

Here's the good news for you: every time we've surfaced a True Purpose that we believed was a terrific win–win for humans — a more honourable objective for the category, more pride and career fulfilment for the employees, a tangible rippling effect of truth and morality out into society — it has resonated with consumers. And in a way that made us think not just, 'Hey I think people might buy this', but 'Holy crap, this is powerful stuff!'

What we see in our testing of True Purpose is not just a sense that all those unbiased humans out there in consumerland might entertain the possibility of buying your product; we see the beginnings of enormous economic potential. In my mind's eye I see a snowball already tumbling down the mountainside, gathering pace and growing.

Like the dairy company I wrote about in chapter 5. It became crystal clear in the 90 minutes of our co-creation sessions that mums didn't just approve of the idea of a small, purpose-driven dairy company making better products for the majority of working families, they *loved* the idea. They wanted it to happen. They'd found something rare and desirable that night and it lit a fire inside them.

'Okay, so great, Mike. That's how you test the commercial viability of your True Purpose if you're a sizeable company with the resources to pay for co-creation sessions and trend studies, and so on. But what about me? I'm just a:

☐ Small-business owner

☐ Startup founder

☐ Person with big dreams

☐ Manager of someone else's small business

☐ CEO of a company with no marketing budget.'

(Tick one.)

Glad you asked. That's what this chapter is about. The truth is, without the means to professionally test the commercial viability of your True Purpose before implementing it, you're going to have to do it on the fly.

testing viability as you go

There's a chain of more than 400 supermarkets in the United States called Whole Foods Market. Today they likely conduct all manner of consumer research and data gathering to pursue their True Purpose of helping people live longer, healthier and happier lives through better quality organic meats, dairy, eggs, fruit and vegetables. But in the beginning they started with just one tiny store in Austin, Texas.

One of the co-founders, John Mackey, tells the Whole Foods Market story in the book *Conscious Capitalism,* written with Raj Sisodia.

The owners had a dream of changing the way Americans eat. The stats on obesity, diabetes and decreasing life expectancy made them sad. What then made them downright furious was the contributing role the big supermarket chains had in this alarming trend.

That sadness and fury was powerful enough to motivate them to put their careers (and houses) on the line and start a new kind of supermarket. One that sold only the freshest organic and free-range foods. A supermarket with a mission to not only sell people food, but to educate them about it too.

It was a huge risk, going up against not only the giants of the American supermarket industry, but all the massive brands that sold products through them. Making it harder was the fact that with only one store and tight budgets, they couldn't afford to professionally test the commercial viability of their higher ideal.

So they decided to work harder than any other small-business owner they knew and make every day a consumer test. Every product they sourced was monitored for sales from day 1. They stood and watched which direction customers went when they first walked in, how they walked around the store, where they hovered and where they walked straight on. They asked for constant feedback on their product range, displays and service.

They used the ultimate co-creation techniques in the ultimate co-creation location: their own store. They did a lot of observing and a little bit of asking (which is always the right ratio). They left their egos at the door and were prepared to act fast when their on-the-job research threw up a potential commercial barrier to fulfilling their True Purpose.

For example, they discovered that sales would be too low to sustain a business if they didn't include some non-organic products in their range. This was a crucial early lesson for them and valuable wisdom for you: they had to seemingly compromise the purity of their True Purpose in order to turn it into a thriving business. I say seemingly because they didn't betray their True Purpose — they simply realised they had to stretch out their own timeline for success.

You see, in 1980 when they opened that first little store, most Americans thought organic food was for hippies. It was harder to find, more expensive and often ugly. The shiny, perfect produce they saw every week at their local supermarket was good enough and hey, an apple's an apple, right? What's more, many shoppers were enjoying the rise in convenience foods such as pre-sliced fruits, and peeled and packaged microwavable vegetables. Many of which were now being produced by the big food brands. Sure, they ended up having colours, flavourings and preservatives to extend shelf life and aid visual appeal. But consumers ignored the long-term health implications and convinced themselves this stuff was fine, aided by ad campaigns by the big food brands showing fresh green fields and dewy fruit tumbling through the air in slow motion.

So you could argue that the guys in that first Whole Foods Market were being pretty naive to think their little store could magically change all that habitual behaviour overnight.

They already knew that in their catchment area the numbers of consumers pre-disposed to buying organic produce was just too small. Sure, they could run a small neighbourhood supermarket on those numbers, but what concerned them more was that unless they appealed to all those grocery buyers who currently didn't think about organic food, they would fail in their ultimate purpose: to help society become healthier. Not just their suburb, not even just Austin, Texas, but the whole of the United States — and perhaps even the world.

This ultimate destiny drove them to do something they originally thought they'd never do: sell non-organic items alongside their beloved organic products. It was a hard decision, but their thinking was spot on: 'If we don't sell some grocery lines that are non-organic but popular with regular shoppers, we will never generate enough customers to make our True Purpose a viable business. And if we can't make this a viable business we can't change the way America eats'.

So they didn't give up; they simply set up a parallel product strategy and stretched out their timeline for success. And they made a deal with themselves: as soon as their business was consistently profitable, as soon as they started to grow and open more stores, as soon as their workshops and online videos and media interviews started opening the minds and wallets of Americans to a better way of eating, they would start to drop those non-organic products from their stores.

That, to me, sounds like a good deal. And a smart way to start a purpose-led business in the absence of sophisticated consumer research.

At my company, Meerkats, we learned a similar early lesson. We called it 'meeting the client where they're at and taking them to Plus One'. Meaning: let's not take such a lofty stance from the outset that we go over the heads of our intended customers. Let's not try and make a business from offering something nobody wants (or realises they need). Instead, let's give people what they want first, then dedicate ourselves to elevating them step by step to a higher ideal. Let's not be philosophical snobs, but empathetic coaches.

You see, we wanted to change the role of advertising agencies in the business world. We wanted to use our insight and imagination to create change, not just advertising (which we saw as a weakening force in free enterprise). We wanted to prove to our clients that the real creativity may well be in their business model, or products and services, or internal culture. At the time, however, almost every large brand would only give you a shot at their business strategy if you also handled their entire marketing budget. So my partner and I acknowledged that if we went out on day 1 and only offered creative business solutions we would likely remain a consultancy of two people, working on very small brands for a long time. And that wasn't going to help change capitalism for the better.

To fulfil the ultimate potential of our True Purpose we had to access the larger companies with the means to fund a different kind of branding. We also wanted to prove our philosophy on the big stage with highly visible brands so we could create successful case studies that other companies wanted to follow.

So we decided, like the founders of Whole Foods Market, to meet the customer where they're at — requesting ad campaigns — and work harder to prove to them that perhaps there's a better way (truth from the inside of a company out into the world). It takes an enormous amount of ego control and patience. It takes a constant honest monitoring of your progress in order to ensure that this compromised position doesn't suck you into giving up on your dreams. And it takes making some hard decisions when you feel your customers aren't genuinely coming around to your point of view.

In Meerkats' case, we'd choose not to pitch for certain companies if we felt they weren't even interested in going to Plus One. Likewise, we eventually resigned clients who said they were interested, but constantly resisted our efforts to provide creative business solutions outside of advertising.

You wouldn't have to do any of this if you had a rich patron funding your True Purpose until it became viable. But it's often the smartest decision you can make if you need to earn an income while trying to change the world.

Smart, purpose-led business owners learn fast that being right doesn't necessarily mean being successful. You never give up on your purpose. But you have to sometimes play the long game in order to fulfil it.

So look carefully in your first weeks and months of leading your purpose-driven business for the right balance between the world you want to create and the world that exists today. Decide in your own mind what's smart flexibility in order to one day achieve your True Purpose, and what is a fearful betrayal of your ideal. Be aware of that line. Every day.

check your toolbox

As well as doing your own on-the-job observational research every day, also ask yourself, 'Am I sure I can't access *any* of those testing tools Mike writes about?'

Read the first part of this section again and think real hard about whether or not you can do any of that consumer research and learning yourself. Sure, maybe not to a professional level. But check for any online studies about buying trends in your category. If you're an existing business, run your own customer feedback surveys. Study your sales data with a microscope.

And hey, try running your own co-creation sessions. With friends and family. People from your book club, football club, bingo centre. Invite them round to your home or office, give them some beer and pizza and ask them stuff like this:

'If you heard about a company that stood for this <insert your True Purpose>, how would you expect them to show up in the world?'

Or the other way round:

'If you heard about a company offering this service <insert your purpose-driven business model>, what would you think that company stood for?'

Of course, take their well-meaning comments with a big pinch of salt (and their nit-picking) and look for the lean-in and heated conversation as described above.

Make sure you only ever use the information you gather as an adjunct to your own. Don't ever let others decide for you. It's a reality check, not a board meeting.

testing on meerkats

I can vouch for this approach because before we opened the doors to our new company, Meerkats, my fellow co-founder and I ran our own co-creation session with family and friends. We ran it just like the ones we had conducted for large clients at our previous agencies. Albeit in my partner's back shed and with a beer and a slice of pizza in lieu of any cash payment.

We had wanted to test a theory that would become a core promise for our new ad agency: that consumers in our small regional market were just as smart, choosy, technologically savvy and socially aware as anywhere else in the world. There was a common myth at the time among ad agencies that consumers in my home city were somehow less sophisticated. In a connected world where consumers were sharing information, we thought that was a dangerous assumption.

So we tested it. We decided on the kind of societal cross-section that accurately reflected the local populace. We picked any and all friends and family and friends of family that matched our preferred profiles. We created a bunch of provocations and prompts that would explore our theory. And we conducted our sessions. Just like you can.

We knew that many of our attendees would be nervous for us and so might be tempted to go along with what they thought we wanted to hear. So we shaped the sessions as a chance to contribute to a thought, rather than answer Yes or No questions. And then in the sessions, rather than take their word as gospel we watched their body language and noted energy changes in the group on any particular point.

In the end we felt our toe-in-the-water research had been just as telling and trustworthy as any professionally led qualitative study. For the validity of a core theme. To add some robustness to our opinion study, we hired a research company to run a cheap online survey of a few hundred local residents. These kinds of surveys are available in most markets, are usually conducted over a single weekend and are surprisingly affordable. So if you were looking to add some cold, hard figures to your own soft human research, I'd recommend you try this.

(23) the circle as a compass

Once you've enunciated your True Purpose, The Circle can become like a magic compass that helps you stay on track towards what's going to ultimately fulfil you as a human, and most likely bring financial reward as well.

This concept can be best illustrated by telling you the story of a very unusual business.

TOMS shoes

Californian Blake Mycoskie is a very driven entrepreneur. Before he even got out of his 20s he'd founded a door-to-door laundry business, an outdoor advertising company and an online driver's education service. And sold them all for good money. He'd also competed in *The Amazing Race*, the TV show that takes couples on an incredible global journey of physical and mental challenges.

After all that he then decided to travel to Argentina to learn how to play polo. As you do. While there, Blake met a woman who provided free footwear to the poor in rural areas. Blake went along on one of her trips and was blown away. He didn't realise a simple pair of shoes could make such a huge difference to the lives of the children of poor farmers.

In one village, Blake saw two boys who had only one pair of shoes between them. Which meant they had to take turns going to school, because students were required to have footwear. Giving that family a pair of shoes for each child triggered tears and hugs and immense gratitude.

Blake was so moved by the experience that he decided to use all his skills as an entrepreneur to pursue a different outcome. He wanted to see if the standard way of doing business, which generated profit for the betterment of the owners, could be applied to generate profit for the betterment of the needy. In a self-sustaining way that didn't require grants or donations.

He started a for-profit company called Shoes For Tomorrow with a unique business model: they would make a simple, fashionable canvas shoe for the cool young people living in California, but the business model (manufacturing costs and pricing) would be designed to make two pairs for that one sale price, with the second pair being given free to the needy children of Argentina.

Not a bad win–win huh?

You may have seen this one-for-one model used in restaurant chains and other business categories recently, but Blake was the first to use it. His idea took off and the company — now called TOMS, short for Tomorrow's Shoes — grew and grew.

At the end of the first season they had sold 10 000 pairs. Which meant 10 000 free pairs of shoes to the children of Argentina (and soon beyond). Which meant thousands of poor families were able to send their children to school, to make a living, to be healthier.

Five years later, TOMS had sold their 10 *millionth* pair and was now a massive company, with annual growth of more than 300 per cent and a hierarchy of management teams, sales and distribution departments, PR divisions, and so on.

It was around this time, when most business owners would be retiring on their phenomenal success, that Blake had a major problem. He had become disillusioned. The team of execs he'd hired to run his company were beginning to get bogged down in bickering and conflicting business strategies. They were implementing what they believed to be commonsense processes and systems based on the companies they had come from. They were identifying competitors in the shoe market that they needed to respond to. In short, they were acting like a big traditional shoe brand.

Worst of all, several long-term employees were leaving for the energy and excitement of new startups elsewhere. And Blake secretly felt like leaving with them. So he took a sabbatical to try and pinpoint the root cause of his disenchantment.

He realised it was because his True Purpose was getting off track. That magic compass that had originally guided him to a bold new business model, which almost every traditional business person had said wouldn't work, had been quietly put away. His company had subtly shifted from the purpose of 'use the proven methods of capitalism to generate a win–win for the privileged and the needy, for the betterment of not just the wealthy but for all humankind' and morphed into 'maintain a massive shoe company'.

So Blake dusted off the compass that was his True Purpose, got his management team together and told them this organisation wasn't just a shoe company. He said they were socially driven entrepreneurs using the tools of the free market economy to create more benefit in society.

He said that instead of asking themselves how they could keep selling so many shoes, they should ask themselves what else they could make that delivered that same win–win. Where else in the world was there a need that could be solved using their manufacturing and design experience?

Fast forward to today and TOMS is selling coffee on the same one-for-one basis as shoes, but this time for every bag of coffee TOMS sells, a village in Africa gets a water well. Would you believe that those two things cost the same? Imagine that: for the cost of one bag of quality, free trade ground coffee, an entire village in a poor part of an African country can be given a reliable water supply. If you've ever seen pictures of those amazing African women who walk 20 or more kilometres every day with 40 kilograms of water on their heads, you'll know what an amazing gift that is.

Not only that, TOMS is also using its canvas shoe experience to make handbags and backpacks, and for every one of those sold in a cool boutique in Los Angeles, a pregnant woman in Africa gets a free birthing pack that allows her to hygienically deliver her own baby (as is still the norm in many Third-World countries today), saving countless tiny lives.

Which brings us back to that compass. Without a clearly defined True Purpose to guide his decision making, Blake's dream of owning an inspiring business that changed lives would be constantly at risk. It pointed him in the right direction when he started TOMS and it was still showing him the way years later.

Without that solitary source of guidance, businesses often make decisions based on who has the strongest personal opinion in the meeting, or who is best at scaring everyone about what the competition are up to, or who can convince everyone that they have a surefire way to get a short-term financial uplift. The consistency of a business's entire strategy can ebb and flow based on the strength of someone's personality, instead of the strength of a singular destiny.

Purpose-driven companies follow a far more linear path to success. They ask themselves, 'If a potential customer who knows nothing about our company was told that we stand for <their True Purpose>, how would they expect us to show up? Y'know, if we were genuine about it?'

The answers can often lead to breakthrough new products, bold new service design, and even convention-shattering brand extensions like TOMS.

All the way down the list of typical business decisions, True Purpose can guide your answers like a compass guides an explorer:

- How do we get our staff to actually like our customers so they serve them better?

- How do we get our staff to buy into our business goals?

- How do we get a jump on that clever competitor?

- How do we break this addiction to sales promotions?

- Should we invest in staff training or open another store?

- Should we spend a chunk of money on advertising to entice people to buy our existing products, or spend it on developing a better product?

When facing dilemmas such as these, instead of putting the various possible actions on a dartboard and throwing a dart, True Purpose gives you a smart visionary solution along a predetermined line of thinking. What's more, it does it in a way that puts everyone's personal opinions second to the ultimate objective. For anyone who's spent hours in a heated boardroom trading points of view with other hot-headed execs, you'll appreciate just how valuable this is in propelling a business forward.

one degree matters

Staying on purpose is a daily endeavour. You'll find yourself making principled decisions on matters so seemingly insignificant that other people will sometimes grumble about you being too wedded to this purpose stuff. Or they'll give you that ubiquitous 'anal-retentive' tag. Smile politely and maintain your watchful eye.

Leading a purpose-driven company is like leading a team of explorers to the North Pole. In a blizzard. Get off track by just one degree and even after a few hundred metres you can miss your objective completely. After a hundred kilometres you're in serious trouble of never reaching your destination at all.

Any issue from which you can draw a line of argument back to your True Purpose, no matter how small, is worth solving. No matter how often that means you have to stop everyone in a freezing blizzard and check your bearings again.

give your compass a spin

Give The Circle a test run right now. Grab your 'Purpose on a Page' and go to each of the five points in turn, asking yourself some key questions.

True Purpose:

- Is this a more exciting goal for me than simply making money?

- Is this true for me? Is it my most authentic motivation?

- Can I describe the tangible benefits of this to myself, my family, my staff, my customers, my industry and (maybe) my world?

- Do I love the end goal of this higher ideal so much that I feel compelled to serve it? Does it pull me towards it?

Attraction:

- What kind of people do I hope my True Purpose attracts?

- How would they be different from just any normal employee in this field?

- What kind of culture could we create together?

- What might be some unconventional job titles that better describe the roles we'll need in order to deliver on this purpose?

Innovation:

- What are some of the traditional business practices of our industry that we're going to reject?

- What would we love to replace them with?

- What's an example of a new product or a way of serving customers better that comes from the intent of our True Purpose?

- How do we want to get our message out into our industry? What's our role in having our True Purpose make our whole industry better, not just our company?

Growth:

- What kind of customer would we describe as being aligned with our True Purpose?

- What do we want them to say about us after they experience our product and/or service?

- What kind of customer would we not take on in order to stay true to our purpose?

- Are there customers that we would seek outside of the traditional audiences of our industry?

Reward:

- How are we going to measure success? Money, of course. But what other rewards will we value?

- Which conventional measures of business success do we agree with, and which ones do we reject?

- What is our opinion about short-term rewards versus long-term ones? How long are we prepared to wait to see them?

- What new income streams are possible through our True Purpose? How much money could they make us?

- How does our True Purpose affect the structure and hierarchy of our business?

Answer these questions, and the many others that will undoubtedly spring up as you go around The Circle, and — guess what? — you'll have a new business plan. One that's been created with energy and flow and optimism, as opposed to the worry and fear and self-doubt that usually accompanies drawing up a business plan.

Do this robustly and your snowball is starting to tumble down the mountain. Your True Purpose is already gathering momentum. And before you know it, it'll be an unstoppable force.

purpose is a long-term play

One of the most important things about running a business to an authentic purpose is to accept that you're playing the long game. In effect, you're wagering that the long-term benefits of doing what you believe in and proving to consumers that this is also in their best interests will be more rewarding than the short-term benefits of putting aside your personal beliefs and only delivering to consumers' current needs.

This is the challenge, and ultimately the price, of being personally fulfilled through True Purpose. You see the reality is, if judged only on short-term results, nine times out of ten True Purpose will lose.

I know this for a fact because that's exactly what I used to do for a job. I built my success as a creative director by gaining attractive short-term results for my clients. In the ad industry, it's called *being retail.* And in my part of the world I was something of a retail specialist.

I once got a brief from a bank that wanted to promote their business loans. The brief spelled out all the benefits of their business loans and explained how much this bank understood business owners. It was all very uninspiring and expected. Apart from a lousy half a per cent discount on the rate — which every bank would invariably match — there was nothing new or unique. Not enough to assure that running an expensive ad campaign would trigger the avalanche of new business customers my client was hoping for.

So I kept reading the brief, searching for anything I could use to capture the interest of their audience. I believed humans were essentially self-serving. I had to find something they valued because that would make for a more effective ad campaign than merely presenting what the bank had to offer. The disappointingly abrupt target audience description of 'all small-to-medium businesses' didn't help me at all (don't laugh — at least it was better than the 'all people 18+' description I usually received).

Nor was there any insight in the desired consumer response, which yet again started with some sad fictional consumer exclaiming, 'Wow. I never realised that ...'

Then I read the business objectives. In those days a cool creative wouldn't even bother reading the objectives because hey, we were communicators, not business people. But there in the objectives panel was this sentence: 'We want to generate $200 million worth of business loans from this advertising activity'.

That figure struck me. Two hundred million dollars is a lot of cash! I figured that a bank offering to discount the interest rate on that cash was like them having a sale of money. Like a shoe shop has a sale of shoes.

In my mind I pictured that $200 million sitting on the floor of a huge bank vault with armed security guards standing on either side. And on top of the mountain of moulah was a little sign that read simply 'SALE'.

We turned that image into an entire four-week promotion called The Great Business Loan Sale. We couched it as the first time a bank had ever held what was effectively a disposal sale of cash. We essentially changed the client's message to the public from an underwhelming, 'We have business loans. Anybody want one?' to 'We have 200 million bucks we need to get rid of. Come and get it!'

They did $400 million in two weeks.

Today, as a passionate advocate of True Purpose, I know there's no way that bank could have achieved a similar level of commercial success *in that same time period* by suddenly embracing True Purpose. Being purpose-driven means going right back to your business model and aligning your entire offering to your authentic motive. It takes time. Products need to be improved or reinvented, service design needs to be reshaped, staff need to be retrained (or fired).

If your only aim is to achieve the most sales in the short term, with absolutely no caveat about pursuing your personal values or achieving a positive triple-win for you, your customer and the world, then going the wrong way around The Circle will beat the right way.

This is my honest explanation of the grey area in the black and white of truth versus greed. No matter how much I pontificate about the future of capitalism being in purpose-driven thinking, if you tell me that you only have four weeks to achieve business success and you don't care about what happens after that, then I'll still look you in the eye and tell you researching what people want and appealing to their lesser selves will work better than the longer process of proving to them that what you genuinely believe they need is better.

And hey, I'm totally cool with admitting that because even though it's true, I'll happily tell you in the same breath that I don't recommend you do it. You see, if you choose that route, you've got to keep doing it, every four weeks, over and over ... forever. And that's going to cost you a lot more money in marketing and media and research. And staff burnout. And consumer trend studies. And competitor reports. Because this path makes you eternally vulnerable. You're going to be working to top up the customers coming in the front door while they pour out the back door. And everybody knows, these days, that's not a solid business model. Investors are not interested in that. Staff are not interested in that either.

I also believe this path will cost you personally. I believe it's a bad way to live. I believe when you go home at night and look your children in the eye you'd prefer to show them you can be a capitalist and be proud and happy because you're helping make the world a better place. Because you're telling the truth: you're not hiding anything, you're not tricking, you're not manipulating in order to be successful or in order to make money.

So when naysayers think they've caught me out by claiming that a hard-nosed retail attitude will work better than True Purpose, I say, 'I agree with you. But only for a few weeks. What happens after that?'

(24) the sliding doors effect

To me, the most enduring benefit of having a True Purpose is that it gives you a choice. A choice that wasn't there before.

All you need to do to stay on purpose as you grow your business is to realise that every key decision can now be made in one of two directions: the right way around The Circle or the wrong way. Which is another way of saying: you can stay true to the long-term benefit of your True Purpose, or give in to the erroneous benefits of many conventional business practices.

Look at it this way: you know that film *Sliding Doors* with Gwyneth Paltrow? Her character's boyfriend is cheating on her. When the doors start to close on a subway train the film splits into two paths: one exploring what would happen to her life if she caught the train and went on, unaware of her partner's betrayal, and another exploring what would happen if she missed her train, returned home and discovered her boyfriend with another woman.

To show you the knock-on effects of being either purpose-driven or non-purpose-driven and where the cumulative effects of those decisions eventually lead, let's use that *Sliding Doors* idea. Let's look at a couple of key moments in your life as a business owner when you have typical business challenges to overcome, and let's see what happens depending on your choice of purpose or non-purpose.

This is not science. This is not the result of an exhaustive study. This is my summary of what I've seen for myself across decades of observing dozens and dozens of companies making these decisions. So it's not about facts. It's about how each of these paths resonates with *you*.

As you read each scenario, ask yourself two questions:

- Which path seems to be building a strong, sustainable business? (logic)

- Which path makes me feel better? (emotion)

scenario 1: how do i deliver good customer service?

The first business challenge is about the all-important customer. I deal with so many owners and CEOs who lament the low standards of customer service in their companies. Despite all their training programs and incentives and staff awards.

I believe embracing True Purpose can have a massive effect in this area. And in a way that's both enduring and self-fuelling at the same time.

the non-purpose-driven solution

Without an authentic motive to generate a genuine desire in your staff to serve people, you're left with conventional motivators such as financial incentive or the lure of elevated job status. There are also negative motivators (fear of demotion, job loss, and so on).

I don't think any of these motivators are truly sustainable because they connect with humans in a very fake, detached way. It's like you're making a clinical deal with people, rather than appealing to their better selves. In effect, you're asking them to merely simulate a certain behaviour in return for a reward, instead of inspiring them to behave that way because they want to. It's not their natural behaviour. So, in my experience, it doesn't last.

I'm sure a qualified anthropologist or psychologist would be able to explain to you the factual reasons why this happens. I'm basing my advice on personal observation of hundreds of companies across four decades of work in this area.

Sure, you might occasionally fluke an employee who just loves dealing with people, but the chances are those magic humans will be in the minority.

And yes, you may be a truly charismatic leader who can inspire employees to do the right thing. But what happens when you're not watching? What happens when you have two or three stores to oversee?

I believe the ultimate end game for businesses relying on fabricated incentives is a constant struggle to maintain decent levels of customer service. And that results in:

- low repeat custom

- high customer churn

- high staff churn

- higher training costs

- higher spend on financial incentives

- stress and hardship for the owner.

the purpose-driven solution

Great service comes far more easily to a purpose-driven company for two key reasons:

- You and your staff buy into a higher ideal that drives you from your heart, not your brain. Some would even say a True Purpose drives them to perform better from deeper down, in their soul. You're not just serving a person, you're serving the potential of an idea to change the world. This truth generates enormous wells of energy and resilience to help sustain good service.

- A purpose-driven company will attract likeminded customers as much as likeminded staff and investors.

This all helps create an attitude within purpose-driven companies that hey, customers aren't that bad. What's more, you and your staff are far more likely to want to make a customer happy because it doesn't just make a sale, it inches you all closer to your higher objective.

The results are:

- high repeat custom

- low customer churn

- high staff retention

- lower training costs

- lower levels of financial incentive.

scenario 2: how can i drive sales growth?

The single most vexing question of any business owner's life. I could write a whole separate book explaining why I think most businesses are lousy at being ambidextrous when it comes to long- and short-term sales. They seem to be either in branding mode or sales mode and can't see that these are one and the same thing, just with different time scales.

Once you know your True Purpose, you're presented with a choice that makes this distinction much clearer for you — a choice you may not have realised you even have.

the non-purpose-driven solution

Without a core powerful truth of triggering genuine innovation in their products or services, many business owners are tempted to generate those much-needed extra sales via the conventional methods, such as marketing and sales promotions.

To replace the customers falling out the bottom, you need more coming in the top. So you offer 40 per cent off. And, hey presto, it works! But when the promotion stops, so do the extra customers. So you do it again. And the same thing happens again. Although this time the new customer numbers are down slightly because your earlier sale reduced the number of available shoppers.

What's more, your competitors are starting to get wise to your tricks and copying you. Before you know it, 40 per cent off is the norm in your entire category. In trying to bribe customers to come and choose your parity products, you've effectively reduced the potential profit margins for everyone.

It's like drug addiction: the more you take, the less of a high you experience, until you have to keep taking the drug just to feel normal.

I've seen this downward spiral happen with my own eyes in clothing, fast food, health insurance, automotive, supermarkets, and more.

Similarly, deciding that you have to advertise your way to a sales increase is just as damaging. Money-first companies spending more on ad campaigns than true innovation ride a rollercoaster of higher sales when the ads are on and lower sales when the ads are off. And the curve is flattening as more and more people get wise to even the most sophisticated marketing techniques and share a brand's true behaviour via social media.

The other death spiral that non-purpose-driven companies fall into is this: if you can't increase sales, decrease the cost of sales. Like the neighbourhood restaurant that you notice is no longer open for lunch Monday to Wednesday. Or the general store that starts closing at 4 pm. Then 3 pm. Or even that huge hardware chain that used to have a friendly chap greeting you at the entrance.

The blunt truth is that all these band-aid decisions are because you're not good enough. And you're not good enough because you're not authentically motivated to be better.

The results are:

- higher cost of sales

- lower margins

- high customer churn

- bickering in the boardroom

- increasing marketing budgets

- lower returns

- fearful, reactive staff focused on competition and margins.

the purpose-driven solution

Profitable, purpose-driven businesses like TOMS, Patagonia, Apple, The Body Shop, Honda, Whole Foods Market, Southwest Airlines, Zappos and hundreds more spend a tiny percentage of their gross income on advertising and promotions compared to their non-purpose-driven competitors.

Their authentic desire to create value in the world drives genuine innovation. And having better products is a far more effective driver of sales than advertising and promotions.

Word of mouth, social media and unsponsored media reviews attract more customers than advertising and promotions because they're more trustworthy forms of endorsement. There's no suspicion of ulterior motive that most consumers have in the backs of their minds as they view ads and sponsorship announcements.

As an owner, viewing advertising as the final option in driving sales—behind product innovation, service delivery and customer experience—is a far more fulfilling, self-fuelling way of doing business than the path described in the non-purpose solution above. It creates momentum and optimism and enjoyment in your culture. It's about building pride, not an expensive marketing department.

The results are:

- sustainable sales growth

- a rising staircase of income growth and pride, not a flattening rollercoaster ride of decrease and desperation

- new markets that grow income exponentially

- a positive, resilient staff focused on growth and possibility.

be your own movie audience

A funny thing happens when we humans sit in a darkened cinema and watch a movie: we see a character's moral choices so much more clearly than we see our own. What's more, we decide very quickly that the short-term benefit that character is gaining from going against their better judgement isn't worth it and that they should trust their gut instinct. Make the brave choice.

We applaud the office nerd who stands up to the bullying boss even though it might cost them their job.

We call out for the Plain Jane to tell the Handsome Jock that she loves him even though she risks social ridicule and rejection.

We urge the unknown amateur sports woman to compete against the world champions even though she risks having her deepest fears of failure realised.

We yearn for the whistle-blower to reveal the political corruption even though he's set for fame and wealth.

We sit in the dark and spot these choices so clearly and quickly. And when those characters we're quietly urging on eventually make the right decision—and they almost always do because hey, that's what movies do—we cheer and clap and feel good. Deep down inside.

So I've often wondered why we don't then see ourselves as characters in our own movies. Why are the big decisions in real life any different? Why do we not trust that good things will come if we follow our own moral compasses?

If there's just one thing you take away from this book, let it be that. Whenever you feel the pang of moral conflict, of money versus truth, of manipulation versus honesty, zoom out, look at yourself on that big screen and ask yourself, 'If I was in the cinema watching this moment in a movie, what would I be hoping that lead character does?'

You'll get your answer in a flash. You just need the courage to act on it.

(25) ten tips for staying on-purpose

My company has guided dozens of organisations through the processes described in this book. Companies, charities, social enterprises, startups, small business, big business and everything in between. We've seen the common roadblocks to success, so here are a few nuggets of wisdom to help you overcome the inevitable setbacks on your journey into purpose-driven ownership.

convention is like gravity

Following an organisational purpose requires more energy because you're pushing away from the norm. All the time.

This is a critical point for you and your staff (and family) to understand. A lot of people think change is a one-time deal — that you work extra hard to make a transition and then you can stop working so hard. Time to relax and cruise again. Being purpose-driven means never cruising. It's like gravity. As soon as you stop actively pushing against that constant force you'll start slipping back down to the ground. And you won't even notice at first. The pull of normalcy, like gravity, is insidious.

Imagine you're a rocket going into orbit. You need to accelerate from 0 to 28 000 kilometres per hour and get to 435 kilometres above the earth in order to break the bonds of earth's gravity. If your boosters stop or even decrease anywhere before you're 435 kilometres up, you'll come back down again.

Keep that image in your mind and imagine the earth is the conventional way of doing business — the wrong way around The Circle. And imagine that what's possible with your True Purpose is out there in space. If you and your team ever stop actively pushing back against convention you'll never achieve your destiny.

So *pushing* is the normal state for a purpose-driven company. Resting on status quo is a slow, insidious death for your dreams. You need to make that clear to people when they join you.

you're now the rebels, not the government

Being driven by an authentic True Purpose that creates good in the world, not just money, is unfortunately not the current norm in business.

Doing that means you're going against convention. A large, established, long-held convention that's so ingrained a lot of people think it's the only way to be.

You're now like the righteous rebel army fighting a corrupt incumbent government that's much larger and better equipped. A government that controls the media and has convinced most of the general public that their way is the right way.

As the rebels you'll feel underpowered. Your victories will be small. But truth and virtue are on your side. Your little army will attract more soldiers. You'll gradually claim more ground and win the hearts of more and more people. You'll unite with likeminded rebels from elsewhere and grow your strength.

But until then you'll only have yourselves to boost your confidence. You'll sometimes look down from your small, wet camp in the hills at the corrupt government officials in their big, comfortable homes and doubt your beliefs. So you must keep believing and put a bright spotlight on any evidence of success.

warning: purpose polarises

I'm no business consultant. I can't help you with manufacturing systems analysis and profitability indicator ratios. But I can offer you some street-smart advice regarding your business plan and, in particular, your projected sales and income.

Be conservative. Your purpose will polarise. It will not appeal to all customers. There's always sacrifice in standing for something.

Like the furniture shop that had to give up the quick bucks from the discount furniture shopper in order to pursue their higher ideal of great design and superior manufacturing. Or the dairy company that decided to turn away from the mass sales of cheap milk in order to prove that it was possible to provide boutique quality products at affordable prices. Each decision meant consciously turning their backs on a segment of the market for the greater good of the long game.

So be patient with the numbers. Build slowly. Start small. Prove your point. Make it commercial, then grow. Play the long game.

naysayers can't help themselves

In the novel *1984* George Orwell wrote, 'In a time of universal deceit, telling the truth is a revolutionary act'. I love that quote. It's so true. I've seen it happen time and again.

What we purpose-driven business owners see as merely embracing common sense or admitting the obvious is often seen by others as dangerous and fearful. Your ideas challenge their basest beliefs and shake their solid foundations. So the natural tendency by many will be to resist your points of view, or at least find fault with them.

This can happen with family and friends, as well as industry peers and occasionally even the passionate staff you recruit to the cause. The basic rule is: the more your thinking impacts them, the more likely it is their fear will come out.

Here's my approach to it.

First, listen carefully for any evidence that what they're saying is true and add it to your thinking — that is, don't be a blind optimist, someone who's actually so fearful of being wrong that you close yourself to the truth. Remember truth is the god of purpose, not correctness. Once I separated fact from fear I learned a great deal from people questioning the validity (and sometimes the sanity) of my purpose-driven thinking.

Second, always take negativity with a pinch of salt. Actually, a huge handful of salt. Naysayers aren't you. They don't see what you see. So they can't be as brave as you. Resist the urge to accuse them of being huge bummers. Resist the heated emotions welling up inside you that may cause you to get huffy and sulky or holier-than-thou. Just listen, learn, smile and move on.

Third, find the energy to fully understand why you're doing something that others are seeing as revolutionary, or naive, or counter-intuitive, or even foolhardy. Use your passion and belief in your True Purpose to fuel the effort it takes to find evidence for your thinking. Then share that evidence. Explain the context to your decision making. Use every moment of potential argument with a doubter as the chance to explain why this is a smart move.

Trust me, it will help cement the logic of your True Purpose for both them and you. I've lost count of how many times I've reminded myself of the value and importance of my mission simply by hearing myself say it out loud to someone else. And by the act of searching for evidence for why I believe in it so much.

At the end of the day, you'll find yourself finishing many of your discussions with sceptics with the words 'trust me' and 'watch what happens'. And that's the way it should be. There's an old saying attributed to Theodore Roosevelt that goes 'Speak softly and carry a big stick'. My version for anyone trying to change the world for the better is 'Argue softly and deliver big results'. Not as catchy, but give it a shot.

value the good feedback

If negative feedback is useful because it provides checks and balances on our logic and strengthens our resolve to prove our purpose is potent, then positive feedback is useful too. And not just because it massages our ego.

As a purpose-driven business owner I've learned that positive feedback has a far greater role over time. That is, it's become more and more useful to me as the years pass, beyond the initial well wishes that gave us strength in those frightening early days of a new business.

What I learned was that positive feedback can actually be another way to keep you on track. If The Circle is like a compass that guides you towards your purpose, then positive feedback is like remagnetising that compass to keep it accurate.

Here's the key: whenever someone compliments you on your purpose, or says they like what your company is doing, say thank you, of course, but then ask them why.

Why do you think ours is a good purpose for a company?

Why is what we're doing here good?

Two things happen. One, you get a quick read on whether the actual experience of your purpose aligns with your original intention, giving you valuable real-world testing of its impact. And two, you occasionally hear a rationale about the benefits of your True Purpose that never occurred to you, giving you added confidence and determination.

Once, one of our designers said she loved what we were doing at Meerkats. When I asked her to explain further, she told me that despite loving graphic design and brand communications at university, she never thought she'd be able to work in the advertising industry because she presumed she'd have to give up so many of her personal values. Like telling the truth and being respectful.

She said that working at Meerkats had already shown her that it was possible to promote brands with integrity. Up to that point, it had never really occurred to me that a whole new generation of talented and creative young people had largely written off our industry because of the deceit and distrust they saw in its conventional behaviour. And that our company had a role in reversing that. That we could help these awesome young minds apply their passions to a rewarding career without compromising their integrity.

That one piece of feedback, once unpicked, made me even more determined to succeed, because now I had in my mind the faces of a whole other group of people who would benefit from it.

The other kind of positive feedback that you want to interrogate is any magazine article, newspaper story, TV documentary, book or blog that supports your point of view. Especially if it deals in a sector of commerce similar to yours.

The conversation around purpose in business is growing globally. There are more and more opinion pieces and case studies appearing in all media channels on this subject. They can not only reassure you that you're doing the right thing, they can expand your concept of purpose so you can explain it better to others, give you valuable facts and precedents you can use to strengthen your presentations and tenders, and occasionally give you the names of people you may want to get in touch with to share experiences.

When we stumbled across the 2013 documentary *The Naked Brand* it was like manna from heaven. We were starving rebels looking for any kind of evidence that our fight was right and here was 56 minutes of well-credentialed proof. Plus exciting new case studies that weren't Apple, soundbites from eminent business leaders, and more.

The key is, even though this was the ultimate positive feedback, we didn't just watch it and feel good. We watched it and watched it and memorised its stats and showed everyone we knew and used clips from it in our client presentations, staff inductions and industry lectures.

Bottom line: don't use positive feedback to simply massage your ego, and don't use negative feedback to simply get angry. Use it to learn and grow and be even more authentic with your True Purpose.

you'll be tempted to go the wrong way

It's going to happen. You'll find yourself going the wrong way around The Circle. It's natural. So don't beat yourself up about it. Just make sure you acknowledge it. Then at least you'll still be making a choice — still running your business consciously.

There are two main situations when it seems more likely a business owner will slip and start going the wrong way. And they both involve money.

financial pressure

In a time of financial pressure, a fear of loss defeats our appetite for change. Anxiety clouds our judgement, weakens our confidence, eats away at our resolve. Let's say you lose a big client or two and suddenly your financial reports are looking sick. There will be a strong temptation to take on a client who is clearly not right for you, or to discount your rates, or to hire cheaper staff.

The very things that people said you were nuts for *not* doing in the first place. But the reasons why those business strategies weren't right for your True Purpose when you started will still apply. It's just that now, with the fear of financial burden looming, you'll find yourself considering them.

'Well gee, I know hiring our sector's smartest minds is going to prove our purpose is potent but we could get three Mac Monkeys for the price of one Smart Strategist. We'd be kind of foolish not to really.'

This kind of backtracking rationale will creep into boardroom conversations. So watch out for it. That's not your authentic purpose-driven self speaking. That's your fearful self. It's okay. Sometimes we have to explore unpalatable options. Just acknowledge that you're consciously thinking the other way around The Circle.

financial windfall

Paradoxically, the opposite of financial pressure can be just as damaging to a purpose-driven company.

Early in our company's history we were wooed by a large retail client worth around two million dollars in billings, which would have equated to around three hundred thousand dollars of annual income for us. We were still a small company of around ten staff and this would have been something of a financial bonanza. And this client was pretty much ready to just walk in the door. No pitch. No lengthy negotiations.

So the temptation for us to go the wrong way around our own Circle was huge. No more bank debt. Computer upgrades for everyone. New desks.

New staff. A coffee machine! And some end-of-year dividends for all the hard work and sacrifice by us owners.

Even stopping to think about it had some of our own staff wide-eyed and slack-jawed. 'What do you mean you're *thinking* about it? This is everything you guys have hoped for! A big branded client!'

But that's the thing with being purpose-driven. Convention is insidious. Going off-purpose is seductive.

After meeting this client, we knew they weren't a good fit for us. They weren't interested in exploring their authentic purpose; they felt they knew their strategy and that we'd simply be a well-paid production house for them. In the end we agreed that we couldn't in all honesty look ourselves in the mirror and say that this client would allow us to prove our philosophies. We knew that taking this client would set us off in the wrong direction around The Circle.

So we said no. We'd just have to wait a little longer for that coffee machine.

And yes, we could have acknowledged that we were about to go the wrong way and said to ourselves 'just this once'. That would still be leading our company consciously, right? Well yes, but you should watch out for the 'just onces'. In his book *How Will You Measure Your Life?* Clayton M. Christensen, Professor of Business Administration at Harvard, tells a powerful story about doing things against your better judgment *just once.*

At Oxford University he was one of the stars of their basketball team. They powered through the season undefeated and were set to play for the championship. The game, however, was scheduled for a Sunday and as a deeply religious man Clayton had promised himself he would never compete on the Sabbath. His teammates implored him to make an exception *just this once.* They argued that this was an exceptionable circumstance that won't ever happen again. And he was sorely tempted. But in the end, he just knew that if he made this decision he wouldn't be able to look in the mirror and see a man of principles. And that would hurt more than winning a pennant.

The reason he shares this story is because he learned that life is actually a never-ending series of exceptionable circumstances. He realised that if he went against his principles that one time he would have ended up doing it his entire life. What's more, in his career as a business lecturer he has seen time and again smart business students with the world at their feet end up bankrupt or in jail because they had repeatedly compromised their integrity *just this once.*

Bottom line: watch out for moments of extreme fear and extreme desire. Make sure you're using the terminology of The Circle to be honest about the decisions you're about to make.

ditch the cookie-cutter stuff

This is a contentious thought, but give it a shot and see if it works for you.

Throughout my career I've witnessed a rise and fall in the popularity of Vision and Mission. And Goals and Values. During each phase of favouritism for those terms, there have been all kinds of new rhetoric about why the new word beats the old word. Or why the new word is adding an important new nuance to the whole process of enunciating ambition. Or why you need a complex mix of all four. And how to place them in the right descending order.

To me, each of those words is asking the same single question: How are we going to create value for the world?

So I personally believe you can throw out all your Vision Statements, Mission Statements and Critical Goals — even that four-word list of Company Values you had printed in computer-cut plastic and glued to the wall in your reception area. A one-sentence summary of your True Purpose can replace it all. Because it will trigger a clear conversation with anyone at any time about how your company is adding value to the world. It'll be clearer, more inspiring and more efficient.

don't compare yourself

(aka 'For God's sake *don't compare* yourself!')

I saw recently that researchers are blaming Instagram for the rise in the world's obsession with keeping up with the Joneses. And the Habibs. And the Xings.

People the world over are increasingly consumed with having the right appearance, wearing the right clothes, eating the right food, listening to the right music, holidaying in the right places and sharing the photos to prove it.

To me, this is a tragic step backwards for humankind. I've never been a fan of comparing myself to the people fear and/or convention tell me I should be like. I discovered early in my career that it leads to perpetual anxiety. No matter how successful you are, or how much stuff you have, you will always come out feeling you're a failure if you compare yourself to others.

I was lucky enough to stumble into a job that paid me a huge salary at a young age. Even though I'm from a lower middle-class background (our family had seven kids and zero cash), I soon found myself mixing with people who had nice houses in the expensive suburbs, drove brand new Mercedes and holidayed in Cannes.

I noticed that I began to expect these things too. What had been an astounding privilege and joy a year or two before quickly became the norm. Sub-par even. A little voice in the back of my head started chattering away about what I needed to possess in order to stay looking like the people who had the things that I deserved to have too.

It's insidious and dangerous. I look out for it now. And I'm more content as a result. I'm me and I'm happy with that. Whatever anyone else wants to do with their life, what job they get, what house they buy, is fine with me. It's just information now, not a trigger.

And that's my advice to you around your True Purpose. Use the discovery of it to drive a life without comparison. The whole magic of purpose is how it creates the motivation to change the world from within you, not from outside influences. It creates new possibilities, not old expectations.

And hey, the truth is that in pursuing your True Purpose you may need to give up some of the shiny things that others have. For a while. You may need to sit at a bar listening to a friend who has cracked a retail scheme that's making them a fortune. You may need to smile and nod as an old work colleague scores a VP gig at a multinational for a phenomenal salary. And stock options.

In that moment you may feel a pang or two of doubt about the path you've chosen, but you should resist the urge to dwell on it. Don't doubt your purpose. You're now the 'monopoly of you' and so comparison to anyone else is inconsequential. You are the only one on your journey.

heads up: effort hurts

I know I said at the start of this book that I'm no Dr Phil and that this isn't a self-help book as much as a field manual for modern business, buuuut … I do feel strongly that change requires effort. And humans have a difficult, often contradictory, relationship with effort.

Dorothy Parker, a prolific author, poet and Academy Award nominated screenwriter once said, 'I hate writing. I love having written'. That beautifully captures my mindset as a purpose-driven business owner. I often dislike having to find the energy to educate a client about truth in business; to create the solution they asked for *and* the solution they actually need; to sit down and explain to an employee how and why their behaviour was against our culture and what they can do about it; to resign a client who has become too much of a philosophical mismatch and do all the hard yards required to replace the lost income. But damn, I'm happy when I have.

Conventional business practices remain the accepted norm because they're easy. Well, easier than unpacking all the component parts, seeing what works and what doesn't, creating a new process, implementing it and then honing it over time. What's more, conventional behaviour provides us vulnerable humans with convenient hiding places for the things that threaten us: what others think of us, our own self-belief, and so on. So challenging convention is not just a question of energy, it's also a brave act.

My co-founder says that applying yourself — and your team — to the many difficult tasks required to make transformational change in an organisation is like parenting. When you're knee-deep in nappies and Lego with one kid screaming and the other pouring maple syrup into the Xbox, you wonder whether it's all worth it. But later that day when you're standing in your child's bedroom, silently watching them sleep you know that being a parent is the greatest, most fulfilling human experience possible. And you're proud of every iota of effort you made that day.

So get ready. Apart from the nappies, leading a purpose-driven company is very similar.

life is about trade-offs

Let's be honest. The purpose of understanding yourself and being true to your most authentic motivations is not to create a bubble of endless perfection and happiness. Life isn't like cereal commercials.

Rather, life is an endless sequence of trade-offs: deciding what you need to give up in order to get what you want. And I believe the measure of a successful life is a matter of how good we are at understanding the trade-offs, choosing them willingly and then, most importantly, owning the outcomes of those decisions.

Choosing friends who always laugh at our jokes and never disagree with us may give us the impression of being popular and successful, but we give up the emotional growth that candid friends can stimulate in us.

Having children can unlock feelings of love from deep inside our primitive selves that we never realised were there, but we give up going out when we want, placing our careers as priority number one, buying that humongous LG wallpaper TV just because we want it — and all kinds of other stuff.

Our troubles begin when we kid ourselves that we can have what we want in life without any sacrifice. So it is in business.

Running a business through conventional corporate practices even when they go against our personal values may get us status and creature comforts, but we give up pride, inner peace and satisfaction.

Running a business through an authentic purpose may get us the personal fulfilment we seek, but we may need to give up that new BMW 6 Series and the corner office.

Each ambition comes with a downside. Each goal is a trade-off of pros and cons. Living purposefully simply means asking yourself, 'Which trade-off would I rather have?'

a final word

The definition of 'capital' is often summarised as 'the financial value of assets'. And capitalism is the current system for acquiring those assets.

But now there's a new kind of capitalism. Where the main asset is you.

Your talent.

Your passion.

Your vision.

You and your beliefs are at the centre of the new kind of free market economy.

You and what's inside your head and heart and soul have commercial value.

Because this allows you to sell authentically to a population fed up with being deceived.

So don't ignore your truth.

Don't waste it.

Surface what genuinely motivates you.

Unleash it on the world.

Use it to add to society, not just take from it.

Use it to prove to Wall Street that there's a way to make money that's honest and fair.

A way that creates enduring value. Not just fleeting profits.

A way that advances humankind towards a future of pride and self-worth.

Thank you.

coaching and conversation

In trying to condense a complex process involving a variety of human emotions into a DIY handbook, I accept there's a risk that I've lost you at some point along the way.

I sincerely hope you've surfaced your True Purpose and taken the first steps to articulate it in words and images and then apply it to your business or social enterprise.

I hope you're newly inspired to pursue what was, at the start of the book, a latent desire buried inside you.

I hope you're now a ball of energy and ideas and can't wait to get stuck into making your True Purpose happen.

But ...

If there's a niggle. Or a block. If there's something you still don't understand. If there's something that just didn't click with you, please get in touch. Seriously.

My email address is mike@meerkats.com.au, or you can post a comment at truthgrowthrepeat.com.

I don't mind being assailed with questions. Whether you're stuck on a particular point. Or can't seem to make the leap from True Purpose to business model. Or maybe you can express your True Purpose in 500 words but not 10. I can help with all that.

You see, my goal is to have this thinking make a difference to more people in order to pursue my own True Purpose of making the world a better place through a fairer, more honest form of capitalism. And if this thinking has inspired you, but you can't implement it, then I won't achieve that goal. I don't want to be just another philosophical guru who purports to want to change the world but is actually most interested in book sales and lecture fees.

So get in touch. Tell me your True Purpose, show me your Protest sign, copy and paste the wording of your 'For too long now' statement or 'Dear World' letter. I want to see them. Especially if you've hit a barrier to pursuing them. Hey, if you're lucky, this book will be a complete flop and I'll only get three emails. I'll have all the time in the world to chat with you!

You can also contact me via LinkedIn: Mike Edmonds, Co-founder. Meerkats: The Brand Leadership Company

recommended reading

This book is the sum total of all the observations and learnings my business partner and I have made about humans and organisations in the 10-plus years we've been together. And indeed, from all 40 years of my working life in the marketing industry.

Every theory, system, method and mantra I've shared with you has been tested in the real world, with real companies and real humans. That's very important to us, coming as we do from an industry that's notorious for making promises on behalf of brands that then fail to deliver on them. But we can't take all the credit. Much of the initial spark for our procedures came from people more insightful than us.

Here's a list of the authors and filmmakers who've influenced us and their key work in this area.

Conscious Capitalism **by John Mackey & Raj Sisodia**

This is the more practical, case study bible for anyone interested in running a purpose-driven business. It shares the experiences of many companies, but particularly of Whole Foods Market, the organic produce brand that grew from one store to more than 400 and who at the time of writing had just been acquired by Amazon for $18 billion. It's the quintessential story of the commercial viability of pursuing an authentic motive in business.

Discover Your Authentic Leadership and *Discover Your True North* **by Bill George**

Although George's background is in leading large corporations, the lessons here are invaluable to anyone who wants to be a CEO. Even if it's the CEO of a fish'n'chip shop, or a small tech startup. It may use case studies like Walmart, Microsoft, GE and Pfizer, but the lessons about authentic leadership are closely aligned with our teachings on truth in business. And so are relevant to any size of business anywhere in the world. George opened a door in our minds that helped shape our thinking. I'm willing to bet it will for you too.

Grow **by Jim Stengel**

This book sets out to test the commercial viability of companies driven by an authentic purpose. Specifically, those centring their business on improving people's lives. It's a robust ten-year research project of more than 50 000 brands and concludes that purpose-driven businesses are growing three to ten times faster than non-purpose-driven businesses. Stengel is highly regarded in this field and this book should be in your top three first reads.

Firms of Endearment **by Raj Sisodia, Jagdish N. Sheth & David Wolfe**

Co-authored by one of the authors of *Conscious Capitalism*, this book also sets out to establish the practical value that comes from being purpose-driven. The authors found, for example, that companies which align their corporate behaviour to a genuine motive to make the world better have average annualised returns three times greater than the average listed company on the American stock market. A particularly valuable book to have if you need to convince any doubters about the commercial viability of True Purpose.

How Brands Grow by Byron Sharp

A terrific book with a feisty premise that a lot of marketing beliefs are based on myth and bluster. Sharp sets out clear evidence for why brand loyalty is not as prevalent as people think. He also questions the marketing industry's addiction to the promotion of broad brand values over the creation of genuine value from better products and services. Right up my street.

How Will You Measure Your Life? by Clayton M. Christensen with James Allworth & Karen Dillon

A brilliant book that puts this whole crazy working-for-a-living thing into perspective. There is a normal-sized paperback of several hundred pages, but I actually prefer the tiny snapshot edition brought out by Harvard University Press. In just 30 pages, Christensen lays out a set of personal guidelines that have helped him find meaning in life, not just in business. You'll see many parallels with going the right way around The Circle.

Start with Why by Simon Sinek

This is the theoretical bible for anyone interested in running a purpose-driven business. It sets out the rationale for understanding your authentic motivation in commerce. It's also well worth typing 'Simon Sinek' into your YouTube search window. You'll find dozens of insightful videos from lectures and interviews ranging from 2 minutes to 2 hours. All of it great stuff.

Story Wars by **Jonah Sachs**

Like the two titles listed below by David Taylor, this book is primarily related to branding, but at such a deep level that it overlaps with organisational purpose. All the great books on branding do. Because the best brand image is the one that authentically reflects the truth about a company. Jonah explores how all good storytelling connects with a primitive need in all of us, and shows how the immutable rules of storytelling can be applied to branding a business.

The Brand Gym and *Brand Vision* by **David Taylor**

These two books are about helping you manage your brand to improve business performance. Connecting the word 'brand' to words like 'business' and 'performance' was quite refreshing when the first title was published in 2003. We admired this work at Meerkats because it contained practical methods to unlock brand meaning within a company, and from a very human perspective. The second title was published in 2006 and takes the idea further, exploring a more visionary approach to branding.

The Cluetrain Manifesto by **Rick Levine, Christopher Locke, Doc Searls & David Weinberger**

This is a truly fascinating book. On the surface it's a treatise on the rise of social media. But I actually found it to be an accurate explanation of the new consumer and their shaky relationship with capitalism. The first dozen pages are worth the cover price alone, as the authors set out 93 short, powerful rules for communicating with people in the 21st century.

optimism vs blind optimism

I'd definitely recommend reading all these books if you're looking to add practical, dispassionate, commercial weight to a debate that can get quite emotionally charged. Especially if you need to convince a business partner, a bank manager, your husband, your wife or a lifestyle partner.

But a word of caution. I differ with these authors on one small but crucial point: their description of purpose-driven as mostly about 'doing good'. As I mentioned in chapter 2, purpose doesn't always mean worthiness. I strongly believe that True Purpose is first and foremost about telling the truth about what authentically motivates you in business, and then (hopefully) maturing that philosophy into an ultimate win–win–win for you and your staff, your customers and society in general. I believe truth is the key to the image of capitalism being reborn in the eyes of our next generations of business owners and consumers.

So proclaiming that purpose is only about being worthy is, in my opinion, blinkered. Trying to convince doubters that consumers will only want to buy from companies that are doing good in the world is a doomed argument. There's just too much proof that fickle, contrary consumers have all kinds of reasons for buying things. Yes, even the savvy young Millennials who despise the devious capitalist world the Baby Boomers have dumped them in.

Sure, more and more consumers are choosing brands that satisfy needs which are beyond the basic human requirements of hunger, thirst, safety, a sense of belonging, and so on. They are increasingly buying from companies that meet self-actualising needs. That is, companies that reflect personal values such as honesty and integrity and equal rights, or that care for the environment. In societies where more and more have most of their primitive needs met, consumerism will naturally mature in this way. But be careful. As worthy as that is, the numbers aren't in our favour yet. There are still way more consumers who are necessarily more self-serving. Their lives have not yet afforded them the privilege of consuming for self-actualisation.

I think this is a critical truth to admit. We lovers of purpose must be very careful not to get too starry-eyed or we risk losing this fight to the smart pragmatists of Wall Street who understand those numbers. So I urge you to be a realist first and a truth-driven dreamer second. It's the only way we can take on conventional capitalism and make it better.

There's a great scene in the movie *The Theory of Everything*. A young Stephen Hawking has just established his genius by presenting a university paper on The Big Bang Theory. His idea about the beginnings of the universe is the toast of the academic world and rapidly becomes the accepted principle. But when someone asks him, 'What are you going to do now?' he replies, 'Why, disprove it of course'.

As a realist, I love that. A vital part of being authentic is a constant readiness to have your beliefs be disproved. Your goal is the truth, not being right.

'The Naked Brand': a 1-hour documentary produced by Jordan Berg & Jeff Rosenblum, co-founders of Questus, an advertising agency in the United States

This is the best hour you'll spend this week. We saw this documentary and immediately ordered a DVD copy for all our clients. We hired a small cinema and showed it to all our staff. And we show segments from it in all our university lectures and new business presentations. It sets out the reasons why people no longer trust ads or the companies behind them. It explains how free enterprise is transparent now and what you can do about it. The message to corporate America is clear: if you want to succeed, tell the truth.

YouTube

Any talk by Simon Sinek is worth watching. On YouTube there are dozens of short clips from interviews and presentations that make great reminders of the core values of purpose.

Search for Alan Watts, too, and you'll get some inspiring clips and monologues from the 1960s that still hold true today.

that other name on the cover

This book would not be possible without Ronnie Duncan, my founding partner in Meerkats. He's the strategic Yin to my creative Yang. Ronnie's visionary thinking has helped me evolve not only as a creative director but as a person.

As a boy growing up in Edinburgh, Scotland, Ronnie would spend most days after school wandering the corridors of Edinburgh's many brilliant museums. His endless curiosity about how humans work led him to become a brand strategist in the marketing industry, where he could be paid to do what he loved: understanding those strange, contrary and wonderful tribes of people we call companies and diving inside the minds, hearts and souls of the humans who buy things from those companies. Then finding the sweet spot between them.

A lot of people see Ronnie as a professor. I guess that's because his manner is intellectual and his accent is still quite British. But he wouldn't be so skilled at his craft if he wasn't also such a big softie. His endless curiosity about human behaviour may come across as clinical and scientific, but his motive is to help people live better lives. To find fulfilment and happiness in ways that are fairer for everyone. I've learned an enormous amount from him about both business strategy and human possibility.

Ronnie and I formed our company, Meerkats, in 2004. What began as a new-age advertising agency offering a more honest kind of marketing campaign has evolved into a creative business solutions company working on business models, service design, product innovation, recruitment strategies, store fit-outs, and so on. All borne of an authentic purpose.

The results for our clients have been so potent that Ronnie and I felt compelled to expand the numbers of people our thinking was helping. On top of sharing our methods with a handful of companies every year through a professional service firm, we decided to make them available to millions of business owners all around the world via publishing, social media and educational events.

Being candid with each other as always, we admitted that writing a book together would not be ideal. We're likeminded in our thinking, but hugely different in our application of that thinking. Ronnie is a 'fermenter' who loves to spend weeks down the rabbit hole sitting with a thought. Whereas I'm a 'doer' who wants to get great thinking out into the world as soon as its value is evident.

We also feed off each other's intellect and chat for hours and hours on this stuff. We knew that if we tried to pen a book together we'd spend more time blue-skying and debating than typing. So we agreed that each of us would pursue our own titles and use the other as a sounding board and first draft editor.

So in short, this book may be written by one person, but the thinking within it is the result of two minds.

about the author

Mike Edmonds is the Chairman and Co-founder of a brand leadership company in Perth, Australia called Meerkats. His goal is to ... wait, this isn't working for me.

For some reason, the convention in publishing is to write *About the author* in the third person. I've never understood this. It seems detached to me. I want to talk to you as I do throughout the book — from me to you, in a normal voice as a (fairly) normal person.

So, let me start that again.

Hi. My name's Mike and I'm the Chairman and Co-founder of a branding company in Perth, Australia called Meerkats. My co-founder Ronnie and I describe our company's job as liberating the commercial value of authentic human motivation by helping organisations find their True Purpose. Unlike ad agencies, we create way more business solutions than ad campaigns. And for the past 13 years we've been doing just that for large corporations, small challenger brands and not-for-profits in almost every category of free enterprise.

As a result, Meerkats has grown too, attracting the biggest brands in our market and building a happy team of smart professionals who, like me, want to change the perception of our industry from wacky cowboys to trusted advisors. We've been named Agency of the Year 3 times and have won awards for strategy and effectiveness around the world. (I usually don't like blowing my own trumpet, but the publishers said this is where I need to establish my credibility with you. Hopefully you're very impressed).

Until recently my role at Meerkats was The Creative Guy. To understand what I did, picture a simple two-circle Venn diagram: one circle contains all the objectives a company has and the other contains all the things consumers want. I worked at the tiny point where they overlapped. I was like an interpreter, sitting between two foreign countries and mediating terms of trade. I was pretty good at it too, winning all kinds of shiny statues and framed certificates at advertising festivals around the world, sitting on award panels in Cannes, Dubai, London and Sydney and being invited to lecture at seminars in Auckland, Bangkok, Jakarta and others. I was running my own company, making good money and traveling the globe.

Pretty sweet, right? Well about two years ago, Ronnie and I realised we weren't happy. As we watched the results our clients were achieving and saw how our methods not only changed a company's fortunes but changed the lives of the people in them — for the better — it occurred to us that we were helping only a tiny percentage of the business community. At best, in any one year Meerkats will work with around half a dozen medium-to-large organisations to surface their True Purpose and then help them implement it (through creative business modelling, new products and services, employee communications, brand platforms, marketing strategies, and so forth).

Six companies a year. We realised this wasn't nearly enough. Our ultimate goal is to reinvent the idea of capitalism as an honourable concept in society and it was clear to both of us that we weren't going to achieve that if we only influenced six companies a year. So, we decided to hand the day-to-day running of Meerkats to our younger (and often smarter) senior staff and spend more of our energy getting our thinking out into the world. Like, get our tools and methods into the hands of more business owners so they too could grow and succeed in a more honourable way like our clients were.

Being the insanely curious strategist that he is, Ronnie felt he firstly needed to know more and went off to research the future of commerce. Being the impatient writer that I am, I figured we already knew enough to start helping thousands more business owners. So, I got to work condensing the philosophies, tools and methods that we offer our clients and turning them into a do-it-yourself manual that any business owner could access anywhere in the world for the cost of a paperback.

Voila. The result is the book you're reading now. I hope you'll find it more usable than the many theoretical titles available today on organisational purpose. For one important reason:

I want you to be successful, not just enlightened.

In the business world today I see and hear so much conversation about the need for authentic corporate behaviour. And yet I witness the overwhelming majority of companies still making these same mistakes:

- Presenting an experience of their brand in marketing that differs from the experience of their brand in the real world.

- Pretending to be motivated by the same personal values as their potential customers.

- Over-promising on product and service quality despite the internet giving everyone the ability to share the truth.

- Thinking that their staff will overlook these untruths because they're somehow easier to hoodwink than consumers.

Ring any bells? Clearly the world doesn't need another purely academic book on organisational purpose. It seems that simply understanding the reasons why consumers gravitate to authentic motive isn't making enough of a change in the real world. Too many company owners are nodding and agreeing, then putting the books down and getting back to the conventional business practices as described above.

I felt that in order to break these deep-seated habits, business owners needed simple tools, not complex theories. They needed a step-by-step playbook to help them find *their* true purpose and then implement it. And they desperately needed a candid heads-up about some of the real-world obstacles that will invariably rise up in front of them as they do.

Cool Mike, but why are you the one to write it?

Good question. I think it's for the simple reason that I am a fierce practitioner, not a theorist. I have spent 40 years in the front lines of free enterprise: the marketing industry. Unlike what you may have seen on Bewitched and Mad Men, success in the marketing industry is not about what you make for your clients (wacky ad campaigns), but what you make happen (sales results).

To be successful business owners ourselves, Ronnie and I couldn't just create theories, we've had to create real growth for real companies in the real world. Five percentage points more market share. Ten percentage points less customer churn. Higher disposition to purchase. Lower cost per acquisition. In our game, if you sound impressive but don't deliver results, you're history.

This is good for you. Because the book you're reading now has been written with an uncompromising commitment to usability. As a Creative Director addicted to telling the truth to my clients *and* the consumers they want to attract, I've spent my entire career turning esoteric theories about consumerism into street-smart tools, gauging the short and long-term results and fine-tuning them so they genuinely work better and better.

Put simply, I wanted this book to not just make sense, but to make something happen. I guess my only question for you now is, 'What do you want to make happen?'

index